&
DESPERADOS

J. J. Harlin, alias "Off Whee...

Hedges, Billy The Kid, Billy ...

Pock-Marked Kid, Caribou Brow...

Dirtyface Mike, Hoodoo Brown...

Pawnee Bill, Kickapoo Georg...

Johnnie Behind the Rocks, ...

Mysterious Dave, Hatchetfa...

Texas George, Durango Kid...

Mike, Kim Ki Rogers, Char...

Nigger Bill, Curley Moor...

The Kid The Second, Pret...

Dick, Wink the Barber, ...

Doubleout Sam, Dutch Pe...

...ndsome Harry...

in, Little Jac

French Pete, Dutch Charlie,

d Laughlin, Scarface Charlie,

ack-Knife Jack, XXXXXX

peck Sam, Beefsteak Mike,

it, Broncho Bill, Solitaire,

d the Hack Driver, Split Nose

the Swede, Webfingered Billy;

ightfingered Jack, Chuck, Bil

Dick, Forty-five Jimmy, Lucky

Mike, Silent Henry, XXXXXX

Curley Bill, Black Kid, King

e Dance Hall Rustler, Big Geor

J. J. Harlin, alias "Off Wheeler;" Saw Dust Charlie, Wm.
Hedges, Billy The Kid, Billy Mullin, Little Jack the Cuter,
Pock-Marked Kid, Caribou Brown, French Pete, Dutch Charlie,
Dirtyface Mike, Hoodoo Brown, Red Laughlin, Scarface Charlie,
Pawnee Bill, Kickapoo George, Jack-Knife Jack, Johnie
Johnnie Behind the Rocks, Flyspeck Sam, Beefsteak Mike,
Mysterious Dave, Hatchetface Kit, Broncho Bill, Solitaire,
Texas George, Durango Kid, Red the Hack Driver, Split Nose
Mike, Kim Ki Rogers, Charlie the Swede, Webfingered Billy,
Nigger Bill, Curley Moore, Lightfingered Jack, Chuck, Billy
The Kid The Second, Pretty Dick, Forty-five Jimmy, Lucky
Dick, Wink the Barber, Red Mike, Silent Henry, Danket
Doubleout Sam, Dutch Pete, Curley Bill, Black Kid, King-
fisher, Handsome Harry The Dance Hall Rustler, Big George
The Cook, Jimmie The Duck, Cockeyed Dutch, kittieDu
Little Dutch The Detective, Smooth, Ruck Flapjack Bill,
Buckskin Joe, Tennessee, Brocky Faced Johnnie, Picolo
Johnnie, Pistol Johnnie, Big Foot Mike, China Jack,
Pinkey, Happy Jack, Big Burns, Cold Deck George, Hop-
fiend Bill, Pegleg Dick, Rosebud, Sandy, (Red Oaks),
Dutch the Gambler (Jim Ramsey), Red-face Mike, Dummy the
Fox, Red River Tom, Holdout Jack, Short Creek Dave,
Skinny, Long Vest George, Smokey Hall, Baldfaced Kid,
Cockey Bill, One Armed Jim the Gambler, Smukuy One Armed
Kelley, Lord Locke, Long Lon, Maroney the Peddler,
"Shakespeare", Chuck-a-luck Betts, Hog Jones, Hog-foot
Jim, Bostwick the Silent Man, Hurricane Bill, Pawnee
George, Blondy, Shotgun Bill, Scotty, Big Murphy, Box
Car Bill, Little Jay, Kentuck, Tommy the Poet, Sheeney
Frank, Shorty, Skinny the Barber, Elk Skin Davis, Broken
Nose Clark, Soapy Smith, Squint-eyed Bob, Stuttering Tom,
Repeater Shan, Buttermilk George, Billie-Be- Damned, and
Candy Cooper, Pancake Billy, Cockeyed Frank, Rattlesnake
Sam, Kansas Kid.

Facsimile: Outlaw names, NMFWP, WPA #88, NMSRCA

OUTLAWS
&
DESPERADOS

A New Mexico Federal Writers' Project Book

Compiled and Edited
by
Ann Lacy and Anne Valley-Fox

SUNSTONE
PRESS
SANTA FE

Sunstone books may be purchased for educational, business, or sales promotional use.
For information please write: Special Markets Department, Sunstone Press,
P.O. Box 2321, Santa Fe, New Mexico 87504-2321.

Book and Cover design by Vicki Ahl

Library of Congress Cataloging-in-Publication Data

Outlaws & desperados : a New Mexico Federal Writers' Project book / compiled and edited
by Ann Lacy and Anne Valley-Fox.
    p. cm.
Includes bibliographical references (p.   ).
ISBN 978-0-86534-633-8 (pbk. : alk. paper)
1. Frontier and pioneer life--Southwest, New--Anecdotes. 2. Frontier and pioneer life--
New Mexico--Anecdotes. 3. Outlaws--Southwest, New--Biography--Anecdotes.
4. Outlaws--New Mexico--Biography--Anecdotes. 5. Southwest, New--Biography--
Anecdotes. 6. New Mexico--Biography--Anecdotes. 7. Southwest, New--History--
1848---Anecdotes. I. Lacy, Ann, 1945- II. Fox, Anne Valley. III. Federal Writers' Project.
New Mexico. IV. Title: Outlaws and desperados.
 F786.O94 2008
 364.309789'09034--dc22
                                2008001475

Published in

WWW.SUNSTONEPRESS.COM
SUNSTONE PRESS / POST OFFICE BOX 2321 / SANTA FE, NM 87504-2321 /USA
(505) 988-4418 / ORDERS ONLY (800) 243-5644 / FAX (505) 988-1025

For Jess and Joaquin
and Ezra and Kalu
with love.

CONTENTS

DISTRICT TWO: *THE TRAGEDY OF PAINT HORSE MESA / 191*

Acknowledgments

We wish to thank the New Mexico State Archives and Record Center, the Museum of New Mexico Palace of the Governors Photo Archives and the Fray Angélico Chávez History Library, Santa Fe, New Mexico, for the use of their collections.

We are grateful to the Archivists at the NMSARC for their nimble assistance with our research.

And we greatly appreciate the continual inspiration and support of our friend and colleague Elise Rymer.

Editors' Preface

A few years ago at the New Mexico State Record Center and Archives, we donned the white gloves brought to us by friendly archivists and began to peruse Works Project Administration files documenting the life and times of Territorial New Mexico. Before we knew it, the cool, quiet research room seemed to be filling with gun smoke; the walls rang with shouts of outlaws pulling off a train robbery; a sheriff's posse thundered between the library tables in hot pursuit of a notorious outlaw they fully intended to hang by the neck from the limb of a cottonwood tree.

As researchers, we knew we'd struck a mother lode with this collection. Inside folders labeled "WPA 1936-1939" we discovered hundreds of articles pecked out on old upright typewriters by New Mexico writers determined to make a buck by their wits, not incidentally documenting some of their state's historical highlights. Many of these articles depicted hair-trigger encounters between various factions in the New Mexico Territory during the last decades of the 19th century into the early 20th: cattle rustlers vs. ranchers, bad men vs. good sheriffs, bad sheriffs vs. good-hearted outlaws, "gentle townspeople" vs. "notorious desperados." Here and there, groups of Apaches or Mexican *banditos* dashed across the pages, making their mark on the pages of New Mexico history.

Inside its covers, the land of *Outlaws & Desperados* is a dangerous place, where greed and violence—both random and intentional—prevail. Many of the central players described in these stories appear as cruel and often racist characters. It's a man's world, where winner takes all. In this collection, cameo appearances by women—Silly Sally; the sassy matron from Lamy who cooks for Curley Bill; a girl who escapes the Apaches and takes refuge in Silver City—are rare occurrences. The macho culture of "Gunfight at the O.K. Corral" that dazzled the silver screen in the 1950s seems tame compared to the tales of risk and outrageous bravado found in these pages.

Some of the accounts resound with zany playfulness or instances of heroic self-sacrifice. The language is often colored by the vernacular of the day. For example, from "Devil Dick's Career and His Ignominious End": "And say Dick was figurin' on startin' a brand new graveyard with Baldy and Shorty and Lem and Long Tom throwed in as headstones." We remind ourselves that such casual narrative tends to mask the *gravitas*—feelings of fear, grief and loss—that surely underscored the lives of those who lived and died in Territorial New Mexico.

Though the NMFWP writers represented in this collection came from various backgrounds and lived in different parts of the state, their surnames indicate that they are predominantly Anglos. History told by one ethnic or cultural group is biased by definition:

many viewpoints are left out of the telling of the story. We know that where a person stands has everything to do with their vision and point of view. That said, readers may appreciate the fact that a group of writers in the 1930s devoted themselves to rescuing a set of stories of New Mexico for the rest of us.

Writers enlisted for the New Mexico Federal Writers Project represent a range of linguistic abilities and proclivities. The prolific writer, N. Howard (Jack) Thorp, perhaps best known for writing and collecting cowboy songs, left behind a highbrow life in the east for the "Wild West." He apparently preferred the view from the saddle to that of the lecture hall (he may have attended Harvard from 1883 to 1886), as he spent the rest of his life in New Mexico, making a name for himself as a cowboy writer and storyteller.

Outlaws & Desperados includes more submissions from N. Howard Thorp than any other writer, narratives that read as if he was spinning a yarn around a campfire. A born romantic, Thorp made free with opinionated pronouncements. Toward the end of his piece about the Dalton brothers' demise ("The Dalton Gang's Last Hold-Up"), he submits, "I hold no grief for those who are professional hold-ups, but a kid like Emmett Dalton's admiration for an elder brother is quite easily understood, for Bob Dalton certainly had plenty of dash and nerve, and in the eyes of the kid was enshrined as a hero."

W. M. Emery, who wrote with a more philosophical, elegiac tone, concludes "The Fate of a Horse Thief" with this: "So the horse thief was buried where he had fallen, and occupies an unknown grave within a few feet of the well traveled road, and the autoists who whisk past the place in their fine cars today, little dream of the tragedy that took place in that beautiful spot less than a half a century ago."

Field writer Elinor Crans organized her articles around dialogue, sometimes in Spanish. From "Bad Hombres": "'Plenty of bad men in the old days,'" explains Filipiano, my aged informant. '*Si*, plenty then—plenty now—plenty always.'"

Reyes N. Martinez used Spanish phrases liberally, and translated them for the reader. Mrs. Frances Totty wrote with a general disregard for formal structure, as if in a rush to get her informant's story down on the page, while Kenneth Fordyce displayed a "just the facts" exactness. In "Crime Did Not Pay in '73," he writes, "The cowhand, Helling, proved rather obstinate for he was convinced that lynching was too good for the murder of his former employer."

Administrators for the Federal Writers' Project divided New Mexico into four approximate quadrants—Northeast, Southeast, Northwest and Southwest—and we have followed suit as a way of organizing a voluminous body of material. Though project writers sometimes submitted newspaper articles or excerpts from published books, their most lively submissions are those based on the reminiscences of New Mexicans who lived during territorial times or were passing down stories in the oral tradition.

Journalistic standards of 1936-1939 were looser, less grammatically formalized than they are today, and it's not always clear to the reader which remarks come straight from the informant and which are shaped by the artist. Our solution to this quandary was to attribute the by-line for each submission (with one exception, a story by Colonel Jack Potter) to the NMFWP field writer and to specifically credit the informant or narrator—those old-timers who fueled most of the stories—at the end of the article.

As manuscript editors, we were torn. Would it be better to publish the original articles with their idiosyncrasies intact, or to correct obvious errors of spelling and punctuation to deliver a smooth read? We came down in the center, with a policy of constructive minimalism. For instance, we decided that if a comma was placed so that it obscured the writer's meaning (many of these writers exhibited an inordinate fondness for commas), we would move it or remove it altogether. We chose to correct misspellings of common words but generally left proper names alone, as well as extraneous capital letters and quotation marks.

Typos presented a similar quandary, as we had no way to distinguish a slip of the typist's fingers from intellectual intention. Similarly, we wondered if changes that were sometimes handwritten on the rough-typed manuscripts had been added by the writer or perhaps by an editor in the bureau office. Since we couldn't know, we made judgment calls on a case-by-case basis. Our hope was to preserve as much of the flavor of the times and of the writer's personal style as possible short of allowing the language to lapse into obscurity. N. Howard Thorp's reports all ended with the words at one time beloved by youthful narrators, "The End." We left these in place for your enjoyment. We also refrained from adding missing italics or accent marks to Spanish words. And where it wasn't obvious to us who was speaking within a particular narrative we left the passage intact, as the reader's guess is at least as good as our own.

We hope you will read these accounts with wonder and enjoyment, as we did. Whatever the vagaries and variables regarding accuracy and authorship, these records provide us with a one-of-a-kind record of thrilling and dangerous times in the "wild and woolly" territory of New Mexico.

About the New Mexico Federal Writers' Project

March, 2008, marked the seventy-fifth anniversary of President Franklin D. Roosevelt's New Deal. The Great Depression that came on the heels of the stock market crash of 1929 threw the country's financial institutions into chaos and put many people across the nation out of work. In 1933, FDR inaugurated his New Deal administration, a comprehensive program designed to stimulate the country's economy while lending a hand to the unemployed.

At a time when many people were down on their luck during the Great Depression, the New Deal's New Mexico Federal Writers' Project (NMFWP) employed writers around the state to record the extraordinary history and lore of New Mexico. The Federal Writers' Project was one of a number of white-collar relief projects of the Works Progress Administration (WPA) that put Americans back to work. In addition to the Federal Writers' Project (FWP), the projects included the Federal Art Project, the Federal Music Project, the Federal Theater Project and the Historical Records Survey.

The New Mexico Federal Writers' Project was officially launched on August 2, 1935, under the direction of poet and writer Ina Sizer Cassidy. Between October, 1935, and August, 1939, a cadre of field writers wrote stories, collected articles, conducted interviews and transposed documents for the public record. Although each of the 48 states across the nation launched their own Federal Writers' Project, New Mexico was seen as geographically and culturally unique. From his office in Washington, DC, the national director of the Federal Writers' Project, Henry G. Alsberg, urged New Mexico project writers to emphasize the state's visual, scenic and human interest subjects in the project's guide, *New Mexico: A Guide to the Colorful State*. "Try to make the readers see the white midsummer haze, the dust that rises in unpaved New Mexican streets, the slithery red earth roads of winter, the purple shadows of later afternoon . . . ," he urged.

New Mexico field writers apparently felt a similar enthusiasm, for they recorded New Mexico's vivid lore and scenic locale in thousands of documents to preserve the state's colorful past for future generations. Their subjects ranged from the colonial New Mexico days of the 1600s and 1700s to the beginnings of the 1900s—from horse-drawn cart to car! Their many lively selections included firsthand oral accounts and remembrances by settlers and residents who were alive during New Mexico's Territorial times and "lived to tell the story."

The NMFWP field writers plumbed the local resources in four prescribed areas of New Mexico, as follows: District One: Taos, Colfax, Union, Harding, Quay, Guadalupe, San Miguel, and Mora counties; District Two: Curry, Roosevelt, Lea, Eddy, Otero, Lincoln, De Baca, and Chaves counties; District Three:

Santa Fe, Rio Arriba, San Juan, McKinley, Valencia, Bernalillo, and Sandoval counties; District Four: Socorro, Dona Ana, Luna, Hidalgo, Grant, Catron, and Sierra counties.

Although parts of the state were more heavily weighted with field writers than others, taken together their subject areas included Native American lore and accounts of encounters with Anglos; Hispano folklore; trails and settlement; the Mexican Revolution and Pancho Villa's raid on Columbus, New Mexico as well as detailed descriptions of the state's geography and demography, landmarks, and travel routes.

In 1939, under the WPA's reorganization, the New Mexico Federal Writers' Project became the Writers' Program. By that time, Aileen O'Bryan Nussbaum had replaced Ina Sizer Cassidy as director. In Washington, DC, Charles Ethrige Minton supervised the New Mexico Writers Program until its closure in 1943. Through its tenure, the New Mexico program produced *Calendar of Events* written by project writers and illustrated by Federal New Mexico Art Project artists as well as *Over the Turquoise Trail* and *The Turquoise Trail*, two anthologies of New Mexican poems, stories, and folklore. A major achievement of the FWP was an American Guide Series publication entitled *New Mexico: A Guide to the Colorful State*, first published in 1940.

NMFWP field workers had a treasure trove of sources to draw from and they mined them well: Old-timers with a colorful heritage and culture and those who entered the territory as early explorers; diarists and journalists; poets and artists; miners, ranchers and cowboys; farmers and merchants; lawmen and outlaws; anthropologists and folklorists—all the many travelers, *paso por aquí*, who animate New Mexico history.

The efforts of the NMFWP field workers have left us a rich compilation of documents stored in various collections in New Mexico, including the New Mexico State Archives and museum and university collections. The Library of Congress in Washington, DC also holds copies of many of the manuscripts. Now, with the New Mexico Federal Writers' Project book series, seventy-five years after FDR launched the New Deal, a substantial number of these readings have found their way out of archival folders and into print for the public's interest and enjoyment.

Introduction

The American Southwest is a big landscape where the eye can see far and one's spirit roams unfettered. It is a place dominated by sky where the wind blows strong, and the light of day reveals hues of great beauty, while the dark night blossoms with stars. It's drier than the long-dead bones scattered along ancient trails where ghost chants are still carried in the wind.

Back in the 1970s, I was following these ancient trails in hot pursuit of folksongs and lore to record in an attempt to fill in a few of the many gaps in the written history of the region. Thus, I recorded Hispano *corridos* and *inditas*, narrative ballads that recall events in the lives of *la gente* as they eked out existence in this exquisitely beautiful but harsh environment. Many of these narrative ballads recall kidnappings by Indians, gunfights, murders and hangings that reveal the violence that dominated the region that became known as the New Mexico Territory.

One day, I met a tall, vigorous *viejo* by the name of Cruz Alvarez who invited me into his adobe home near the plaza in La Mesilla, New Mexico. He spun vivid accounts of the days of his youth when lawlessness prevailed throughout the territory. When Señor Alvarez was a boy, many Civil War veterans were barely middle-aged, and echoes of the Indian wars rebounded off canyon walls. He spoke fondly of Pancho Villa whose raid on Columbus, New Mexico left several dead and wounded kindling legends that still fire the lore of the Mexican Revolution.

I paid him a final visit as he lay on his deathbed. He grinned at me and said, "¡Adios, y buena suerte!"

The life of Cruz Alvarez began when the west was yet wild. For centuries, New Mexico had been witness to frequent, often deadly encounters between peoples of different cultures who guarded their homelands against interlopers, raided their neighbors, squabbled over territorial boundaries, defended their deities against an alien god, waged all-out wars. The centuries of conflict resulted in horrific bloodshed hewing a model of violence that contributed to the cultural paradigm. It was into this milieu that the American outlaw of the latter half of the nineteenth century rode into prominence.

By the 1850s, the New Mexico Territory was included within the boundary of the United States, and was accessible by horse, by mule, by wagon, by coach, and by foot. In the 1870s, the "iron horse" trailed though the landscape on iron rails. Even so, the wild west was remote enough and lawless enough to tempt many to try their hands at banditry. Other tough-minded men followed the Mexican tradition of cattle-ranching, thus cattle barons drove great herds of long-horned cattle from Texas into the Territory, often violently displacing Hispano sheep ranchers, shooting them dead, not bothering to bury their remains. Access to waterholes was brutally contested and became battle zones for gunslingers that had gained zeal and expertise during the Civil War.

There were also hostile Indians to fight to the death, their lands to claim by right of westward expansion shaded by the semi-divine right of manifest destiny. Apaches and Navajos fiercely defended their homelands to the extent that U.S. military detachments continued to pepper the New Mexico Territory with forts well after the Civil War. During the period from 1850-1900, almost every full-grown male living in the New Mexico Territory toted a gun.

Some lived on the side of the law while others preferred existence outside the law. Many straddled the fence. Professional outlaws rustled cattle, held up stage-coaches and wagon trains, robbed banks, stole gold and silver from miners who were more successful than the Spanish colonists of earlier centuries. It was common for outlaw gangs to tie the reins of their horses to their saddle horns and gallop into town, their hands free to shoot their pistols, rifles and shotguns mostly skyward, but sometimes taking out a dog or chicken, occasionally plugging a lawman. Many were boisterous, others almost genteel, and almost all took their pleasures at the expense of the local citizenry.

Many were caught, tried and hanged. Others were caught and lynched without benefit of a trial. Some died in gunfights. Still others avoided the law and retired into respectability. Such was Clay Allison, a rebel Civil War veteran who rode in from Texas and became known as one of the great gunfighters of his day. He is recalled as never having shot a man to death without provocation. His death toll is estimated at between ten and forty. He quietly retired to his farm and died one day when he fell off his wagon and broke his neck.

There was a distinction between a gunfighter, and a gunman hired as an assassin to kill in behalf of his employer. There were gunfighters of both Anglo and Hispano descent. One of the most famous self-appointed lawmen was Elfego Baca from central New Mexico who was said to have single-handedly held off eighty Texans for thirty-six hours. His practice was to rein in outlaws within forty-eight hours of their crimes. He hand-wrought his first lawman's badge well before he was elected sheriff.

One of the most villainous outlaws of the late nineteenth and early twentieth centuries was "Black Jack" Ketchum. With the appearance of the railroad in the 1870s, outlaws were provided with yet another compelling and intellectually challenging venue. "Black Jack" was one of the masters of the train hold-up. He and his gang terrorized the countryside around northeastern New Mexico. While many outlaws were said to have comported themselves as gentlemen most of the time, "Black Jack" and his gang were downright mean all of the time. "Black Jack" was finally wounded in the arm in an unsuccessful train hold-up, and the arm had to be amputated. At his trial, he was sentenced to death by hanging.

The story goes that to ensure that this infamous outlaw was properly hung to death, the carpenters in Clayton, New Mexico constructed a gallows that was higher than usual. At his request, "Black Jack" was given a new pair of boots to climb the thirteen stairs in preparation for his final descent. His last words were, "I am dying with my boots on. Please make it snappy as I'm in a hurry to take possession of the place the devil has reserved for me." As the story goes, the noose was placed around his neck, the trapdoor sprung, and the force of his descent snapped off his head. The attendant physician is said to have taken needle and thread and sewn it back on.

Corporate outlawry gained a hearty foothold with the presence of the Santa Fe Ring of politicians and developers whose nefarious shenanigans extended from the end of the Civil War to the mid-1880s, and was masked behind the veneer of legislation and respectable business practice, a tradition that continues to this day. Post-Civil War carpetbaggers who moved into the territory to make a fast buck, and then move on, founded a heritage still present in the southwestern landscape. Colfax and Lincoln Counties that bordered the eastern edge of the New Mexico Territory were rife with skullduggery that involved elected and appointed government officials including then Governor Samuel B. Axtell. Merchants and ranchers fought bitter feuds and contributed to a level of lawlessness that eroded the boundary between law-abiding citizens and desperados of many hues. This was the milieu of William "Billy the Kid" Bonney who was said to have killed a man for every one of his twenty-one years of life. Billy was finally shot and killed by lawman Pat Garrett who later became part of a business consortium that included cattle-baron John Chisum. There are ethical laws and there are laws of convenience. These distinctions continue to prevail.

Indeed, the New Mexico Territory of the last half of the nineteenth century was a danger zone. New Mexico was admitted to statehood in 1912, and gradually the citizenry quieted down to the extent that lawlessness was mostly contained. In 1929, the stock market crashed, plunging America into the Great Depression. In an effort to restore the national economy, President Franklin D. Roosevelt initiated the New Deal that included the Federal Writers' Project. In New Mexico, field writers fanned out around the state to listen to stories of New Mexico's flamboyant territorial days by those who lived them.

Many who were yet alive during the 1930s had been born when America was wrestling with itself during the Civil War, and remembered its grim history, as well as the subsequent Indian wars, and the coming of droves of cattle and cattle ranchers who claimed the landscape where water was rare and springs, streams and waterholes were sometimes defended to the death. These culture-bearers, including the young Cruz Alvarez, recounted many of their stories to WPA writers who interviewed them, and thus provided an immensely rich archival trove of lore.

This anthology is filled with stories and commentaries recounted by people who knew Billy the Kid, Black Jack Ketchum, Clay Allison, Elfego Baca, Pancho Villa and many others whose nicknames spice the colorful and dangerous cultural mosaic of the New Mexico Territory of the nineteenth and early twentieth centuries. These stories tell it as it was, or at least as it was recalled by those who witnessed the lifespan of the legendary wild west that dominates much of the imagination of American culture, and spawned the contentious apothegm: "When guns are outlawed, only outlaws will have guns."

—Jack Loeffler
Los Caballos
Autumn, 2007

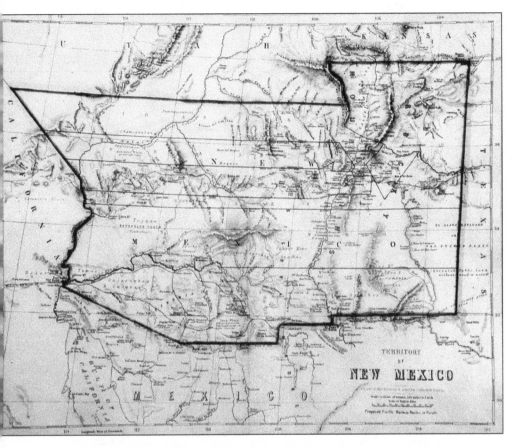

Territory of New Mexico, ca. 1857 by A.D. Rogers (artist), A. Keith Johnston (artist), Courtesy Fray Angélico Chávez History Library Map Collection, Palace of the Governors, Museum of New Mexico

DISTRICT ONE: CURLY BILL

"Now, hush your trumpet," he said,
"and pass the griddle cakes or I'll kill you."

(from "Curley Bill" by N. Howard Thorp)

Black Jack, "Tom Ketchum"

by
L. Raines

B lack Jack, the leader of the worse gang of train robbers and one of the worst criminals of his day, had the distinction of dying with his boots on. His depredations spread far and wide, but his most daring robberies were confined to northeastern New Mexico. It is in this section of the state that he attempted his last and most unusual robbery.

In August of 1899 Black Jack planned to hold up the fast mail train of the Burlington Railroad near Folsom, New Mexico. His plan called for careful action. He and his men were to board the train at Folsom as incidental passengers, and ride south as far as the Sierra Grande, to a point where the train makes a sharp downhill turn. At this curve they were to order the train stopped and proceed with their haul.

Black Jack's lieutenants, however, misunderstood the instructions. Instead of boarding the train at Folsom they climbed to the summit of the mountain to await the arrival of the train at the site for the hold-up. Black Jack, a man of boundless courage, saw his instructions had miscarried but proceeded to attempt the robbery alone.

At the proposed point he ordered the train stopped. He slipped back to the baggage coach, where the mail clerk had speedily concealed himself behind the mailbags with his rifle. The battle which followed resulted in Black Jack's defeat. At the first volley he stumbled to the ground, a load of buckshot in his right arm. The gangster's companions were interested observers of the one-sided struggle but were in no position to come to their leader's aid.

In a few hours the wounded outlaw was rushed to a hospital in Trinidad, Colorado, where the surgeons, seeing the danger of blood poisoning, amputated his arm.

In the Trial which followed, Black Jack was found guilty and was sentenced to hang. The execution was to take place in Clayton, the county seat of the county where the crime was committed. Fearing Black Jack's associates might attempt a rescue, the authorities constructed a high wooden corral inclosing both the courthouse and the jail. Armed men were stationed around the corral during the trial and until the day of the execution.

As a last wish granted to him, Black Jack was given a pair of new boots which he wore on his last fatal walk. As he ascended the thirteen steps leading to the scaffold he remarked, "I am dying with my boots on. Please make it snappy, as I'm in a hurry to take possession of the place the devil has reserved for me."

Source of Narrative: Mack Taylor.

Black Jack Ketchem

by
D. D. Sharp

Black Jack Ketchem, killer, bandit and train robber, was as bold, vicious, and probably as greatly feared in those parts of the State where he operated, as any of the much more widely published outlaws of the old West.

Black Jack, whose real name was Thomas E. Ketchem, came to New Mexico from Texas about 1890 when he joined one of the trail herds which in those days was Clayton bound. Ex-Governor Hinkle says that while Tom and his brother Sam never worked for him, they were with his outfit and wagon at a time when he was running the C. A. Bars. Tom also worked for the L. F. D.'s (Phelps White), the Bar W (Ortons), and Governor Hinkle recalls that he went up the trail once with the Cross S outfit (Segrists).

Ten years before this, Tom and his brother Sam had already been in trouble and left San Saba County, Texas, with several men of bad reputation, one of whom was Will Carver, alias G. W.

Franks. The Sheriff of San Saba County was after him for killing Jap Powers.

Black Jack was a handsome man and proud of his ability to shoot true with both hands. He was tall, with a head of black hair, black heavy mustache, dark eyes, high forehead, large ears close against his head, with a long face and well-shaped nose.

The first murder attributed to him in New Mexico was killing Levi Herzstein near old Liberty, a few miles north of the present town of Tucumcari about 1891. Herzstein was a storekeeper and postmaster. His store was robbed and he started after the robbers with a small posse of three or four men. They came upon Tom and Sam Ketchem in a draw along the Canadian River. The two were seated before a campfire and Herzstein and his men covered them with rifles. Tom and Sam threw up their hands but managed to grab the rifles as they ducked under the horses' necks. They killed Herzstein and then fled toward the Taos hills west of the town of Cimarron to join his gang that was composed of Will Carver, Ezra Lay alias McGinnis, Dave Atkins, Red Pipkin, Bob Hayes, William Walters alias "Broncho Bill," and Ed Bullin. With them also was a young woman who posed as Bullin's wife. She is known only as Laura Bullin.

Before Tom joined the trail herd to Clayton he and his brother had worked for large cattle companies in southwestern New Mexico, the "Diamond A's" and others in that section. From 1897 until they left that section the Black Jack gang were accused of almost every kind of crime, pillaging and murder.

After the two brothers killed Levi Herzstein and rejoined their gang in the Taos mountains, they learned that Carver had been "scouting round," quietly investigating opportunities around Clayton. Business there was good. The season's wool sales had just been made and there was no bank in Clayton then. There were also sums of cash expressed almost daily to the gambling houses at

Clayton, which were doing good business also.

When Tom came in to take charge it was soon planned that a train robbery would be profitable. On the night of September 3, 1897, Black Jack boarded the southbound train at Folsom. Crowfoot was engineer, Cackley, fireman, and Harrington, conductor in charge of the train.

Five miles out of Folsom when the train reached Twin Mountain, Black Jack dropped from the tender and covered those in the engine cab with his gun. "Stop her," he demanded and Crowfoot did so.

Black Jack marched the two back to the express car and Cackley called for the messenger to open up. Sam Ketchem and Will Carver joined Black Jack and a fourth member of the gang waited in the shadows with horses.

When the messenger protested he did not know the combination of the safe he was struck on the head with a Winchester and five sticks of dynamite were placed on top of the safe and a quarter of beef thrown atop them for tamping. When Conductor Harrington heard the explosion and came forward with his lantern Black Jack ordered him to go back and put out his light, or get it shot out.

Three thousand five hundred dollars in silver and greenbacks were taken from the train.

After this train robbery the gang went back into the southwestern part of the Territory to carry on their crimes. There were many operations along the Arizona line, a train holdup was made at Grants, another at Steins Pass, a bank in Nogales, Arizona, the general store of Weens and Anderson at Sepia, and Rogers and Wingate were murdered at Camp Verde, Arizona, in July 1899.

Probably the strangest coincidence in outlaw activities took place soon after. The gang which Black Jack commanded robbed the C & S train at Twin Mountain three times. Conductor

Harrington was the conductor each of those times, but another coincidence is involved to make this fact interesting.

Sam and Tom decided to split, the men staying with Sam while Tom rode back to northern New Mexico as a lone bandit. At Camp Verde, July 2, 1899, Black Jack murdered Rogers and Wingate, then pressed on to Twin Mountain to attempt single-handed a holdup of the C & S passenger train at the exact spot he and his gang had robbed it in 1897.

By remarkable coincidence this same train had been held up on July 11, by Sam and the men who had remained with him. When Black Jack arrived on August 16th at the same spot to make his daring single-handed attempt, he was entirely unaware that his brother had robbed it but a month before and had died in the Santa Fe Penitentiary July 24th.

Black Jack boarded the engine's tender at Folsom, August 16, 1899, just as he had done two years before. He rode there until the train reached Twin Mountain, then he dropped into the cab and commanded engineer Kirchgraber to stop his train. Then he marched the engineer and fireman back to the rear of the express car next to which was the combination mail and smoking car. En route, Scotty Drew, the express messenger, was forced to join them. Fred Bartlett, mail clerk, put his head out the door to see what was going on. Black Jack shot him through the jaw with the admonition to "get your damned head back in there."

Kirchgraber, Drew and the fireman reached the rear of the express car and were commanded to uncouple it from the next coach. It had jammed and wouldn't yield. Black Jack threatened and the trainmen tried to move the coupling.

While this was going on Conductor Harrington got down his double-barreled shotgun and crawled through a small opening at the bottom of the partition between the smoking room and the mail compartment, pulling his gun after him. There he found mail clerk Bartlett suffering from a shattered jaw. Harrington went on to the front door of the wooden coach, opened it a tiny bit and peered out; there between the two cars stood Black Jack urging the engineer to make haste in uncoupling the two cars. "In the dim light," Harrington relates, "I plainly saw the robber who moved quickly about exhorting his prisoners to do his bidding. The four men were perhaps ten feet from me, the trainmen standing close together in line with the bandit."

"Hurry, damn you," came the gruff admonition of the robber. Kirchgraber and Drew were making sad headway with the couplings.

Presently Drew, who was standing back of the engineer and directly in front of the robber, moved forward.

"Here, Jose," he said, "I'll help you." The form of the robber was exposed.

"I wanted to hit the bandit in the heart. It had to be done quickly. I knew that as I opened the door my appearance would be noticed by the robber, who faced me. I aimed as best I could."

There followed an exchange of shots. Eleven buckshot entered Black Jack's arm. Black Jack's bullet just clipped Harrington's sleeve. "His buckshot jiggled my aim," said Black Jack later. "I'd have killed him if he'd waited a fraction of a second. I had a bead on his heart, but he jiggled my aim."

Black Jack fell, but managed to crawl away into the dark.

"I tried a dozen times to mount my horse and failed," Black Jack explained afterwards.

The passenger train moved on to Clayton. Next morning the crew of a freight train passing Twin Mountain found Black Jack lying near the right of way. Engineer Waller disarmed him and took him on to Trinidad, Colorado, where his shattered arm was amputated. In Trinidad, Ketchem attempted suicide by taking the bandages from his arm and tying them around his neck.

New Mexico, Arizona, and the entire West breathed more easily. The press applauded the intrepidity displayed by Conductor Harrington. Two awards of $1,000.00 each were paid to Harrington, one by the United States Government and the other by Wells Fargo and Company. Several other awards had been posted, but were never paid.

Arizona wanted to try Black Jack and made requisition on Governor Miguel A. Otero, but Governor Otero wanted him in New Mexico. In 1899 Jeremiah Leahy, a leading lawyer of Raton, New Mexico, was District Attorney for the Fourth Judicial District of New Mexico which included Union County where the three train holdups had been committed.

That same year William J. Mills was Chief Justice of New Mexico and Union County was in the judicial district over which he presided. Black Jack had been kept in the penitentiary at Santa Fe as a precaution, since there were many rumors of jail delivery by his gangs. In the late fall of 1899 he was taken from Santa Fe to Clayton under heavy guard to stand trial. Great interest in the trial drew reporters and other visitors to the little cow town.

Alighting from the train at Clayton, Black Jack looked about him. "Say," he said to one of the guards, pointing to a frame building on the main street, "that's where Charlie Meridith had his saloon, I used to play poker and buck monte in there. Frank Martinez was agreeable-like to play with, though Sam could beat him any time dealin' monte. I used to keep my rifle in the back room at Charlie's when I was up from Roswell with the trail herd in 1891. Give me that old gun now, and a little start. With one arm gone, I'd get away."

"This is right smart pleasant quarters," he said on entering the jail, "but I'd a heap rather be out on the Perico eatin' dinner at the chuck wagon along with them Jingle-bob rowdies of Phelps's, White's and Cap Day's and Jim Kinkle's bowlegged wild bunch from the Pecos Valley. We sure had good times in this burg durin' trail days."

April 23, 1901, Black Jack was again brought from Santa Fe, this time to be hung at Clayton. Persistent rumors of interference by his old gang caused Governor Otero to send Captain Fort to Clayton to take charge of the execution. Fort was a well-known lawyer of Las Vegas. On the morning of April 26, 1901, Black Jack was to be hung, but a spurious telegram purporting to be from Governor Otero delayed action until twelve minutes past one that afternoon, when Ketchem was escorted from jail to the scaffold by Sheriff Garcia and several guards and deputies. He waived permission to address the crowd. He stood erect, left hand chained to his side. His head was uncovered. Deliberately he took his place on the trap, looked downward to see if he was standing in the proper place. The guards bound his legs. The hangman's noose was drawn down and placed about his neck. Black Jack moved his head from side to side assisting in its proper adjustment. The black cap was then pulled down over his head and tied. Sheriff Garcia picked up a hatchet. "Are you ready?" he asked.

"Ready. Let her go," Black Jack said cheerfully.

The ax fell, severing the rope that held the trap door. Black Jack's body shot downward, descended two or three feet, paused, then dropped to the ground. The noose instead of merely breaking Black Jack's neck, had decapitated him.

Two hours afterward a spring wagon drawn by one horse carried the body out of the village to the place it was to be buried. The head had been restored to its body and the pine coffin was lowered into an unmarked grave. But later a row of stones was placed around it.

In 1933 the body was disinterred and removed from its lonely location to the Clayton Cemetery where it has been marked with a monument and identifying inscription. After thirty-two years in its grave, the remains were well preserved. The jet black hair and mustache had turned to maroon red, the black suit was reddish gray, a pair of slippers disclosed that he had not been buried in his boots as had been thought. Over the stump of his right arm his coat sleeve was still neatly folded.

Mr. Albert W. Thompson, an old timer at Clayton and from whose booklet, "The Story of Early Clayton, New Mexico," much of this story had been selected, has gone to a great deal of trouble in tracing out the end of each member of Black Jack's gang. I am copying his tabulation below. Thomas E. Ketchem, leader, hanged at Clayton, New Mexico, April 26, 1901.

Sam Ketchem died in the penitentiary, Santa Fe, July 24, 1899, from wounds received while resisting arrest.

Will Carver, alias G. W. Franks, shot in Sonora, Texas.

Dave Atkins, reported to have been arrested in Wyoming and in 1899 taken to Texas on murder charge.

Red Pipkin killed in a saloon, Silver City, New Mexico.

Jack Rollins, said to have left his sordid companions, and betaken himself to Texas where all trace of him was lost.

Bob Hayes, shot and killed, Deer Creek, Pleyer Valley, New Mexico. Buried at Separ.

Ed Bullin, shot near Steins Pass, New Mexico, December 1897 while attempting to rob a train.

William Walters, alias Broncho Bill, captured in Socorro and tried for murder. Found guilty. Sentenced May 23, 1899, to New Mexico penitentiary for life. Pardoned 1917. Not long after fell from a windmill tower, southern New Mexico, and was killed.

Ezra Lay, better known as McGinnis, tried for murder in Raton and sentenced to penitentiary for life. Discharged 1906.

The Hanging of Black Jack Ketchum, Clayton, NM, photograph by W.A. White, 1901, Courtesy Palace of the Governors (MNM/DCA #128886)

Murders in Early Clayton

by
D. D. Sharp

"Like all settlements of the far west in early times, Clayton was not exempt from shootings and needless murders. Most of the murders were committed by so-called bad men, gamblers, and saloon habitues while under the influence of liquor. Cowboys riding to town from round-ups, cow camps and cattle trail wagons, usually indulged in drinking, bucking monte, faro, roulette and other games of chance, which had their tempting places in saloons of the town. The cowboys who in scores rode into Clayton in the 1890's and 1900's did on the whole little damage to themselves or to the others. Their departure from the village after a few hours' recreation was usually proclaimed by wild coyote-like yells and generous volleys from their guns, but so far as I can recall, few men were injured in these frolics. Quiet soon followed the din raised by the riders of the range."

Sheepherders who visited Clayton in early times were

almost exclusively Spanish-Americans, commonly referred to as Mexicans. With several months wage to his credit, upon arrival in town from sheep camp, the herder cashed his checks, proceeded at once to a saloon, took a few drinks of *agua-diente*, and was soon in a blissful state of serenity. This condition was accompanied with a spirit of reckless generosity, which was hard for the bystander to escape.

"The Mexican game of 'monte' was the sheepherder's passion. Monte was played with cards whose faces were different from common playing cards; a queen in the monte deck was represented by a woman on horseback. The ace of clubs by an impersonation of a club, which looked like the 'big stick' so often pictured in the Theodore Roosevelt days. Monte cards were made in New York and sold by the Dougherty Company, and though they were in general used at the gambling tables in Clayton forty years ago, I have not seen a deck of them for years.

"It is needless to say that, after a night in the saloons, the tipsy herder quickly got rid of his money and, sobering up after a few days in town, returned to his pastoral duties, for which he was paid $14.00 to $16.00 per month."

Some of the killings Mr. Thompson records of this early time are as follows:

"One of the first killings was that of 'Red' (name unknown), bartender in Charlie Meridith's saloon, which stood on the site of the present gas company office. The shooting of a cowboy, Mike Beals, in a small barber shop on the lot now occupied by the Corich pool hall. In 1891 a young man was shot in the dining room of the Clayton House because of jealousy over a waitress. Louis Finger, a resident of the Tramperos country, fell from his wagon and was killed while descending a hill. Carl Gilz, a prominent rancher of the Pasamonte country was killed in front of the present Eklund Hotel, by a bullet intended for someone else."

Mr. Thompson records the murder of two Chinese laundry-men as follows. "A most revolting double murder was committed in Clayton about 1896 when two hardworking Chinese laundry-men were slain in the story and a half house which occupied the site directly opposite (south) of the present Baptist Church. The two foreigners were peaceable, industrious fellows, and extremely popular in the little community. The following is a report of the affair as published in the Denver Republican:

"'A bloody hatchet, red to the end of the handle, a railway coupling pin on which was also blood, two Chinamen, one with half the top of his head cut off, leaning in a recumbent position against a table, and the other, in a room adjoining, on the floor lying in a pool of his own blood, with three gashes in his neck and the left side of his head beaten to a jelly, was a discovery made this morning by a patron of the laundry in which the two Mongolians lived and worked. A more brutal and revolting murder was perhaps never committed and the town is tonight shocked over the affair, the solution of which may remain for some time a mystery.

"'This morning about ten o'clock, John Spring, proprietor of the Clayton House, had occasion to visit the laundry, a story and a half frame building with three rooms below and an attic above. He opened the door of the largest of the lower rooms and lying in front of him, bathed in a pool of blood, lay one of the victims of last night's murder. Spring quickly announced his discovery and a crowd was soon surrounding the home of the unfortunate Chinamen.

"'On entering the house the first body was found on its face near the door with a gash on the head and three small wounds from a knife on the neck. Passing on to the kitchen the dead man's companion, Lee Hop, was discovered in a most ghastly position, resting against a box which served as a table. On this box were a hatchet and small knife, both covered with blood. Hop's head was literally smashed to a jelly. Both men were dressed in overalls and rough shirts and were without shoes or stockings, which pointed to the fact that they were about retiring when the murders were committed.

"'The pockets of the murdered man in the kitchen were turned inside out, but on the person of the first discovered victim, eight dollars were found in a small pocketbook in his overalls. Tonight the country is being searched and parties on horseback are riding far and near, trying to get track of the assailants. A reward of $500.00 was quickly raised this morning by citizens of Clayton, and Governor Thornton has been wired asking him to offer a like amount for the apprehension of the assassins.'"

For a day or two after the discovery of the murder no clues were found. Mr. Thompson was a member of the coroner's jury. After a day or two of investigation the jury found evidence pointing to a Mexican who was working as a kitchen hand in the home of John C. Hill.

Antonio Lenta, this young man, said that it had been planned to rob the Chinamen who were supposed to have a considerable amount of money hidden around the place. Murder had not been intended. About midnight Lenta, who was intimate with the Chinamen's quarters and who had been befriended by them, knocked on the door and was admitted with his five companions. Lenta disappeared from Clayton but the other four were tried, convicted and sentenced to the penitentiary at Santa Fe, and later pardoned. . . .

Excerpts from Albert W. Thompson's "Early Clayton, New Mexico"—published by the Clayton News in 1932.

Tom Tobin

by
Helen S. Speaker

om Tobin, one of the last of the famous trappers, hunters, and Indian fighters to cross the dark river, flourished in the early days, when the Rocky Mountains were a veritable "terra incognita" to nearly all, excepting the hardy employees of the several fur companies and the limited number of United States troops stationed in their remote wilds.

Tom was an Irishman, quick tempered, and a dead shot with either rifle, revolver, or the formidable bowie-knife. He would fight at the drop of the hat, but no man ever went away from his cabin hungry, if he had a crust of bread to divide; or penniless, if there was anything remaining in his purse.

He, like Kit Carson, was rather under the average stature, red-faced, and lacking much of being an Adonis, but whole-souled and as quick in his movements as an antelope.

Tobin played an important role in avenging the death of

the Americans killed in the Taos massacre, at the storming of the Indian pueblo, but his greatest achievement was the ending of the noted bandit Espinosa's life, who, at the height of his career of blood, was the terror of the whole mountain region.

At the time of the acquisition of New Mexico by the United States, Espinosa, who was a Mexican, owning vast herds of cattle and sheep, resided upon his ancestral hacienda in a sort of barbaric luxury, with a host of semi-serfs, known as Peons, to do his bidding, as did the other "Muy Ricos," the "Dons," so called, of his class of natives. These self-styled aristocrats of the wild country all boasted of their Castilian blue blood, claiming descent from the nobles of Cortez's army, but the fact is, however, with rare exceptions, that their male ancestors, the rank and file of that army, intermarried with the Aztec women and they were really only a mixture of Indian and Spanish.

It so happened that Espinosa met an adventurous American, who, with hundreds of others, had been attached to the "Army of Occupation" in the Mexican War, or had emigrated from the States to seek their fortunes in the newly acquired and much over-rated territory.

The Mexican Don and the American became fast friends, the latter making his home with his newly found acquaintance at the beautiful ranch in the mountains, where they played the role of a modern Damon and Pythias.

Now with Don Espinosa lived his sister, a dark-eyed, bewitchingly beautiful girl about seventeen years old, with whom the susceptible American fell deeply in love, and his affection was reciprocated by the maiden, with a fervor of which only the women of the race from which she sprang are capable.

The fascinating American had brought with him from his home in one of the New England states a large amount of money, for his parents were rich, and spared no indulgence to their only son. He very soon unwisely made Espinosa his confidant, and told him of the wealth he possessed.

One night after the American had retired to his chamber adjoining that of his host, he was surprised, shortly after he had gone to bed, by discovering a man standing over him whose hand had already grasped the buckskin bag under his pillow which contained a considerable portion of his gold and silver. He sprang from his couch and fired his pistol at random in the darkness at the would-be robber.

Espinosa, for it was he, was wounded slightly, and, being either enraged or frightened, he stabbed with his keen-pointed stiletto, which all Mexicans then carried, the young man whom he had invited to become his guest, and the blade entered the American's heart, killing him instantly.

The report of the pistol awakened the other members of the household, who came rushing into the room just as the victim was breathing his last. Among them was the sister of the murderer who, throwing herself on the body of her dead lover, poured forth the most bitter curses upon her brother.

Espinosa, realizing the terrible position in which he had placed himself, then and there determined to become an outlaw, as he could frame no excuse for his wicked deed. He therefore hid himself at once in the mountains, carrying with him, of course, the sack containing the murdered American's money.

Some time necessarily passed before he could get together a sufficient number of cut-throats and renegades from justice to enable him wholly to defy the authorities; but at last he succeeded in rallying a strong force to his standard of blood, and became the terror of the whole region, equaling in boldness and audacity the terrible Joaquin, of California notoriety in after years.

His headquarters were in the almost impregnable fastnesses of the Sangre de Cristo Mountains, from which he made his invariably successful raids into the rich valleys below. There was nothing too bloody for him to shrink from; he robbed indiscriminately the overland coaches to Santa Fe, the freight caravans of the traders and government, the ranches of the Mexicans, or stole from the poorer classes, without any compunction. He ran off horses, cattle, sheep—in fact, anything that he could utilize. If murder was necessary to the completion of his work, he never for a moment hesitated. Kidnapping, too, was a favorite pastime; but he rarely carried away to his rendezvous any other than the most beautiful of the New Mexican young girls, whom he held in his mountain den until they were ransomed, or subjected to a fate more terrible.

In 1864 the bandit, after nearly ten years of unparalleled outlawry, was killed by Tobin. Tom had been on his trail for some time, and at last tracked him to a temporary camp in the foothills, which he accidentally discovered in a grove of cottonwoods by the smoke of the little camp-fire as it curled in light wreaths above the trees.

Tobin knew that at the time there was but one of Espinosa's followers with him, as he had watched them both for some days, waiting for an opportunity to get the drop on them. To capture the pair of outlaws alive never entered his thoughts; he was as cautious as brave, and to get them dead was much safer and easier; so he crept up to the grove on his belly, Indian fashion, and lying behind the cover of a friendly log, waited until the noted desperado stood up, when he pulled the trigger of his never-erring rifle, and Espinosa fell dead. A second shot quickly disposed of his companion, and the old Trapper's mission was accomplished.

To be able to claim the reward offered by the authorities, Tom had to prove, beyond the possibility of a doubt, that those whom he had killed were the dreaded bandit and one of his gang.

He thought it best to cut off their heads, which he deliberately did, and packing them on his mule in a gunny-sack, he brought them into old Fort Massachusetts, where they were speedily recognized.

Information from "The Old Santa Fe Trail," Col. Henry Inman, pp. 358-361.

Uncle Dick Wooton
"Uncle Dick's"
Toll-Road on Raton Pass

by
Helen S. Speaker

The Raton Pass, through which the Old Santa Fe Trail ran, was a relatively fair mountain road, but originally it was almost impossible for anything in the shape of a wheeled vehicle to get over the narrow rock-ribbed barrier; saddle horses and pack-mules could, however, make the trip without much difficulty. It was the natural highway to southeastern Colorado and northeastern New Mexico, but the overland coaches could not get to Trinidad by the shortest route, and as the caravans also desired to make the same line, it occurred to Uncle Dick that he would undertake to hew out a road through the pass, which, barring grades, should be as good as the average turnpike. He could see money in it for him, as he expected to charge toll, keeping the road in repair at his own expense, and he succeeded in procuring from the legislatures of Colorado and New Mexico charters covering the rights and privileges which he demanded for his project.

In the spring of 1866, Uncle Dick took up his abode on the top of the mountains, built his home, and lived there until two years ago, when he died at a very ripe old age.

The old trapper had imposed on himself anything but an easy task in constructing his toll-road. There were great hillsides to cut out, immense ledges of rock to blast, bridges to build by the dozen, and huge trees to fell, besides long lines of difficult grading to engineer.

Eventually Uncle Dick's road was a fact, but when it was completed, how to make it pay was a question that seriously disturbed his mind. The method he employed to solve the problem I will quote in his own words: "Such a thing as a toll-road was unknown in the country at that time. People who had come from the States understood, of course, that the object of building a turnpike was to enable the owner to collect toll from those who traveled over it, but I had to deal with a great many people who seemed to think that they should be as free to travel over my well-graded and bridged roadway as they were to follow an ordinary cow path.

I may say that I had five classes of patrons to do business with. There was the stage company and its employees, the freighters, the military authorities, who marched troops and transported supplies over the road, the Mexicans, and the Indians.

With the stage company, the military authorities, and the American freighters I had no trouble. With the Indians, when a band came through now and then, I didn't care to have any controversy about so small a matter as a few dollars toll! Whenever they came along, the toll-gate went up, and any other little thing I could do to hurry them on was done promptly and cheerfully. While the Indians didn't understand anything about the system of collecting tolls, they seemed to recognize the fact that I had a right to control the road, and they would generally ride up to the gate and ask the permission to go through. Once in a while the chief of a band would think compensation for the privilege of going through in order, and would make me a present of a buckskin or something of that sort.

My Mexican patrons were the hardest to get along with. Paying for the privilege of traveling over any road was something they were totally unused to, and they did not take to it kindly. They were pleased with my road and liked to travel over it, until they came to the toll-gate. This they seemed to look upon as an obstruction that no man had a right to place in the way of a free-born native of the mountain region. They appeared to regard the toll-gate as a new scheme for holding up travelers for the purpose of robbery, and many of them evidently thought me a kind of freebooter who ought to be suppressed by law.

Holding these views, when I asked them for a certain amount of money before raising the toll-gate, they naturally differed with me very frequently about the propriety of complying with the request.

In other words, there would be at such times probably an honest difference of opinion between the man who kept the toll-gate and the man who wanted to get through it. Anyhow, there was a difference, and such differences had to be adjusted. Sometimes I did it through diplomacy, and sometimes I did it with a club. It was always settled one way, however, and that was in accordance with the toll schedule, so that I could never have been charged with unjust discrimination of rates.

Soon after the road was opened a company composed of Californians and Mexicans, commanded by a Captain Haley, passed Uncle Dick's toll-gate and house, escorting a large caravan of about a hundred and fifty wagons. While they stopped there, a noncommissioned officer of the party was brutally murdered by three soldiers, and Uncle Dick came very near being a witness to the atrocious deed.

The murdered man was a Mexican, and his slayers were Mexicans too. The trouble originated at Las Vegas, where the privates had been bound and gagged, by order of the corporal, for creating a disturbance at a fandango the evening before.

The name of the corporal was Juan Torres, and he came down to Uncle Dick's one evening while the command was encamped on the top mountain, accompanied by the three privates, who had already plotted to kill him, though he had not the slightest suspicion of it.

Uncle Dick, in telling the story, said: "They left at an early hour, going in an opposite direction from their camp, and I closed my doors soon after for the night. They had not been gone more than half an hour, when I heard them talking not far from my house, and a few seconds later I heard the half-suppressed cry of a man who has received his death-blow.

I had gone to bed, and lay for a minute or two thinking whether I should get up and go to the rescue or insure my own safety by remaining where I was.

A little reflection convinced me that the murderers were undoubtedly watching my house to prevent any interference with the carrying out of their plot, and that if I ventured out I should only endanger my own life, while there was scarcely a possibility of my being able to save the life of the man who had been assailed.

In the morning when I got up, I found the dead body of the corporal stretched across Raton Creek, not more than a hundred yards from my house.

As I surmised, he had been struck with a heavy club or stone and it was at that time that I heard his cry. After that his brains had been beaten out, and the body left where I found it.

I at once notified Captain Haley of the occurrence, and identified the men who had been in company with the corporal, and who were undoubtedly his murderers.

They were taken into custody, and made a confession, in which they stated that one of their number had stood at my door on the night of the murder to shoot me if I had ventured out to assist the corporal. Two of the scoundrels were hung afterward at Las Vegas, and the third sent to prison for life.

The corporal was buried near where the soldiers were encamped and it is his lonely grave which frequently attracts the attention of the passengers on the Atchison, Topeka, and the Santa Fe trains, just before the Raton tunnel is reached, as they travel southward.

Information from "The Old Santa Fe Trail," by Col. Henry Inman, pages 347-351.

Uncle Dick Wooton
The Daylight Stage-Coach
Robbery

by
Helen S. Speaker

In 1866-67 the Indians broke out, infesting all the most prominent points of the Old Santa Fe Trail, and watching for an opportunity to rob and murder, so that the government freight caravans and the stages had to be escorted by detachments of troops. Fort Larned was the western limit where these escorts joined the outfits going over into New Mexico.

There were other dangers attending the passage of the Trail to travelers by the stage besides the attacks of the savages. These were the so-called road agents—masked robbers who regarded life as of little worth in the accomplishment of their nefarious purposes. Particularly were they common after the mines of New Mexico began to be operated by Americans. The object of the bandits was generally the strong box of the express company, which contained money and other valuables. They did not, of course, hesitate to take what ready cash and jewelry the passengers might happen to have upon their persons, and frequently their hauls amounted to large sums.

When the coaches began to travel over Uncle Dick's toll-road, his house was made a station, and he had many stage stories. He said:

"Tavern-keepers in those days couldn't choose their guests and we entertained them just as they came along. The knights of the road would come by now and then, order a meal, eat it hurriedly, pay for it, and move on to where they had arranged to hold up a stage that night. Sometimes they did not wait for it to get dark, but halted the stage, went through the treasure box in broad daylight, and then ordered the driver to move on in one direction while they went off in another.

"One of the most daring and successful stage robberies that I remember was perpetrated by two men, when the east-bound coach was coming up on the south side of the Raton Mountains, one day about ten o'clock in the forenoon.

"On the morning of the same day, a little after sunrise, two rather genteel-looking fellows, mounted on fine horses, rode up to my house and ordered breakfast. Being informed that breakfast would be ready in a few minutes, they dismounted, hitched their horses near the door, and came into the house.

"I knew then, just as well as I do now, they were robbers, but I had no warrant for their arrest, and I should have hesitated about serving it if I had because they looked like very unpleasant men to transact that kind of business with.

"Each of them had four pistols sticking in his belt and a repeating rifle strapped on to his saddle. When they dismounted, they left their rifles with the horses, but walked into the house and sat down at the table, without laying aside the arsenal which they carried in their belts.

"They had little to say while eating, but were courteous

in their behavior, and very polite to the waiters. When they had finished breakfast, they paid their bills, and rode leisurely up the mountain.

"It did not occur to me that they would take chances on stopping the stage in daylight, or I should have sent someone to meet the incoming coach, which I knew would be along shortly, to warn the driver and passengers to be on the lookout for robbers.

"It turned out, however, that a daylight robbery was just what they had in mind, and they had a success of it.

"About halfway down the New Mexico side of the mountain, where the canyon is very narrow, and was then heavily wooded on either side, the robbers stopped and waited for the coach. It came lumbering along by and by, neither the driver nor the passengers dreaming of a hold-up.

"The first intimation they had of such a thing was when they saw two men step into the road, one on each side of the stage, each of them holding two cocked revolvers, one of which was brought to bear on the passengers and the other on the driver, who were politely but very positively told that they must throw up their hands without any unnecessary delay, and the stage came to a standstill.

"There were four passengers in the coach, all men, but their hands went up at the same instant that the driver dropped his reins and struck an attitude that suited the robbers.

"Then, while one of the men stood guard, the other stepped up to the stage and ordered the treasure box thrown off. This demand was complied with, and the box was broken and rifled of its contents, which fortunately were not of very great value.

"The passengers were compelled to hand out their watches and other jewelry, as well as what money they had in their pockets, and then the driver was directed to move up the road. In a minute after this the robbers had disappeared with their booty, and that was the last seen of them by that particular coach-load of passengers.

"The men who planned and executed that robbery were two cool, level-headed, and daring scoundrels, known as 'Chuckle-luck' and 'Magpie.' They were killed soon after this occurrence by a member of their own band, whose name was Seward. A reward of a thousand dollars had been offered for their capture, and this tempted Seward to kill them one night when they were asleep in camp.

"He then secured a wagon, into which he loaded the dead robbers, and hauled them to Cimarron City where he turned them over to the authorities and received his reward."

Information from "The Old Santa Fe Trail," Col. Henry Inman, pp. 351-354.

Biography of Guadalupe Lupita Gallegos

by
Bright Lynn

For many years Mr. and Mrs. Gallegos ran a small store at San Ilario. Their store stood close to the main road and almost every traveler who passed stopped in to buy something and to pass the time of day. One day Mrs. Gallegos returned to the store from a visit with one of her neighbors. Her husband was in the front of the store talking to an American cowboy in Spanish. When her husband saw her come in he called to her and said, "Lupita, I want you to meet a friend of mine. This is Billy the Kid."

Mrs. Gallegos says that she had always been a brave woman but when she found herself actually face to face with Billy the Kid she almost fainted. The Kid seemed to be in a talkative mood for he started telling Mrs. Gallegos about his adventures and for emphasis he drew his gun and shot a couple of holes in the ceiling. The neighbors all came running to find out what all the shooting was about but upon finding it was Billy the Kid they all started running the other way.

The next time Mrs. Gallegos saw Billy the Kid she was in the store by herself. He came in, bought some things, and left. Mrs. Gallegos says that he was always very courteous and that he was, in her opinion, a real gentleman.

Mrs. Gallegos knew Sostenes, a member of Billy's gang, very well. His parents were good people and lived in Los Alamos. As far as she knew Sostenes was always a good boy and it was hard for her to believe that he would turn outlaw. When he did turn, however, he turned with a vengeance. Mrs. Gallegos was acquainted with an old man who was half blind and he told her the following incident:

One day while he was traveling on his burro, Billy the Kid and Sostenes rode up. Sostenes said, "Billy, let's kill this old blind man just to see how old blind men die."

"Let him alone," commanded Billy. "He's doing us no harm." The old man thought his day had come, and when Billy prevented Sostenes from killing him the Kid became the old man's hero.

Mrs. Gallegos knew Silva, the notorious bandit, very well indeed, for he worked for her husband one year carrying trading stuff from Las Vegas to Santa Fe. She says that he was considered a respectable citizen then. She describes him as tall and handsome, rather fair of complexion and light of hair. Years later when Mrs. Gallegos was living at Los Alamos she and the neighbors used to see a mysterious person dressed in a black cap and cape with a black cloth over his face walking by the side of the river. Everyone suspected it was Silva and afterwards they discovered it was he.

Silva had his headquarters at the home of a woman named Cruz, a respectable lady on the surface, who used to come often to Mrs. Gallegos's house to visit. Of course no one knew at the time that her home was being used as a headquarters of such a notorious band of outlaws as the Silva gang.

Source of Information: Mrs. Guadalupe Gallegos. Corrected copy sent in Nov. 8, 1938.

Vicente Silva and His Gang

by
Isidora C. de Baca

My grandfather, Titibio C. de Baca, has often told me of the crimes of the notorious Silva gang, one of the most vicious groups of lawbreakers in the Southwest and certainly the most depraved band of cutthroats that ever infested Las Vegas. My grandfather's cousin, Manuel C. de Baca, has published an account of Silva's gang.

My maternal grandfather has also told me stories of the crimes for which the gang was responsible. He said it was terrifying to go out in the morning and see hanging on trees the night's victims of Silva's bandits.

Vicente Silva was born in Bernalillo County, New Mexico, in 1845. His parents were poor but respectable, but they were unable to send their son to school. From his childhood he had a very innocent, pleasant expression, which he kept throughout his life, blinding many people as to his true character.

Silva came to Las Vegas around 1880 and lived there until 1895. He married Dona Telesfora de Sandoval.

He opened a saloon and afterwards established a pool hall. Having been in that business for two years he had made a great number of friends in Las Vegas and nearby places. These men spent their time in Silva's gambling place; they were called *vagas* (lazy loungers) by hardworking citizens.

By the end of 1892, Silva had organized a society of bandits, which he called *La Sociedad de Bandidos de Nuevo Mexico*. There were thirty members.

The hiding place which Silva operated, largely under police protection, was at Ojo del Monte Largo in the mountains of Santa Fe County. It was used for the hiding of stolen cattle and horses. The place was discovered by Refujio Esquibel, who found there a number of his missing horses. He was about to bring suit against Silva, but Silva made his escape as soon as he found his retreat was known.

Believing that one of his gang had betrayed him, Silva called a meeting of all his men. On the night of October 22, 1892, nonmembers of the society who were drinking in the canteen were amazed to hear Silva announce that the canteen was to be closed for the night; amazed because the place was kept open day and night.

Everybody left the saloon. Members of the gang went around Moreno Street in West Las Vegas, entering the saloon through the back entrance. Among them was Patricio Maes, whom Silva suspected of being the traitor. The bandits surrounded Maes and accused him of treachery. He protested his innocence and promised to prove that he was blameless. Silva, however, told his men they could not afford to take the risk of letting an enemy live; Maes must be got rid of.

They decided to hang him. He was taken to the bridge

over the Gallinas River and was prepared for execution. When he knew it was his last moment he asked pardon of God. The bandits drew the rope taut and, when they were sure Maes was dead, disappeared.

The following morning Silva gave the alarm that a dead body was suspended from the bridge, commenting loudly upon the boldness with which the crime had been committed and assuring his aid in bringing the murderer to justice.

Now that they felt safe from treason within their ranks, the gang grew bolder. Their depredations increased both in number and in daring as time went on.

Silva's most horrible crime, and the one which meant his own undoing, was the stabbing of his wife, Telesfora S. de Silva. Telling her that he wanted her to join him at his ranch near Los Alamos he succeeded in getting her to leave Las Vegas with him. When they arrived at the ranch he asked her for some money for a trip to Taos. Mrs. Silva had very little money and felt she should keep it to care for her own needs; but she reluctantly gave it to her husband. Then he questioned her about her jewels. This time she rebelled, telling him she suspected he wanted her jewels to give to his mistress. Silva became enraged, struck her, told her she was going to pay for the harm she had done, accused her of betraying the gang's secrets, and, in high excitement and frenzy, pulled a dagger from his belt and stabbed her.

When his men arrived he ordered them to wrap the body of Mrs. Silva in some rags and take her to a place he had prepared for her burial. The men silently bore out the body, put it in the ground, and shoveled dirt over it. Then they returned to the house. Silva's face was still red with anger. Fearing that they would in time meet the same fate, the men interchanged meaningful looks. The bravest of them, Antonio Jose Valdez, walked on the left side of the captain and suddenly shot him in the left temple.

Silva fell, mortally wounded. The men waited only to bury him by the side of his wife and dispersed to their homes in Las Vegas and Los Alamos.

The murders were discovered and the gang was finally broken up.

Source of Information: Baca, Manuel C. de, "The History of Vicente Silva and His Forty Bandits," Spanish-American Publishing Co., Las Vegas, N. M., 97 pp., 75¢. In Spanish.

VICENTE SILVA.

Vicente Silva in an 1896 illustration, Courtesy Palace of the Governors
(MNM/DCA #143691)

Las Vegas

by
Malaquinas Baca

On or about the 26th day of the month of May, 1893, the city of Las Vegas was shocked when hearing of the most atrocious crime committed within 6 or 8 miles east of town, at the commonly called Alto Colorado, on the road leading to the "Cuesta de Olgin" (Olgin Hill).

Benigno Martinez, sheep owner, and Juan Gallegos, the shepherd of the flock, two of the most inoffensive and law abiding citizens of Begaso, San Miguel County, had been brutally murdered; both men were that day herding the flock of sheep and lambs numbering about 2500 head, which Martinez owned and had been able to own through hard labor, when the black hand of a brutal and inhuman assassin by the name of Cicilio Lucero in cold blood shot and brutally murdered the two men at the sheep camp.

Lucero the assassin was married, and was the cousin of

Martinez the sheep owner; the said Lucero and his wife were living at the house of Martinez, and as such cousin, was granted many favors by the deceased, treating him and his wife with all due consideration, as a relative and friend.

The day before committing the crime, Lucero had been at a nearby Railroad station called Watrous, about 15 miles from the place of the crime, and had made all possible efforts to contract for the sale of a flock of 2500 head of sheep and lambs, but whether he had been able to make the deal, no one seemed to know.

The next day on or about sunset, he went to the sheep camp, and without any motive or reason he deliberately shot his cousin Martinez dead, and then he killed Gallegos the shepherd; not satisfied with firing into them the bullets that had ended their lives, he crushed the head of each of his victims so badly that their brains could be seen; the rifle with which he killed them was found a few days afterwards at his house, and the butt of the rifle had blood and brains on it, which indicated he had used the rifle in crushing their heads.

To further increase the sadness of such a horrible and brutal crime, committed in cold blood, he took a rope, tied the rope to the neck of one camp burro and tied both feet of the victim, and doing the same thing to the other victim whereby both bodies were dragged by the burros all night until the next morning when they were discovered near a lake where the burros had gone to water.

A man by the name of Juan Aragon was passing by towards Las Vegas, saw the flock of sheep and no herder, but noticed that the burros were dragging something; he went close to where they were, and to his horror found the horrible crime that had been committed. He immediately hurried to Las Vegas and notified the sheriff (who at that time was Don Lorenzo Lopez) of the crime he had discovered.

The sheriff and a great crowd immediately went to where

the bodies had been seen, and there, to their amazement found the unrecognizable bodies of the two victims, untied them from the burrows, took them to the city, where a coroner Jury viewed the bodies and held a postmortem examination and preliminary investigation; and there the identity of the victims, who were full of blood and mud, through letters in their pockets were recognized as those above mentioned.

Excitement was general in town, and hundreds of people went to view the bodies; who upon seeing them, bloody, muddy, and disfigured, swore vengeance if the murderer should be caught.

When the preliminary examination was held according to law, it was clearly ascertained that Cicilio Lucero the cousin was the murderer; he was arrested at his house, where the rifle used in the double slaying was found; he was placed in the county jail located in West Las Vegas; the next day at 2 o'clock P.M., he was taken before Judge Wooster of East Las Vegas, and the preliminary was postponed until 7 o'clock P.M. For some reason or other the hearing was not held at the set hour. At about 10 o'clock P.M. of the same day, an infuriated crowd of citizens, numbering about 500, gathered in the neighborhood of the City Jail, and then and there battered the City Jail door, took Lucero out and lynched him from a telegraph post, leaving him hanging till next day at sunrise, as an example to others who dared to commit such brutal crimes.

Biography: Salome Garcia

by
Carrie L. Hodges

A native-born citizen of New Mexico, and one who always had the interest and welfare of his state at heart, was Salome Garcia, one of Union County's most prominent citizens.

Mr. Garcia was born at Los Alamos, San Miguel County, New Mexico, in 1859. He chose to follow the life of a rancher and his ranch was stocked with well-kept herds of both cattle and sheep. He followed this chosen profession until the year 1900, when he was elected to the office of Sheriff of Union County from 1900 to 1901.

During the year 1901, it was his painful duty to perform the task of executioner at the hanging of "Black Jack" Thomas E. Ketchem, one of New Mexico's most notorious outlaws, on April 26, 1901. It was Sheriff Garcia's axe that fell upon the rope that held up the trapdoor upon which "Black Jack" stood, the result of which sent this criminal to meet his final judgment.

After successfully filling the position of Sheriff, Mr. Garcia retired to his ranch home near Pasamonte, just below the H.T. Ranch, where the reminder of his days were spent, and where he passed away August, 1926.

Mr. Fructuoso Garcia, son of Salome Garcia, relates this incident in the early life of his father:

When Mr. Garcia was a small lad of about ten years, there came to camp, just across the Creek from his father's home, a band of Navajo Indians. At this time the Indians were just at the point of becoming civilized, and yet held a grudge against the Spanish people, and it took only an imaginary gesture or word to put them on the "warpath."

All was peace and quiet during the night, and when morning came the Chief and other men-folk of the band left camp, leaving behind the Squaws and children. An Indian boy of about the same age as Mr. Garcia came down to the creek, and upon seeing the Spanish boy playing on the opposite shore, decided to join him. They played happily for awhile but alas, the wrestling sport seized them, and in their rough and tumble play, the Spanish boy (Salome Garcia) accidentally threw the Indian boy, at which he ran home, screaming and gesticulating. And alas, again, for Salome Garcia. When the Chief returned to camp and heard how the boy of his race had been "abused," he immediately held council with the elder Garcia and told him the only way the injustice to the Indian boy could be repaired would be for the Spanish boy to allow the Indian boy to strike him across the mouth as punishment for what he had done; otherwise, there would be war between the Indians and the Spanish.

Although the supposed "injustice" was the result of play, the Garcias realized the only way out was to accept the terms of the Indians, so the Indian boy was allowed to strike him across the mouth, and all was peace again, the injustice repaired, and the Indians went their way.

Mr. Garcia relates another incident which took place one night when his father was cooking supper and making "Fried Biscuits" over the fire. He noticed his biscuits were disappearing almost as fast as he fried them. He was unable to account for this and was seeking a solution to the mystery when he noticed a fine wire hook descending through the chimney of the fireplace and manipulated so quickly and silently as to be almost unnoticeable. Quite naturally he investigated, and found an Indian perched upon the roof. It was he who was stealing the biscuits.

Mr. Garcia relates another encounter with the half civilized Indians: His father was herding some 3000 head of sheep for a rancher, when he was approached by two Navajo Indians on horseback. They demanded a sheep from him to supply themselves with meat. Mr. Garcia refused their request, trying to explain the sheep did not belong to him. The Indians did not argue the question, but began riding around him in a circle, unloosing their rawhide lariats. They then rode up to him, one on either side, and began lashing him with the lariats, the keen, strong rawhide cutting his flesh cruelly. Up and down he jumped and circled trying to escape, but to no avail. No avoiding those long, tortuous thongs, so he told them to take all the sheep they wanted. However, one animal seemed to meet their requirements, so they took just the one and went their way.

Mr. Garcia, cruelly gashed and welted, his wounds bleeding, painfully made his way to the ranch and reported the incident, and was told by his Boss to never again risk his life by refusing the Indians their request.

Such were the usual events our pioneer friends were called upon to endure, that New Mexico, today, be a habitable place for mankind.

All data furnished by courtesy of Fructuoso Garcia, Clayton, New Mexico, and Assessor of Union County, son of the late Salome Garcia; interview, October 9, 1936.

Bandits of New Mexico

by
N. Howard Thorp

Among the most interesting of the many points of historical interest in the vicinity of Las Vegas are the ranches formerly owned by Vicente Silva. These were used as hideouts for his gang, and for the many bunches of stolen cattle, horses and sheep which from time to time these outlaws accumulated.

One of the ranches, the Ojo del Monte Largo, "The Spring of the Long Thicket," lay to the west of Las Vegas, and in a very rough mountainous country, and on account of its inaccessibility was almost impervious to any surprise attack from Sheriffs or others.

The second ranch was known as Coyote; it was in Mora County east of the La Cueva ranch. Both of these figure frequently in the life of Vicente Silva and his gang of outlaws.

The difference between Pantaleon Mera—whom I have

already alluded to in a previous article—and Vicente Silva, was that Pantaleon killed principally for robbery, while Silva was a stock thief. If anyone interfered with his operations, he and his gang did not hesitate to put those who were in his way under the sod; and either by threats or terrorism, were for years in absolute control of several counties.

Vicente Silva was born in the year 1845, in Bernalillo County, New Mexico, and for many years afterwards lived in the town of Old Las Vegas where he owned a saloon, dance hall, and gambling joint, the toughest of all the tough joints of that time.

His family consisted of his wife Telesfora de Sandoval, an adopted daughter named Emma—about whom more later—and Telesfora de Sandoval's brother, Graviel Sandoval.

In the year 1892 the county of San Miguel was overrun with outlaws and the night which passed without a crime being committed was rare.

All stockmen in the counties of San Miguel, Guadalupe, Mora and Santa Fe suffered great losses. Stock was stolen, haystacks burned and miles of barbwire fences were destroyed, while anyone objecting was visited by a band of masked riders, was taken from his home and disappeared.

The head of these riders was Vicente Silva, who, not satisfied with the profits derived from his saloon and gambling house thought he would take the short cut to riches through robbery. Although there were many others in the counties above mentioned who belonged to the gang, the following men were the most active members. Julian Trujillo, Jose Chaves y Chaves, Eugenio Alarid, Martin Gonzales y Blea alias El Moro, Manuel Gonzales y Baca, Guadalupe Caballero alias El Lechuza, Dionisio Sisneros alias El Candelas, Antonio Jose Valdez alias El Patas de Mico, Ricardo Romero alias El Romo, Jose F. Montoya, Florentino Medran, Francisco Ulevare, Remijo Sandoval alias El Gavilan,

Nestor Herrera, Manuel Maldonado, Livrirado Polanes, Patrico Meas, Procopio Real, Acasio Real, Zenon Maes, Nestor Gallegos, Nicanor Gallegos, Hilario Mares, Marcos, Varela Gabriel, Pital Genvovo Avila alias El Cachumeno, Cicilio Lucero, Jesus Vialpando, Juan de Dios Tomas y Sostemo Lucero. The first three men mentioned were members of the Las Vegas police force.

This gang was always afraid of betrayal by some discontented member. The first one to be hung for imaginary treachery was Patrico Maes, who after a meeting of the gang was condemned and hung one night to the bridge crossing the river in the town of Las Vegas. The second one to be killed was not a member of the gang, he was Silva's brother-in-law, Graviel Sandoval, who knew too much and was thought to be talking concerning the gang's operations.

The next thing of moment was when Vicente Silva fell in love with a woman named Flor de la Pena, "Flower of the Rocks." As his legal wife did not take kindly to the idea, Vicente by various ruses decoyed her to the ranch called Coyote, where he proceeded to dispose of her. The adopted daughter at this time (was) placed in a school at Taos.

The next robbery was the store of an American named William Frank who lived at Los Alamos on the Mora River. Besides stealing what money he had, and provisions, they took all his accounts books and not knowing what accounts were due him, they practically broke him. Near this point of Los Alamos, the gang had another hideout, which was used for stolen stock, and to hole-up-in when things in Las Vegas got too hot.

These masked riders would often at night ride through the streets of Las Vegas or Santa Fe, terrifying the people, eventually stopping at the home of someone they wanted, who after being taken would disappear; these were usually people they were assured were interfering with their operations.

Times in San Miguel county became so terrible that at last the Citizens called a meeting, and sent a deputation to Santa Fe to confer with the Governor, who immediately offered a reward of a hundred Dollars each—dead or alive—for every member of this gang of outlaws.

One of the members, Manuel Gonzales y Baca, who for some offense was then in the Las Vegas jail, sent for a Lawyer named Manuel C. de Baca for a consultation. He offered, if guaranteed immunity from prosecution, to disclose the names of all the outlaws concerned. As additional witnesses were required, Lisandro Montoya, Manuel Maldonado and Hilario Mares gave themselves up, and with the exception of the two who left the country all were arrested, tried and sentenced to from ten years to life in the Penn.

The names of the two who escaped were Jose Chaves y Chaves and Jesus V. Vialpando, but more concerning these later. Manuel Gonzales y Baca and the other three who gave themselves up confessed to all the crimes committed by the gang and told how, when Vicente Silva killed his wife in the ranch house of Coyote he called the others in, and told them to carry the corpse over to the Campo de los Cadillos about a mile from the ranch, so named as it was an arroyo growing many cockleburs. They did as told, and broke down the bank of the arroyo to conceal evidence of the burial. Vicente followed them and when their task was completed, he took off a money belt and handed each of his men a ten dollar gold piece.

His gang was very much discontented with the way they had been treated, they doing all the dirty work, and Vicente getting all the money. As Vicente turned to put on his belt one of the men, nicknamed Patas de Rana, "Frog legs" shot him and after dividing up the money, buried him in the same arroyo as his wife.

In the meantime the two outlaws who had escaped from

Las Vegas, Jose Chaves y Chaves and Jesus Vialpando, stole a bunch of horses, taking them to the mining camp of San Pedro where they sold them. In a few days—being broke—they started towards Las Vegas, and on the road met up with a fourteen-year-old boy, who having a horse and saddle followed them. Deciding to go by Ojo la Baca "Cow Springs" when within a few miles of it they made camp and being without food they killed a steer and hung the hide on a bush. Early the following morning a man followed by a dog rode up, and recognizing the brand on the hide as his, stood by the fire and began asking questions as to why they had killed his steer. One word brought on another when both of the outlaws opened fire, killing the stranger who fell into the fire. The dog being scared by the shots ran away, but one of the men shot at and wounded him slightly. They then piled brush and wood upon the fire trying to hide all evidence of the crime. Leaving the boy, who had accompanied them, they saddled their horses and left.

The dog made his way home to the ranch and carried on at a great rate, partly on account of his wound and the fright he had received.

After the dog became normal he started back to where he had left his master, the ranch people—mounted—following.

'Tis a rough country covered with heavy brush, but in time the dog led the ranch folks to where he had last seen his master. Sniffing his way through the brush, the dog arrived where the fire had been, which disclosed nothing but a pile of burnt logs and ashes.

As they got off their horses the boy who had been left by the outlaws came out of a thicket where terrified by the happenings he had been hiding and told the story of the brutal killing and burning of the body, which later was identified by a shoe which had not been entirely consumed by the fire. The man who had been killed was Tomas Martinez, well and favorably known in Cow Springs and the surrounding country.

A posse was quickly formed, the trial of the fugitives picked up and followed into Las Vegas, where they were identified by the boy they had left behind.

As the crime had been committed in Santa Fe County they were taken there, tried and convicted on a charge of first-degree murder, and eventually hung by Sheriff Cunningham, which put an end to the notorious bandidos de Nuevo Mexico.

The End

Old Days in Las Vegas, New Mexico

by
N. Howard Thorp

Before the railroad entered Las Vegas, the Barlow and Sanderson stage line carried mail and passengers daily from Santa Fe, and was held up once or twice a week by bandits, who robbed the passengers, and cutting open the mail sacks took anything which might prove of value.

After one of these holds-ups, a clerical looking man named Parker, with a long black beard—who owned and ran a Hotel and livery stable in Las Vegas—reported that four young men—the number that robbed the stage—came to his Hotel, and on each of the robberies rented a two horse platform spring wagon and drove into the country, returning with the team in a lather and tired out. They had left his Hotel, but he was confident he could identify them. After leading a posse on a search for several days the trail was abandoned. Parker was afterwards proved the robber, and was hung.

Mr. Lute Wilcox, who in 1879 was the owner of the Las Vegas Optic, gives the following account of a little affair happening at that time.

Dutch Henry's gang of four men rode in from the Pan Handle of Texas to "get" Joe Carson, at that time the town Marshall of Las Vegas, against whom they held an old grudge dating back to a misunderstanding they had with him in Ft. Worth Texas. This gang was composed of Tom or "Dutch" Henry, John Dorsey, Jim West, and Bill Randall. They took possession of a cabin in the hills near Mora, county seat of Mora county, and lived off the country. They once entered the old town of Las Vegas, and drove off with a new buggy and team of horses, leaving word that if the owner wanted them he could come and get them. This sort of thing continued for some time, but no one seemed anxious to go after the gang.

One night when they entered Las Vegas, Joe Carson told them to lay aside their guns in accordance with the custom of those times. They replied they could manage their affairs and needed no advice.

That night Joe went to George Close's dance hall to enforce the order.

The gang was dancing with the fairies, and there opened up a lot of gunplay. As Lute tells the story, he was working in his office getting out copy for the Optic when Mrs. Carson stuck her head into his office and cried, "I believe Joe has been killed, as I heard a lot of shooting in Close's dance hall, and I know Joe went there to arrest those Texicans."

We rushed out to the rear of the dance hall, and stumbled over something. I struck a match and Mrs. Carson fell upon the form of her husband.

A large crowd had assembled in the open space between the Close dance hall and Mrs. McDonald's restaurant. We packed Joe into Dr. Severson's drug store but the man was dead, of course, with so many shots in him. The Mrs. was hysterical, and carried on frantically, but eloped a few weeks later with the Justice of the Peace, Woodo Brown, to the Indian Territory.

Mysterious Dave Matthews and Dave Rudebaugh were in the fight, and damaged the outlaws considerably. One of the gang had been left outside to hold the horses, his name was unknown and he evidently escaped in the darkness. An operator named Costello, an innocent bystander, was killed and a number wounded. None of the dance hall girls were hurt, for as Lady Maude, and Cock Eyed Liz declared, it was all in the day's business.

Of the outlaws, Bill Randall was killed and Jim West badly wounded. Tom Henry was unhurt and John Dorsey got a bullet through his leg; these three were captured while trying to make their escape, and were locked up in old town jail. A few nights later they were taken out by the vigilantes and strung up to the windmill in the middle of the old town Plaza. Bonfires were lighted, and most of the population of old and new town were present.

Mr. Charles Ilfeld was there in person, and a few years ago stated that there were four men hung at this time. It seems that all the social events in those days, such as church events, dances, and hangings took place at old town; new town felt very much slighted, and quite overlooked.

But regarding this particular hanging, the merchants of the old town plaza seemed quite provoked and held a meeting of protest. Their report stated their windmill had cost them six hundred dollars, and now, just think of it, they would have to dig up sixty dollars more to remove the infernal thing as a nuisance incompatible with the peace and dignity of the dear old plaza.

This Las Vegas quartet—who had paid the penalty—were still at the end of their respective ropes, as the stage rolled in full of passengers. As the stage passed the old windmill on its way to the Hotel, one of the passengers—evidently a woman—let out a shriek. The driver plied his whip and the stage dashed up to the curb with a woman struggling with a man and screaming, "Let me go! Take me home! Take me home! I will never live in this God-forsaken country!"

These two were Mr. and Mrs. A.M. Conklin from Arkansas, who later settled in Albuquerque. Mr. Conklin afterwards moved to Socorro where he was killed by Abran and Onofre Baca, but that is another story.

Every coach arriving meant recruits for the underworld and crime flourished.

Six miles from Las Vegas are the famous Hot Springs—equipped at the time I speak of, 1879, with an old time lot of bath houses—and a Hotel of which Scott Moore and his wife were proprietors. The good table they set was noted all through the west, and especially on Sundays, when their Hotel was always crowded, they often having to set a second table to accommodate their guests.

The Scotts finding they were entertaining two of the most conspicuous outlaws then in the west—Jesse James and Billy the Kid—brought them together, and they became friends.

Jesse James or Mr. Howard—as he was then known—was prospecting and preparing to move to a new country, and after meeting Billy, and sizing him up, made him a tentative offer to join forces and hit the trail together. Although both were outlaws with standing rewards out for their capture, their lives and activities were entirely different. Billy was never a train bank robber, nor a hold-up in any sense of the word. His only peculations had been stealing and branding other people's cattle, a common diversion of that time, and not considered much of a crime if you could get away with it; it was much the same as bootlegging is today. The offenses for which he was now wanted were entirely traceable to the so-called Lincoln county war. On account of the difference in their status, and of the fact that to join Jesse James was too big a proposition for him, Billy declined enlisting in his services.

Jesse James's half brother John T. Samuels confirms all the above and also states Jesse's nickname was Dingus, which he always called him.

A very unfortunate happening occurred about this time involving the Scion of one of the most influential families in New Mexico, Don Miguel Barrela of Mesilla New Mexico. He had come from home after merchandise with five big freight wagons drawn by eight mules each. He had completed his purchases; his wagons were loaded and in camp ready to start south the following morning. He had then decided to go into Las Vegas, and as a farewell do a little stepping out.

Meeting up with a companion, they started drinking, which presently ended up by Miguel Barrela shooting an apparently inoffensive citizen, Patrisio Ortega. As the man fell, an American sprang from a door at the side of a narrow street with an old fashion musket in his hands which he used as a club. With a terrific blow over the head, he knocked the murderer insensible. An officer in the plaza hearing the shot was on the spot in a moment and took charge and with the help of the prisoner's companion they dragged him to the jail but a short distance away. The doors were hardly locked behind them before a crowd filled the street in front of the jail, yelling, "Hang him! Hang him!"

Don Desiderio Romero was then Sheriff of San Miguel county and word reached him of the riot at the jail. Not waiting to assemble a posse, he came on horseback dashing at full speed and plunging through the crowd, with a forty-five in each hand guiding his horse with his knees.

Reaching the jail he stopped, and using his guns as clubs he drove the crowd from the jail yard, threatening anyone who carried a gun if he did not drop it he would kill him. His voice and face as well as his actions indicated that he meant business.

It was certainly an exhibition of pure nerve, though for all his bravery that night a mob overpowered the jailor, took the prisoner out, and hanged him to the very much abused plaza windmill.

Hanging Windmill on the Plaza, Las Vegas 1879-80, Courtesy Palace of the Governors (MNM/DCA #14386)

Curley Bill

by
N. Howard Thorp

Curley was known as the leader of the San Simon outlaws and cattle thieves, and for some years held undisputed sway over that locality, situated in Cochise County, Arizona, and bordering on the western line of New Mexico. Their operations extended well into New and Old Mexico, the livestock stolen in New Mexico being drifted into Arizona, those from Arizona being marketed in New Mexico and across the border to the south.

There was hardly any deviltry or meanness this gang would fail to attempt, and usually succeeded. Curley's gang was composed of some thirty or more followers, who, beside the theft of horses and cattle, held up stages and banks and committed highway robberies with impunity. They became such a menace that President Arthur issued a proclamation declaring them outlaws, so anyone who dared could shoot them on sight.

There are so many different tales told concerning Curley Bill's origin that they are confusing, though I have been told—on seemingly good authority—he came from the old Indian Territory, where so many hard characters first saw the light of day.

Bizby, like Galeyville, Arizona, has passed out of existence, so we shall follow Curley Bill—after the breakup of his gang—into New Mexico and view his life and his demise.

In looks Curley Bill was homely, in fact as ugly a man as is often seen and seemed to delight in his appearance, as it distinguished him from all other homely men one might meet. Just make the statement that you had seen the ugliest man in the world, and you would undoubtedly have run across Curley Bill. He had bright red hair, which looked as though it had never been combed, his face was freckled, seamed and wrinkled, thereby rendering his countenance when he frowned, terrible.

Badly wounded by a saloon keeper called Charley, or "Pizen" Baker, Bill left the San Simon country and we next find him running a saloon at where Lamy, New Mexico, now stands, near a place noted for its good meals during the early stage days and the construction of the A.T.&S.F. railroad.

A short distance south of the eating house, Curley Bill had his saloon, a two-room affair made in sections, so it could be easily moved to new locations as the grade work on the railroad progressed. Nailed to some posts in front was a large sign which read, LIQUID REFRESHMENTS FOR ALL NATIONS SOLD WITHIN "CURLEY BILL," DRINK ARTIST AND PROPRIETOR "WELCOME." Such was the setting we find Curley in where he made his last and fatal stand. Hard man and killer that he was, it seems strange he should have met his end at the hands of a tenderfoot.

At the end of the construction work there were hundreds of tents and small houses for the graders; the Engineers had their camp also while running the line and furnishing the grade stakes for the railroad.

Among the engineers was a young German named Shultz, a quiet and inoffensive chap. Somehow, especially when drunk, Curley Bill seemed to have selected him as an object for his ridicule and abuse. Whenever Bill happened to see him, Shultz was sure to receive a sample of Bill's profanity. One morning Shultz went to the shack of a post office to mail some letters to his home in Germany. Bill happened to meet him, and as usually cursed him and told him to leave camp, and leave at once, for if he did not the next time he saw him he would shoot him on sight. The young Engineer made no reply to these threats, but studied over the outrages he had to submit to. This treatment to a well brought up young fellow was most humiliating, and drove him almost to distraction. The usual hangers-on of construction camps, wishing to curry favor with Curley Bill, like a pack of hungry dogs took up the hue and cry and added their abuse.

However, the engineer seemingly unconcerned resumed his work, unaware that possibly it was his last day to live, and before night he might join the unmarked graves of those who had fallen before Curley Bill's six-shooter.

Most of them were friendless graders, full of Bill's bad whiskey which had sent them on the proud "fight." Bill's usual plea of self-defense had previously always cleared him at the inquests, so he had never faced an indictment for murder, and it was common knowledge that he had plenty of skill in securing the right sort of testimony and in handling the jury so as to have returned a verdict of justifiable homicide. Bill planned that the Engineer, armed, would seek him out and so seem the willful aggressor; or at least so it would appear from the testimony of Bill's satellites, with which he was always surrounded.

Bill figured so as to have all the advantage, and the worst

that could happen to him was to spend a few hours in the custody of the Sheriff until released; but the best laid plans of mice or men go oft astray. Shultz determined no longer to submit to Curley's abuse, and late in the afternoon went to his saloon, and sent in word for him to come out and settle their difficulties, and the one remaining alive would go to supper when presently the bell rang.

Bill sent a taunting reply to the Engineer's message, and stated he would soon send him to Kingdom come. Bill was amazed upon looking out to see Shultz standing with his gun in his hand out in the open awaiting him, and immediately began shooting at the Engineer from the inside of the saloon, firing from various and different positions in the hope of hitting him. Shultz was placed at great disadvantage in not knowing the location of his enemy. However, he saw presented a chance, a shadow passing a crack of the half-open door as it swung on its hinges. His shot scored, and Curley Bill had received a mortal wound. A crowd gathered around; he was still conscious and cussing with all his usual vigor. Bill had killed many a man, and it was now his turn to die with his boots on. "Boys," he stated, "I wouldn't mind taking this trail if I had only sent that dirt-scratcher ahead, to tell the devil I was coming."

The news of Bill's death was cheerful information to the proprietress of the eating house, whom he had often abused. She said that Bill ought to have been "rounded up" long before; that at breakfast that very morning, Bill had been very drunk and quarrelsome, and she had told him he was just a skulking tinker in Tarantula juice, and if he did not behave himself she'd throw him into a kettle of hot water. "What reply do you suppose that brute made to me, who was serving him the best breakfast in the land? He said, 'You old rendezvous of a starvation outpost, you ought to change your base, your old man ought to close this hash house and enter you in a beauty show. The very idea.' he says, 'of that ten-story neck of yours bobbing around this shack, with your delicate hands bigger than a double circus ring and those scrawny legs of yours longer than the Suez Canal, and those feet of yours bigger than the State of Texas, would in a beauty show make you a sure winner. Now hush your trumpet,' he said, 'and pass the griddle cakes or I'll kill you.'"

The lady continued, "I'm proud to know you, you old sign board of a cheap distillery, and so I kept passing the compliments to him, when my husband who was in the next room thought there was a battle going on, and needed him to come to my support, so he drew a double action six-shooter from my work basket but his hand shook so he shot himself in the knee. Bill thought someone was shooting at him through the wall, and did not even stop to eat his hot cakes.

"I think you must have seen my husband," she stated. "Didn't you meet a pair of grey horses hitched to a dead-axe wagon with a man stretched out on a pile of straw? Well, the driver was taking him to Santa Fe to see the doctor. There is one thing my old man has learned; he can shoot himself, even if he can't hit anything else. Bill has kept my old man in terror for months, but he couldn't scare me one little bit."

The wounded man arrived safely in Santa Fe, but lockjaw set in and within a week our landlady became a widow.

Shultz the civil engineer surrendered to the authorities; he was exonerated by the coroner, possibly because Bill was not there to fix him. He returned to his work. He was never again molested by the bad men of the border, for his reputation had been established. Curley Bill is planted just south of Lamy, surrounded by a few of his other victims.

The End

Bill McGinnis
The Nerviest Outlaw of
Them All

by
N. Howard Thorp

Of all the bad men and outlaws who in the past made New Mexico their "stamping ground" none, for pure nerve, approach the record of Bill McGinnis whose number in the New Mexico Penitentiary was 131. Received August twenty-fifth 1899, sentenced to life imprisonment for murder and train robbery, he was pardoned on January 10th, 1906.

The first time he appeared in the limelight was when, in company with Perry Tucker, Jim Lowe "Butch Cassidy," he appeared on the San Francisco river in western Socorro County and went to work for an outfit as bronco buster, one of the best. The average old-time buster, or staumper, as they frequently termed themselves, were needlessly rough and cruel with the young horses they were breaking, not only cruel with their spurs, but by beating them over the head with a loaded quoit. However Mac, as he was called, gentled his horses without being cruel. He was a handsome young fellow, tall, dark, and well built. With a good education, it was evident he came from good people, and I believe started in the train and other robberies through a love of excitement and adventure.

Tom Caphart known as "Franks," Bill McGinnis, and Sam Ketchum held up the train on the Colorado Southern road, near Folsom, New Mexico, getting away with considerable money, popularly supposed to have been between thirty and thirty-five thousand dollars. These three had left another man thought to have been McGonigal to look after two pack horses left in Cimarron canyon. As soon as notified, a strong posse had left Trinidad, Colorado, and gone by railroad to Raton, where getting horses they at once started for Cimarron, where although they found that the bandits had already passed that point, picked up their trail, and being joined by more men, proceeded to follow them. They eventually located their camp and were able to creep up to it. There were four bandits and one of them had been shot as he was going after water carrying a canteen—this was McGinnis. Several of the posse recognized him. As they saw him roll into the arroyo they supposed he had been killed. As soon as McGinnis fell, a heavy volley was directed at the posse.

It seems, as afterwards became evident, that the posse was not only badly scared but very much demoralized; despite the fact that two of the bandits were wounded they had very much the best of the fight. The Sheriff posse consisted of eight men with the advantage of surprise and the wounding of two of their opponents. The two remaining members of the party who had not been wounded had not only whipped the posse off but had killed three of them and wounded a fourth. This victory had been so complete they had been able to carry their wounded and all their equipment away with them. One of the bandits, Sam Ketchum, had only ridden twenty miles before he quit, the result of a broken arm; he simply did not have any grit. He had a hanging ahead of him if caught, and a little thing like a broken arm should not have stopped him. McGinnis escaped, though badly shot by the posse's first attack, but he, Franks, and McGonigal somehow got away, leaving no trace behind. Sam Ketchum was found, arrested and taken to Santa Fe. As for Mac and his partners, they seemed to have disappeared into thin air.

It was over a month later that Mac was arrested. Tom Caphart brought the news, having just ridden over from Lincoln county, some three hundred miles from where the fight took place, which he and Mac had had in the Cimarron Canyon in Colfax County. Tom had arrived on the San Francisco river after midnight of the night before, his horse and himself thoroughly played out, and had at once gone to Jim Lowe's camp in the W.S. horse pasture; and now the two were hustling around to procure bail in case Mac's offense was bailable. Several ranchmen offered to go bail if it would be accepted.

Tom Caphart, whom the authorities knew as Franks, gave the following account of how Mac had been taken. In telling about Mac, Tom did not allude to the cause of Mac's trouble; he just stated Mac had been wounded four times, two shots passing completely through his body. Owing to the long rides he had to make in order to get away from his pursuers, and not being able to give proper attention to his wounds, he was in a very weak condition when they got to Lincoln County where they had intended getting work.

Mac laid out in the hills to try and recover, while Tom looked around for a job and made trips to the nearest settlement in search of provisions. He didn't think it well for him and Mac to be seen together, for Mac's description was in all the papers, also a pretty fair picture of him, while so far no mention had been made of Tom, nor any attempt to publish a likeness of him. In the papers was a very vague description of a man they called Franks, which gave his height and complexion and which might possibly have been recognized as him. It seems there was an isolated cabin not far from Mac's camp whose owner always made them welcome when they stopped in.

When Mac's wounds were better and ceased to hurt him they decided to go back to Socorro County and get a job on one of the ranches where they had formerly worked. Tom did not get a job where they were, and Mac could not, owning to the publicity given him in the papers and placards with large rewards posted everywhere, copies of which had been mailed to all Peace officers in New Mexico.

So they decided to go to the San Francisco River, as their only haven of refuge. They agreed to meet at their friend's cabin the next day, and in the meantime Tom rode off to get provisions, ammunition, and other necessaries as they might need on their trip. They figured it would take them a week, as they would have to cover half the width of New Mexico, dodge ranches, and water at night, and not show themselves more than necessary. But luck seems to have failed them. It appeared that some horses had been stolen quite recently in that neighborhood and the Sheriff was out with a party looking for the thieves. The cabin and its owner was under suspicion of being a hold-out of horse thieves. The result was, the Sheriff and his party made a raid and took possession of the place before sunup on the very morning that Mac and Tom had arranged to make use of it. The Sheriff's idea was that the horse thieves were using it as a rendezvous, and they held the owner prisoner and concealed themselves in the cabin until such time as the thieves would turn up.

The first to arrive was Mac. As he had no cartridges for his saddle gun; he left it on his saddle when he hitched his horse, and there was only one cartridge in his six-shooter when he walked in among them. Mac was surprised upon entering, when he found himself covered and told to throw up his hands. His idea was that he was wanted for the train robbery. He was not going to give up voluntarily. He jerked his gun and shot one of them through the wrist, then having no more cartridges went at them with his fists, and knocked three of them cold. They were compelled to beat him into insensibility before he would give up. It was only after they had him tied and saw his wounds, which were not yet healed, that they suspicioned who he was. The Sheriff, it seems, had a description of him, with the offer of the five thousand dollars reward.

When they were sure they had the right man, they gave up all idea of capturing the horse thieves and took Mac to the nearest railroad point. All this Tom learned from the owner of the little ranch when he arrived an hour or so later. There was nothing Tom could do single handed, so he at once headed for the San Francisco River to find Jim Lowe "Butch Cassidy." How he managed to cover the three hundred miles and how many fresh horses he stole to enable him to cover the distance in three days may never be known, but the fact remains that he did it. In a few days the newspapers appeared in Alma, telling the details of the capture. It said Mac had put up a desperate fight with his bare hands against tremendous odds, and they only identified him when they saw the shirt which he was wearing was covered with blood, and the partly healed wounds; he was wearing the same shirt he had been shot in at the time of the robbery. One can't help contrasting Mac's nerve with that of Sam Ketchum who quit before he had gone thirty miles, and afterwards died in Prison.

Mac had ridden over three hundred miles with four bullet holes in his body, had been unable to change his bloody shirt for a month, had no bandages or medicine and little to eat, and still fought the posse like a tiger, until by main force they overpowered him. Whether right or wrong, Mac, as the posse had to admit, was a brave and nervy man.

The End

Clay Allison, "Gunfighter"

by
N. Howard Thorp

One of the most noted gunfighters of west Texas and New Mexico was Clay Allison. I make a distinction between gunman and gunfighter, the former being practically a murderer, while the latter always gave a foe a chance for his White Alley; in short, a gunfighter was not a hired killer.

Allison was born in Tennessee, in the year 1840, in the town of Jackson near the battlefield of Shiloh. At the beginning of the civil war he joined the Confederate Army. At the conclusion of the war he became, like Quantrell, Belle Starr, and her brother Shirley, the James boys and many others a Guerrilla and kept up a constant fight against all northern sympathizers.

In appearance, Clay Allison was a striking figure. He was well over six feet two inches in height and weighed a hundred and ninety pounds. Like most all "Braves" he had blue eyes, which seemed—in some way—to be the distinguishing mark of a killer.

His face was large, with a very prominent nose; he wore his hair long, covering his shoulders, while his mustache was large and dropped below his chin. For a big man he was very quick in his movements, though crippled from having accidentally shot himself in the foot.

There is woven into his early life in Tennessee a story of how someone insulted his Mother and his having killed the party for having done so. The same reason was given for Billy The Kid's stormy career, where one of the facts regarding the over-dramatized Billy was that his mother and stepfather wore out many a shingle on him, trying to keep him out of the saloons and tough joints of Silver City at night. No! We will omit any hero stuff concerning Clay Allison.

It is undoubtedly true that Clay Allison killed many men, though I doubt if even his enemies can accuse him of waylaying, shooting from ambush, or killing by unfair means. His friends state, he never killed anyone where death was not a benefit to the community in which they lived.

How many Allison actually killed is hard to determine, the score seeming to run from ten to over thirty, ten being probably nearer the mark. In comparison, Ben Thompson of Texas seems to be on fair terms of equality, though in comparison with Pantalion Miera of Algodones, New Mexico, he falls far behind. An old Sheriff of northern New Mexico at the time Clay Allison lived there stated that Clay never killed anyone except in self-defense, though I believe the Sheriff was a little prejudiced in his favor. When sober, Allison was agreeable and very much of a gentleman, but when drunk he became dangerous and was always ready to fight on the least provocation. A short time after the close of the Civil War and the end of Guerrilla operations, Allison went west, spending several years in what was then known as the Indian Territory and while there was credited with having fought several duels.

After leaving the Territory and crossing Red River to enter Texas he had a fight on the ferry boat, which was operated by a bad man named Tolbert, a Red River desperado. The fight was with knives and was so intense they both fell into the river. The bath in the cold water seemed to have cooled them off, so they did not resume the battle.

After working as a cowhand on the headwaters of the Brazas River, in 1871 he left for Colfax County, New Mexico, where he started in the cattle business.

While working on the Brazas, he, like all others at that time, was stealing what cattle he could get his rope on; many were of course straight mavericks, others being "made Mavericks." A neighbor whom Clay thought was getting more than his share got to quarreling, so to settle the matter they agreed to fight a duel. Whether the following account of the fight is fiction or not, I do not know, but this is the way the story traveled the range country by word of mouth.

Allison and his neighbor dug a grave and then, bowie knives in hand and stark naked, seated themselves one at each end, agreeing that after the fight, the survivor should cover up the one who was killed with the earth taken out in digging the grave. Allison shoveled in the dirt and shortly afterwards left the country.

In the early seventies, worlds of cattle drifted from the north into Colfax County, New Mexico, but few if any of the cows gathered by the owners in the roundups had any calves by their sides, these—if large enough—having been cut off and branded by Allison and his men. He was now well enough along in the cattle business to be classed as wealthy. Suddenly he sold out and moved temporarily to Colorado. This was on account of having killed several men in quick succession and it is certain he had now made for himself in New Mexico a name as a killer.

About this time, Clay met up with a desperado by the name of Bill Chunk, who happened to be a nephew of Frank Tolbert, the man with whom Clay had had the fight with on the ferry boat. This Bill Chunk held a record of having killed fourteen men, and being jealous of Clay's sudden rise to fame as a gunman, sent him word that he was desirous of adding Clay's name to his list so as to enable him to carve fifteen on the butt of his six-shooter. Chunk's boats didn't seem to bother Clay, who went about his business without trying to keep out of his way.

In those days the Clifton House, a two-story adobe building, stood where Raton, New Mexico, is now located and was a famous gathering place for outlaws, preachers, and citizens of all kinds passing on the north to Colfax County, New Mexico. It was there Clay and Bill met. For a couple of days they drank and spreed around, neither one being anxious to start the trouble that was sure to come. Allison was riding a fine looking horse one day and Chunk, who was also mounted, challenged him for a horse-race. In the race which followed, Chunk's horse beat Clay's and this further fanned the flames of hatred. Presently the dinner bell rang and they entered the hotel, sitting at each end of the table, their drawn six-shooters resting in their laps under the edge of the table. During the meal Chunk dropped his hand to his lap as if to pick up his napkin but really to draw his gun to kill Allison. As he raised his gun from his lap, the sight struck the edge of the table and his shot went wild. Allison fired a second after, hitting Chunk above the eye; his head fell forward into his plate. Allison replaced his pistol and finished his meal.

As the Santa Fe railroad was building west, Allison went to Las Animas, Colorado, which, like several towns, for a few months was the terminal of the line. These towns while terminals collected all sorts of men and women; among this tough element, Allison became a prominent figure. His first trouble was a fistfight with a rival stock buyer named Joe LeFevre. In this Allison seems to have come out victorious.

His next clash was with Charley Faber, the town Marshall. Allison and his brother John dropped into a dance hall; presently the Marshall came in and seeing the Allisons were carrying their guns, the Marshall ordered them to take them off. As everyone else was armed, the Allisons refused. The Marshall then got a shotgun and returned to the hall. Sighting John Allison first he started to fire; but at the same time the two Allisons shot, killing the Marshall, though some of the buckshot from his gun entered one of John Allison's arms and also his side. Clay refused to surrender to the authorities until his brother had been sent to the hospital, and then only under the promise that he would not be handcuffed or chained, both of which agreements—after Clay had given up his arms—were broken. The two Allisons easily came clear at their trial, as public opinion thought Charley Faber's actions proved he was trying to gain a reputation by killing the Allisons.

A man living in Mora, New Mexico, a Doctor Menger—on account of his wearing a silk hat—was Clay's pet aversion, so he proceeded to shoot it off his head. In Cimarron, New Mexico, Allison killed a noted desperado named Pancho while having a drink with him. Standing together at the bar, Pancho began fanning himself with his large hat as if he was suffering from the heat. Presently Allison detected Pancho drawing his gun from his waist sash behind his hat, and killed him before he completed the draw.

With many more shootings Clay went his lucky way; with all his shortcomings he was often on the side of the helpless, as in the case of Old Man Shaw and his daughter, when a mob tried to hang them for having killed the town Marshall when he broke into their home. I might continue to tell of the part Clay took in the Tally killing to bring the murderer to justice. Clay now returned to ranching and from all accounts he seemed to have quit most of his wild ways. His ending came in a most unexpected manner; he broke his neck when falling off a loaded freight wagon which passed completely over him.

The End

Dancing Cowboys

by
Kenneth Fordyce

Men yet living today, who knew Clay Allison, declare that he was not the bad-man of Northern New Mexico that he was reputed to be. Clay was just one of those fellows who would not be imposed upon by anyone. He attended to his ranch, his cattle, and commanded the respect of many of his neighbors.

Clay did have the bad habit of getting drunk. It was easy to start trouble with him when he was drinking but the trouble seldom proved serious.

Clay Allison had a dugout between where French and Maxwell are today and it was used by Clay and other cattlemen when they were in that locality rounding up cattle. It was located over west of the river in the hillside. It was about thirty or forty feet back in the hill and was all one large room. The men kept provisions there and lived there during the days that they worked in that locality. Clay's supplies always included a supply of whiskey (usually about five gallons).

Each evening the men would wash up and eat their suppers, and then the evening would be spent in drinking and dancing. Clay Allison loved to dance. He always saw to it that a fiddler was along. There would be no women but that did not matter, the men would dance around the fire, shouting and singing, and keeping time to the fiddle music.

On one occasion, the cook, who was a fat individual, decided that he would hide out in the grass near the river and sleep, and not dance that night. Some of the men did get tired of dancing every night but Clay loved it and insisted on dancing regularly. It was not long until Mr. Allison missed the cook and he started on the hunt for him. It took Clay almost an hour to find the cook but when he did, that obese individual made up for his rebellion by doing a solo dance which was forced for many hours to the great delight of the host.

Odd individuals, these first men of the west were, some of them, eh?

Source of Information: C.B. Thacker, Raton.

Early Crimes and Tragedies in Northern New Mexico

by
Kenneth Fordyce

The railroad boomer, the drifting miner, and the gun-man of the cattle range were three rough types to be found mixing and mingling with the gentlepeople in Northern New Mexico during the first pioneer days of the 1880s.

Society's restraint on the hair-trigger passions of the lawless element was unusually impotent when old Judge Lynch's court held a session, or the bad men came in contact with too much whiskey. However, the record of local crimes and tragedies was neither better nor worse than that of the average western settlement where plainsmen and mountaineers were joining forces to make homes and a community.

There were many killings between gunmen that worked to a double advantage, the slower on the draw passed out, and the other, passed on. One heavy investor in property on First Street and the owner of a prosperous saloon killed his man and fled, never to be heard of again. Fairmont Cemetery contains the unmarked graves of many bad men today, for whom these green pastures for an easy living had turned a sickly red. Through these tragedies of the '80s and the '90s the respectable element of those throbbing days lived blissfully on, accustomed to the occasional sight of a murdered or injured man, yet contributing as best they could to the support of law and order.

In 1881, a mob of men left Raton late one evening and went down to Otero, five miles south of the city, where a Dr. Washington was taken from the Otero jail and hanged on the railroad water tank for an alleged crime committed in Raton. The details of the affair have not been preserved.

Two other unofficial necktie parties occurred during the first decade. A railroad employee, who had struck a fellow employee over the head with a hammer, was taken to a pinion tree standing in the middle of Miembres avenue (now Park avenue), west of Topeka avenue (now Fifth Street), and near the foot of Goat Hill where he was hanged. When the self-appointed executioners returned to town, the man presumed to have been murdered was found to have revived.

A similar incident of tragic consequences resulted in the lynching of Juan Barela who was whipped into insensibility by a Raton resident for an alleged attack on a girl. Friends of the man, who doubted the truth of the accusation against him, hid Barela in a box car in the lower railroad yards where he was found an hour later by a mob from the East Side (Chihuahua), taken to a cottonwood tree on Raton arroyo east of the round house and strung up, more dead than alive from his beating.

Hanging has been the legal method of execution in New Mexico until a recent date, but only one legal hanging has ever taken place in Raton. On May 25, 1906, David Arguello and John Medlock, a negro, played the leading roles in a double execution which took place on a scaffold built in the alley-way on the west side of the old Colfax County Court House and Jail, which were on North Fourth street and Clark avenue.

Traditional—Jay Conway, Raton.

Dr. T. O. Washington—Deceased

by
Kenneth Fordyce

No one knows just where Dr. T. O. Washington came from, but perhaps he had reasons for not telling as will be borne out by a review of some of his actions.

Dr. Washington had settled in Otero, New Mexico in 1879 and was practicing medicine. He soon visited El Moro, Colorado and brought home a bride who had been a Miss Elizabeth Minger.

The doctor was a quarrelsome person and he frequently got into disputes with those about him. It wasn't long until Dr. Washington had trouble with a neighbor. This time he let his temper rule his actions and during a quarrel of some chickens he stabbed the man twice in the abdomen. Two vicious wounds resulted in the neighbor's death. The man's death resulted in Dr. Washington leaving Otero suddenly. He moved to the Harvey House in Raton.

Dr. Washington was called on to minister to a young woman

in the hotel as she was ill and he visited her several times. During her convalescence the doctor perhaps was lonesome which may have accounted for his untimely advances and unprofessional conduct. The young patient informed her fiancé of the doctor's proposals and this young railroad man was highly incensed. He told other railroad men of the incident and remembering the doctor's recent trouble in Otero the railroad men decided that Dr. Washington was an undesirable citizen.

In those first settlement days of northern New Mexico such men as the doctor and even worse ones were often encountered, and the means of ridding the community of them, as was used that time, was often resorted to. They banded together and started looking for the doctor. The officers who knew of the determination of the Raton group knew that they had no adequate place to keep Dr. Washington safely and so they rushed him back down to Otero and placed him in the jail there.

This removal of Washington did not deter the mob. The men started for Otero at once in mass.

On being informed of the approach of the Raton men, Dr. Washington fainted away and was revived only in time to accompany the angry men who had captured him to the railroad yards.

There without trial, other than the opinions of the men in the mob, Dr. Washington met his death, by means of a rope and the frame work of the water-tank which served as a scaffold.

Thus was the idea of justice in the early days of New Mexico when undesirable citizens could not conduct themselves in accordance with the generally accepted better rules of society.

Source of Information: Mrs. Mary L. Sinnock, Otero 1879, Raton since 1882.

Crime Did Not Pay in '73

by
Kenneth Fordyce

Tony Meloche, one of the better known and more beloved cowmen of the early days of Northern New Mexico, operated a cattle ranch in Colfax county on the Vermejo River near the present site of Colfax, New Mexico.

Tony Meloche, of French descent, settled in Colfax county in the early 60s, having come to the southwest as a wagon-master with a government outfit of some sort. He was a typical pioneer. His cattle interests became very extensive and he had a host of friends.

A notable episode in the life of Tony Meloche was the part he played in the capture of the slayer of his friend, Mike Karney, an old Texas cattleman who was murdered on Mr. Meloche's ranch in Colfax county in 1873.

Karney was operating a ranch with a partner thirty miles east of Denver in 1872 and 1873. He came to Colfax county in

November of 1873, to make up a herd to drive back to Denver. Hugh Helling, a cowhand, came with him.

About a week after their arrival, Helling went after a load of wood one morning. When he returned he found Karney murdered and robbed of the $12,000 in drafts, checks, and money which he had brought with him. It was Tony Meloche who organized and directed the posse which was to hunt down the strange man who had been seen in the neighborhood that same day, and who he believed had committed the crime against his friend.

The posse of eight went in groups of two, each group going in a different direction. Helling and a Mr. Davis set out on the trail of a lone rider which led toward the Red River country. At the old Crow Creek station, they encountered a riderless horse and soon came upon John Cauley who they suspected of being the wanted man. They took him, although he loudly declared his innocence, back to the ranch and turned him over to the sheriff. The sheriff and a very well-known man of the time—Clay Allison—took the man up to the edge of the timber on the Meloche ranch, put a rope around his neck, put him on a horse, and tossed the rope across the limb of a cedar tree. Then they told the prisoner to tell the truth. Allison started to lead the horse away from the tree and the rope began to tighten about the neck of Cauley. The man started to plead and beg for his life and declared that he would tell the truth. He acknowledged his guilt and promised to lead the men to the hiding place where the $12,000 would be found. The sheriff and Allison took him back to Crow Creek and made him dig up the treasure. By that time, lynching parties were gathering. The sheriff deputized every man he could find to assist in getting the killer to the jail at Cimarron.

The cowhand, Helling, proved rather obstinate for he was convinced that lynching was too good for the murder of his former employer. He was finally persuaded to let the law have its way.

Tony Meloche had been active in the round-up of the outlaw, and after the capture, had been one to back up the law in its effort to get the prisoner to jail, so that he might be tried before he was hanged.

Story from Evlyn Shuler, Raton Library, from a clipping—Chronicle News Trinidad.

Black-Balled

by
Kenneth Fordyce

Anyone who lived in Raton, New Mexico, at the time the town was started in 1870 and for a few years after that can tell of the lawlessness which existed there. The old-timers gaze dreamily into the distance and say, "It was plenty wild." They hesitate to talk of those early days and some of the things that happened.

The lawless element drifted in from Texas and other places where they were not wanted and soon there were more of them in Raton than of the law-abiding kind. They were drifters. They were unorganized.

In 1883 the more peaceable citizens had a meeting and decided that it was time to clean up the town. They did not want bloodshed, so they devised the plan which worked very nicely. They banded together, forming a large posse, and quietly and quickly collected the lawless into one group. The determined town-savers mounted their horses and marched the group of lawless on foot before them out of town, up the Raton Pass to the Colorado line, and there turned them loose with a warning that it would be very unwise to return.

It was about ten miles up that long mountain trail to the state line from Raton and after that trip on foot and the very definite admonition "not to return" from those determined citizens, the group decided that they would make their homes elsewhere.

In 1886 another group of the lawless kind had drifted into Raton, one at a time, until the little city was again getting the reputation of being wild. Again the citizens had a meeting and the once successful plan was tried again—with the same fine results.

After this second forceful suggestion, southwestern bad men decided that Raton would tolerate none of their kind and the town remained free of so many of them.

Source of Information: A.E. McCready, Raton.

A Would-Be Bad Man

by
Kenneth Fordyce

For years the exact extent of the Maxwell Land Grant was not known. No survey had been made. The grant officials first were satisfied with twenty leagues of property, the north line of which extended from Tenaja and Eagle Tail Mountains over to the Red River Peak. Then the line was moved northward and ran about where Rio Grande Avenue is today in Raton, New Mexico. Later, through action in Congress at Washington the bounds were extended until the north boundary line was almost to Starkville, Colorado, across the Raton mountains.

Each time that the line was changed and more territory added it took in land on which settlers had come in and settled with the purpose of homesteading. As soon as the grant owned it the squatters, who immediately became anti-granters, were given notice to buy or move. This led to foreclosures, quarrels, threatenings, shootings, etc.

Naturally the grant people needed men to act as deputy sheriffs, enforce the law, put the squatters off or make them pay for their place, or hold sales and sell them out. This job was cut out for that type of individual who thought that he was tough, hard, bad, and a bold gunman from the badlands.

A fellow by the name of Bill Cook came up from Texas and qualified for such a job. He was a deputy sheriff. He recommended himself highly. He was quite a drinker and felt important with his new position. It wasn't long, however, until he became exceedingly unpopular with the people of northern New Mexico who were sympathetic with the anti-grant faction.

Cook had taken part in several evictions. Hearing him boast in the Raton saloons it would have been quite natural to think him a bad one, an excellent gunman, and exceedingly brave.

It is reported that Cook and his riding partner, D. Russell (name believed to have been Dave), who was also a deputy sheriff, were in a group which attempted an eviction in south Raton that failed. A squatter, as they called him, had been given notice to buy, get off of the property, or he would be sold out by the sheriff's deputies. As the deputies rode to the property where the sale was to be held after the owner had refused to comply with the demands, they approached a small hill near the house. Over the top of the hill they could see some twelve or fourteen rifles trained on them. They could also understand the command to halt and about-face. The guardians of the place said there would be no sale of the property. There was no sale. Cook did not do anything about it.

Some time after this event, Cook and his partner Russell were riding up the trail toward Raton and from the trees and rocks some distance from the road two rifles spoke. Russell was hit squarely and killed. Cook was struck but only wounded. He lost no time getting into Raton where he stayed until he was well and able to hit the trail. It was said that the assailants were Mexicans. Several people got credit with the shooting but no one was ever arrested or named in a complaint.

Stories of early day shootings are not always explainable, especially at this late date. So it is with this bit about Cook. He claimed to be looking for a man by the name of Jack Miller. He, as an officer, wanted Miller. He visited the saloons, one at a time, got a drink and sought his man. Frank Cattern knew where Miller roomed, knew that he was at his room, and offered to show Cook where Miller was. They started off together; they went up First Street to a rooming house and climbed the stairs. At the room at the back end of the hall Cattern stepped up to knock on the door, and then Bill Cook shot him in the back with no witnesses present. (So the story goes.) Jack Miller was in his room, so they say; he came to the door but was not taken by the deputy. It was an unexplainable shooting and made the deputy Cook even more unpopular in this section of the country than he had been. It is pointed out that he shot Cattern in the back; again it shows the real character of the early bad men.

Cook decided that he had better get away for awhile, and as there was a fellow that was wanted who was living in a Texas town two or three hundred miles to the south and east, he believed that this was a good time to go over and get him. To show how bad he was, he wrote the man a letter and told him that he was coming after him and if necessary he would come "a'shootin."

Cook got to the Texas town; as he alighted from his train a long Texan stepped from beside the station building with a double barreled shotgun aimed at Cook and pulled the trigger. Thus ended the life of the bad man Bill Cook, ex-deputy sheriff. The killer of Cook walked up to the court house and appeared before the judge, displayed his threatening letter, admitted the shooting and said that he would stand a trial if the judge wanted to have one. It is said that he was never called to court to answer for his deed. Dan Young, brother-in-law of Fayette Gillespie, was at the town in Texas buying cattle when the shooting of Cook took place. He brought the story back to northern New Mexico.

It is said that little grief was felt for the loss of the deputy in Raton and Colfax County, New Mexico.

Source of Information: According to Mr. Judd Lyon; Common Belief. Common belief or general talk among neighbors was meant by "it was said"; during those days when the Grant War was in progress NO ONE wanted to be quoted on any subject. (Mr. Gillespie could not remember the name of the Texas town.) Bits from: Mr. A.E. Fairbanks, Raton; Mr. Fayette Gillespie, Raton; Mr. Judd Lyons, Raton and others.

Raton's First Jail

by
Kenneth Fordyce

Sheriff John Hicks had arrested Rick Rogers—a bad-man from Arizona—several times for drunkenness and disorderliness around the saloons in Raton, back in the early days of the town, but there was no jail. It was necessary to use a box car on the siding for a jail until court convened the following day. The embarrassing part for Sheriff John was that the prisoner would always have made his escape before the court got ready to try him.

Now Rick could be bad, and he promised that if arrested again he was not going to calmly submit as he had before, but that he would take an extra drink to steady his nerves and shoot the molesting officer for his efforts.

The report came to the sheriff one night rather late that Rick was shooting out the lights at the east side saloons and making plenty of trouble.

Sheriff John, with two assistants, discovered Rick's horse tied up on the hill by the cemetery. They decided that the best way to take him was to hide there and wait for him to appear. Soon he came wandering up the hill—none too steady. One of the assistants got impatient and overly nervous, drew his gun, and fired at Rick before he was close enough. He missed. The spurt of fire gave the hiding officers away; Rick fired into the group and wounded the sheriff in the knee. Rick ran, and made his get-away without his horse. The sheriff was badly wounded and his leg had to be amputated.

The result of the affair was that John Lee decided that Raton should have a jail. He was going to build one. By petition, he secured enough two by fours to build a jail. He placed them flat against each other to thicken the walls and make it almost impossible to break down. The jail was finally completed and everyone was pleased and proud of the new "Bastille." Everyone congratulated John Lee and bought him a drink. It shouldn't be said that he got too many drinks (free), but John did get rather disorderly, tried to shoot out several lights, and it was necessary to lock him up for the night. So John Lee was the first man to be confined to the jail which he had built for his fair city.

This jail was used for some time. There is one more part to the story about it. The sheriff brought in a suspected cattle-thief, locked him in the jail, put the keys in his pocket, and returned to the range to get the prisoner's partners, if possible.

While he was gone, someway or other, the jail caught on fire and burned. The helpless citizens, who had no keys to the place, were unable to save the occupant.

That was Raton's first jail.

Source of Information: C.B. Thacker.

124

Northern New Mexico's Bad Man and His Gang "Black Jack Ketchum"

by
Kenneth Fordyce

Black jack may mean a billy in the city, it may mean chewing gum to the 'kids,' but in New Mexico at the mention of the word black-jack thoughts turn to the man who made Northern New Mexico his headquarters and operating center for the activities of his murderous and thieving gang of ruffians. This gang operated during the '90's and their depredations extended into Texas, Colorado, Arizona and as far as Utah. Train robberies and raids were their specialties. The ferocity of their crimes was unequalled anywhere.

The gang was led by Thomas Ketchum, who was known as "Black Jack." Other members of the gang included one of his brothers, Sam Ketchum—the bearded one, Bill McGinnis, Will Carver, George Musgrave and, of course, others who only stayed with the group for a short period of time.

"Black Jack" and his gang had as a favorite place of operations

Northern New Mexico. Cimarron Canyon was a profitable spot. They also favored the country around Folsom, New Mexico. They had many hideouts in the hills all through Northern New Mexico.

Three men determined to catch Black Jack one time, after many posses had tried and failed. They followed his trail for hours and finally found where he had entered a large cave, which was probably a hideout. Being few in number they sent one man for reinforcements, the remaining two never once losing sight of the cave entrance. Just as the reinforcements arrived, and they were preparing to storm the cave, someone in the posse espied Black Jack riding away on his horse several miles across the canyon. They had overlooked the fact that the cave had two entrances.

Turkey Canyon was one place the gang holed up frequently. In fact, near the end of the gang's operations, Turkey Canyon was where some of the members of the gang were captured.

Even to-day, over thirty-five years after the gang was broken, there are those who believe that there is hidden treasure buried in Turkey Canyon. During those thirty-five years, many have gone out and tried to find some of the hidden loot, which 'talk' says is still there. It seems very unlikely though considering the financial condition of the leaders toward the end of their lives.

They found the Cimarron Canyon a profitable place, for the miners of gold from Baldy and Elizabethtown brought their bags of gold dust and nuggets down through that district on their way to market and the railroad center. They were often relieved of their treasurers by "Black Jack" and his gang.

Black Jack and the gang would ride up to a ranch and literally take possession for a day or several days, and their demands upon the rancher were unheard of. They would usually stay until the poor man had met them. All the while they would be using of the best in the house and causing great anxiety with their rowdiness and drunkenness.

In the last years of operations of the gang, it turned to train robberies as a more profitable business. Where the Colorado & Southern comes through the mountains into New Mexico, near Folsom, and continues on southeast to the Texas line, was another favorite place where 'business' was good.

The Ketchum boys, Sam, Tom, and Berry, had been raised together in the Panhandle. Berry chose to stay at home and live a respectable life. Sam and Tom just naturally had to wander, and although they had intended to get work at ranches they soon tired of working and turned to crime. A friendly storekeeper allowed them to sleep in his store one night and they took advantage of his hospitality, robbed him, and left before dawn. When the storekeeper and two others overtook the Ketchum boys the next day, they were killed by the Ketchum boys. That seemed easier to the boys than to be captured. This was their first experience in their lives of crime. Thereafter "Black Jack" and Sam left a trail of blood wherever they went; killings were credited to them through many states, and many men in New Mexico found death when they encountered "Black Jack" and his gang. Their fame grew during a series of crimes, and it was not long until they had gathered about them, men who thought that there was glamour and thrill in the easy, adventurous life of an outlaw.

"Black Jack" chose to stay in Northern New Mexico a great part of the time; crime after crime was perpetrated on the people who had come to the sunshine territory to make their homes. Constant fear of robberies, hold-ups, and raids by "Black Jack" lurked in the minds of the prosperous, and the traveling public. Train robbery became very common. In one section, near Folsom, there had been a half dozen robberies.

Robberies of the trains got so common that on one occasion the train accidentally became uncoupled, and caused great fear and uneasiness, for the passengers just 'knew' it was "Black Jack" and his gang.

In July, 1899, the Ketchum gang held up the passenger and express train but this job was not successful and contributed to the breaking up of the gang. The robbery netted the gang practically nothing, as the express messenger, immediately realizing what was going on, took the valuables from the safe and hid them elsewhere. He had time to do this while the engine and express car were being disconnected and taken down the track a mile or two. For this service to his Company, he received a good beating by the bandits who made good their getaway in the darkness.

A few days later they were tracked down by a posse; in a gun battle one sheriff was killed and two others were wounded. Sam Ketchum, the bearded brother, was also wounded and captured; his wounds caused blood-poisoning from which he died soon after. Sam's death crippled the morale of the gang.

"Black Jack" was greatly depressed by the loss of his brother, and the serious effects it had upon other members of the gang. He was despondent. People liked some outlaws, like "Billy the Kid" and others, who used their gains to bring happiness and joy to the needy. Many doors were open to those men, but he, "Black Jack," could think of no reason why any household should welcome him. In this despondent mood he decided on his future course of action. He had $1,000.00 and he determined to increase it sufficiently by gambling to furnish him a start in some distant land, or if he lost, to pull one more good train job, and in that manner secure money to break away and live where he was unknown.

It is easy to imagine the commotion which "Black Jack's" entrance in Kent's saloon in Folsom made. He was immediately recognized, and the occupants of the place did not know whether to expect a holdup, a killing, or a friendly visit. With a remark about the weather, and a question as to the limit on the game, "Black Jack" seated himself at the gambling table and played; first he won, then he lost; when his $1,000.00 was gone and the dealer had raked in the last chip, "Black Jack" arose, walked out of the place, mounted his horse and rode away.

That left only one way to carry out his plan, one final hold-up. So a few days later "Black Jack" boarded the Denver-Forth Worth express and a short distance out of Folsom he held up the train single-handed. When they stopped the train at his command there was difficulty in disconnecting the express car from the rest of the train, because the train was stopped in a slope, and this gave the express man and the conductor time and opportunity to arm themselves with the idea of driving off the outlaws. Finding only one man, "Black Jack," covering the train crew on the ground, the conductor fired at him with a shotgun. However, his shot was not before "Black Jack" had wounded both the express messenger and the conductor. The buckshot had struck "Black Jack" in the right arm; badly wounded, the outlaw retired. The train crew boarded their train and left as speedily as possible.

Early the next morning posses were at the scene, and "Black Jack," seriously wounded, lying on a nearby hill, and suffering intense pain, was captured. "Black Jack" was placed in the caboose of a train and taken to Folsom. Feeling against the outlaw was so bitter that it was thought wise to leave him immediately, and he was taken to the hospital in Trinidad, Colorado. After a week there, he was removed to the penitentiary in Santa Fe. The arm failed to heal; it was necessary to remove it. No anesthetic was used at the request of "Black Jack" who underwent the ordeal without a murmur. At the penitentiary, he proved to be a good prisoner, with few exceptions.

The next spring a grand jury at Las Vegas, before whom "Black Jack" was taken, indicted him on a charge of robbing a train while armed. He had pleaded 'not guilty.' He was then taken back to Santa Fe to await trial which was to be held in Clayton, New Mexico.

At his trial "Black Jack" was found 'guilty.' He was sentenced to hang for his crimes. After the usual delays, during which time he was kept at the penitentiary at Santa Fe again, the day for hanging was set for April 26, 1901.

An odd thing about Tom Ketchum's views on his life, his activities, and his punishment was the fact that he could not understand, even realizing how many persons he had shot down, why the law should demand his life.

It is told how "Black Jack" refused to eat while in prison the first time. He thought that he would get thin enough to get his one hand through the bars, and get possession of a gun. All went as planned and his arm and hand did get thin, and he did grab a gun from one of the guards, but there were too many others around and his attempt, to subdue his guardians and make his escape, failed.

Although he thought that they would never execute him, he was taken to Clayton and hanged. "Black Jack's" executioners wished to do a thorough job and arranged the scaffold on which he was hanged so that his body dropped farther than was necessary; in fact, so far that the head was jerked off of the body. The official doctor at the scene of the hanging was ready with surgical "needle and thread" and fastened the head back on to the body. He had anticipated the catastrophe.

"Black Jack's" body was buried east of Clayton in a cemetery from which most of the bodies were later removed. In 1933 it was decided to disinter "Black Jack" Ketchum, and place his remains in the new Clayton cemetery. At the announcement everyone planned to be present. On the appointed day a large crowd gathered and the gruesome task had many witnesses. The coffin was in a very good state of preservation. When the air struck it, though, it fell to pieces. Some members of the crowd attempted, and some succeeded, in getting bits of "Black Jack's" clothing or a lock of his curly brown hair. Their success was effort almost wasted, for as the air got to their 'treasures' they fell to pieces.

An odd coincidence happened on the day of "Black Jack's" disinterment. The Colorado & Southern train from the north, which he had so often delayed, failed to arrive in the city of Clayton. Later it was found that a washout was responsible.

"Black Jack" and his gang added color, although undesirable, to the early days of Northern New Mexico. Mention "Black Jack" in Clayton, Folsom, Raton, Cimarron, Ute Park, or any other Northern New Mexico town, and someone is sure to speak up and have a thrilling tale to tell about "Black Jack" Ketchum.

Origin: Gathered from Robert Tomlinson, Raton, Bob Campbell, Raton, Levina Kite. Newspaper articles by George Fitzpatrick from whom permission was secured to use some facts.

American Guide
Kenneth Fordyce   165 Words.

Pioneer --

Daily Robbery.

In the 1880s, when Raton, New Mexico was a small but rapidly-growing railroad city, it is said that the population consisted of railroaders, many of them boomers, working for a stake to enable them to continue their travels, and a tough element, drifters from everywhere, many who had been run out of more particular towns and communities.

This may explain why there were so many robberies. The railroaders were getting good pay and the loafers wanted money. It is said that scarcely a night passed that there was not a robbery or stick-up.

Many of the men sought amusement, entertainment, and refreshments at the very popular dance hall - saloons on the east side, known as Chihuahua. If a man displayed money or had a drink or two more than he could handle, it was a pretty sure thing that he would be waylaid as he re-crossed the arroyo and the tracks on his way home.

Most of this ceased when the citizens got together and marched the worst of the lawless ones out of town, on foot, in 1883, and again in 1886.   Information by Wm. J Howell.

(Raton)

Facsimile: "Pioneer, Daily Robbery," Kenneth Fordyce, March 26, 19—, NMFWP, *American Guide*, WPA #188, NMSRCA

The Law in Their Hands
Kid Menser's Shooting in a Saloon

by
Kenneth Fordyce

A s you cross the Colorado-New Mexico line, come down the Scenic Highway into Raton, New Mexico, and enter that peaceful but busy little city with its broad streets, you never think of looking at the signs or poles to see if there is a dead man hanging on any of them at the end of a rope.

But a few years ago, on a warm June morning, travelers got out of their one-coach train—for travelers rode on trains then— and walked over to First Street, where a crowd had gathered to see the man who was hanging in front of the Raton Bank, where a restaurant is located today. Many of the passengers who visited the scene did not even go into the Santa Fe Eating House that morning; they lacked an appetite.

Today that is the corner of First Street and Clark Avenue. Many people still live who were there on that June 27, 1882, which was the "morning after the night before" when Raton had experienced in real life something which is seen in the movies and read in stories now, and thought of only as an idea that has been created in some author's mind, but really never happened.

In June, 1882, Raton was a small, rapidly-growing railroad town consisting of two strings of box cars, a few log cabins, and some frame buildings, which had been moved up from Otero and rebuilt to house the saloons, stores and businesses, which were even then starting Raton on the road to being a business center for Northern New Mexico. These were mostly located along First Street, close to the railroad which caused its birth and nurtured the village into a real town, then into a city.

About six months before that June night, two partners came to Raton from Texas, Gus Menser and Pete Burbridge. They operated the Bank Exchange Saloon, in what is now the one hundred block of South First Street. An interesting tale followed these men. It was said that they had an enemy in Texas, where they had run a saloon, who insisted on fighting a duel with Mr. Burbridge, who did not choose to fight. There had been trouble. Mr. Menser, after a few drinks, which often got him into trouble, wanted to settle the quarrel and uphold the honor of his partner, so he offered to fight the duel for him. He proceeded to the street, and he and the irate Texan stepped off the twenty paces, turned and fired. The enemy fell mortally wounded. That was the signal for the partners to leave for a new location, and they chose Raton in New Mexico. Pete Burbridge was very grateful to his partner, Mr. Menser, or at least should have been, for taking this great responsibility off of his shoulders, and preserving his honor. This was the pair who now owned and worked at the Bank Exchange Saloon.

Gus Menser, who was sometimes called 'the kid' drank more heavily than ever, and often caused trouble in the saloon. Pete

Burbridge warned him frequently, but it did no good. Finally Pete found it necessary to fire Gus, and throw him out. Gus, being a young man, less than twenty-five years of age and a heavy drinker was hot tempered and thought that something should be done about it immediately. He entered the saloon, accosted Burbridge, demanded reinstatement, made violent threats, and referring to the assistance which he had given Mr. Burbridge in Texas. But all of his pleadings were of no avail. He then demanded that Burbridge come out into the street and settle the matter with pistols and twenty more paces. Mr. Burbridge's distaste for duels again dominated the situation, and Gus decided to shoot it out right there in the saloon.

Pete Dallman, a deputy sheriff who was present, took command of the situation and tried to prevent a killing, but drew the fire of the wronged partner instead. The customers and the bartenders took refuge under the tables and behind the bar while Pete and Gus banged away, damaging many of the furnishings of the bar-room including the skylight and the water system at the bar. One shot was supposed to have hit Gus but it failed to stop him.

Gus fled; and the crowd which then offered its assistance to Pete Dallman could not find him. They searched the boxes and packing cases along the street and all of the building were gone through in an effort to locate this man and put him under arrest.

From in front of the saloon someone espied Mr. Gus among the packing cases at the depot. A shout went up and the chase was on. About this time, the evening train arrived, and it was assumed that Gus would try to get away on it. So the men went from one end of the train to the other looking behind seats, in the wash room, and even under the train. Gus could not be found. It was then decided that he was in the woods some distance beyond the tracks and the search was abandoned for the time being.

Pete Dallman spoke up, said that it was his life that had been endangered, and that the drinks were on him. So the entire crowd repaired to the Jackson Saloon, near the Bank Exchange Saloon, and ordered drinks. For the next hour, the experiences of the previous hour were lived over again, and drinks livened the group considerably. The group then went back to the Bank Exchange Saloon to inspect the damage done there and to witness and mingle with the crowd which was gathering in anticipation of the opening of the show in the Music Hall over the Bank Exchange Saloon. "Louie" Lord was the particular actress appearing at that time in the Music Hall.

As the group was seated in the back of the saloon, who should enter but Menser himself and demand that the bartender serve him a stiff drink.

Menser might just as well have asked for a volley of lead for that is what his request for a drink got him. The men of the group surged forward. Mr. Lattimore was first to engage in an exchange of shots with Gus. He received a wound which took him out of the evening's excitement but from which he recovered some three months later. Realizing that he was definitely on the defense, Gus fled toward the railroad yards just across the depot lawn. The switch engine had just pulled up. Engineer Mulvaney had taxied his wife up to town in the engine from their box-car quarters a mile down the tracks to get some groceries at the Mercantile Store which was located between the saloons. They had just reached the store when the shooting started. Gus, seeing the engine, made for it on the run with the group of pursuers not far behind. He disappeared behind the engine. A Mr. Eldison, one of the top partners, Moulton & Eldison, was first to round the front of the engine, and was met by a bullet from the gun of Gus Menser, which struck Eldison in the esophagus.

As the other men reached Eldison they halted momentarily

to examine their fallen comrade; this gave Gus a temporary advantage. He boarded the engine and attempted to make his getaway on the engine, but fortunately Engineer Mulvaney had left the reverse lever of the engine in a neutral position and the frantic jerking of the throttle was of no avail.

Mr. Jackson of the Jackson Saloon, next to get close to the gunman, was in the engine cab when Gus discovered him. Fearing capture and having sobered enough to realize his precarious position, Gus was determined that his man should not take him. He stuck his gun in Jackson's stomach and pulled the trigger. Jackson fell from the engine cab . . . dead.

Deputy Sheriff Jones from Blossburg had arrived on the scene by that time and decided that it was his duty to take this man. He climbed aboard the engine and made for his man who was dividing his time between trying to get the engine started and snapping his now empty gun at the oncoming Jones.

Discovering that Jones was succeeding in subduing Menser, the crowd surged onto the engine and quickly overpowered the desperate man.

While part of the crowd was taking Mr. Eldison to Dr. J. J. Shuler's office on Park Avenue, just off of First Street, to see if "the doc" could save him, the larger part of the group accompanied the sheriff and his prisoner to the saloon.

Sheriff Jones finally decided that he should shackle his prisoner to prevent further escape and more tragedy. As he stooped to adjust the shackles to the leg of Gus Menser, Moulton, of the Moulton & Eldison partnership which was mentioned before, entered the saloon followed by a large group of Raton citizens. Moulton announced in a loud voice: "We want that man, Sheriff, he shot my partner, Eldison, and Eldison just died . . . bled to death." He drew his gun and the sheriff turned his attention from his prisoner to the new situation which threatened to be serious.

As Moulton approached the prisoner, Deputy Jones found that to stop the determined man and his group it would be necessary to shoot. Jones shot Moulton in the right hand. Moulton quickly grabbed his gun in his other hand and shot the sheriff, wounding him seriously.

Gus Menser, taking advantage of the disorder that this shooting created, jerked off his buttoned shoe and the manacle, dashed out of the back door, and shot into the Williams Butcher Shop. The surprised butcher could only gasp: "Why, Gus, we've been lookin' for you all evenin'." By that time, the crowd had caught up with the fleeing man and started pouring in at both doors. As Gus was unarmed, they quickly took him again.

By this time Mr. Williams, the butcher, had recovered enough to be of some help. He grabbed a rope with which a customer had that day led a pig to his shop to be butchered, and handing the clothesline rope to the leader of the mob, suggested that they might need a good rope. The rope was accepted.

The rope was placed around Menser's neck. The men pulled him out on to the boardwalk of First Street. The captured man dug his feet into the walk and profanely attempted to tell the mob that they were making a mistake and that they would be sorry when he succeeded in getting loose. His threats were cut short for the job had reached a spot where a sign board reached from the buildings to a post at the street edge of the walk. The rope was tossed over the sign and without any ceremony they heaved on the loose end of the rope, and up went Gus—for a moment. The poorly fastened sign gave way; man, sign and rope all crashed to the board walk. This did not stop the group for long. A boy in the crowd was boosted up the post, on which the sign had rested, and he fastened the rope over the top of the post, and again Gus Menser felt the good earth leave his feet. For a few moments he eased the strain of the rope around his neck by holding to it with his hands, but his strength was about gone, his hands gradually loosened, and finally they fell limp at his sides. Thus ended an exciting evening of shooting, killing, and mob-administered law, for the crowd, one by one and two by two, slunk off into the darkness.

You can imagine that a large crowd was present at the first sign of dawn the next morning. The people stood around, talking and wondering what was next on the program.

About this time the morning train arrived. The passengers rushed over to see the man who was hanged by a mob. A photographer had arrived and had taken a picture or two of the dead man hanging to the sign post. Now it was time for the next step. They cut the rope and lowered the body.

It was reported that Gus Menser had had $300.00 in a pocketbook in his coat pocket, but upon searching they failed to find it. The body, of course, had hung there all night, and who can tell what became of the money—if any. A deck of cards, however, was found in his pocket, and they were distributed to the people who were present, as souvenirs.

On further examination it was discovered why the shot fired by Pete Dallman, which was supposed to have struck Menser, had not seriously hurt him. The bullet had hit the large buckle of his suspenders and had only been folded up in the metal.

Two Mexicans had been given a dollar to bury the body. About this time they drove up with their wagon which was drawn by two burros. They had come by Mr. Blackwell's log cabin, which was located on First Street at Rio Grande Avenue, and had gotten the wooden box which he had made early that morning for the purpose. Without further ado or ceremony the body was placed in the box, the lid was set on, and away they went. Their instructions were to bury Gus Menser at the foot of Graveyard Hill, and not up in the cemetery with the other graves.

Mexicans are not too eager to work hard on a hot June

morning, as a rule, and so when the grave was about two feet deep they tired of their labors and decided that the hole was deep enough, although they could not yet put the large box in. They easily remedied that situation by taking the body out of the box and dumping it in the hole. They filled up the shallow grave, and one of them took the box home and made a cupboard out of it. All he had to do was to put shelves in it and it was a good big storage space which pleased his Senora immensely.

For years the grave remained undisturbed, with the exception of the times when the children of the neighborhood would stop to drop a flower or two on it. Finally not so many years ago, Gus Menser's sister came from an eastern state where the family home is and had the bones removed and placed in a coffin and shipped back home where the remains were given a regular burial.

As you drive down the peaceful streets of Raton today, you can turn into First Street and see the spots where these scenes took place, but you will probably see only the modern little city with its bustle and hurry. You will probably note the "cop" on the corner who seems to have all of the present situations in hand, and you will probably feel the safety of our present day order and routine lives. Then you'll think back to the happenings of June, 1882, and wonder if someone didn't just dream about Gus Menser and his partner, Pete, the deputy sheriffs of the 1880's, who tried to preserve order, the mob which had its way, and all of the rest.

The Stockton Gang

by
Kenneth Fordyce

A gang of outlaws called the Stockton gang gave some trouble to the ranchers of northern New Mexico in 1879 and 1880. The gang came up out of Texas and hard-to-tell where from before that. This tale has to do with where they ended.

Mrs. Mary L. Sinnock who was in school in Otero, New Mexico, a town of about 600 people, five miles south of Raton in 1879, remembers the first time that she ever saw the gang of outlaws. The bad men came riding into Otero with their reins tied to the pommels of their saddles to leave both hands free to handle their guns which they fired into the air as they rode at full gallop into the town, thus announcing their arrival to the more timid or law-abiding citizens. Of course, the children all rushed out of the school to see the gang in action. The men were not in sight for long for they soon disappeared into the Otero saloon. After drinks, food, and rest the gang rode away to the east.

A short time later the gang appeared at the McCuistion Ranch, over east near Folsom. Mrs. McCormack, mother of Mrs. O. W. McCuistion, later told Mrs. Mary L. Sinnock of Raton that the men accepted the usual western hospitality of the ranch and sat around after dinner during the early afternoon resting and talking. They told the McCuistions that they were cattlemen and were out hunting. Mrs. McCormack said that she remarked when the men were gone that she had never talked to a more polite and gentlemanly group of men in her life.

Well, they were hunting and it was the cattle business that they were hunting but they were not successful in securing their cattle without payment as had been their custom for some weeks past. Neither would they hold up another store man or rancher who was unable to protect his property, for the group that they visited shortly after they left the McCuistion Ranch was prepared for them and during the shooting all of the important members of the Stockton gang were killed.

So! another gang came to New Mexico to prosper unwisely and unlawfully but found the men who settled the territory a determined lot able not only to come into a wild, unsettled land and make homes but able to protect those homes and establish law and order by eliminating the undesirables who drifted in looking for an easy life and a place to carry on their lawless living.

(The Stockton Gang is not to be confused with "Pap" Stockton, Thyke Stockton, and Tom Stockton and their descendants who reside in northern New Mexico yet.)

Source of Information: Mrs. Mary L. Sinnock, Otero in 1879, Raton since 1882.

Taos . . . The Law Conscious

by
Kenneth Fordyce

The people of Taos County, New Mexico have the reputation of being deeply interested in things political and legal. The day court convenes at the county seat, the day of an election (city, county, or national), the day of an execution, or any other political or legal event calls for the attendance of a majority of the people in the county. They come from far and near, arrive at sunup, and stay until the last bits of the interesting formalities have been disposed of.

Recently at a Raton Kiwanis meeting, Attorney Robert Morrow of Raton and Attorney J. E. Owens of Amarillo—formerly of Santa Fe and Taos—told of tax meetings, foreclosure sessions of court, and regular sessions of court in which they have participated in Taos. They related many interesting and amusing incidents; always present at these legal gatherings was the majority of the population of the Taos district, these people attentive, wide-eyed, and awed by the majesty of the law.

Mr. Luis Martinez of Raton tells a very interesting tale of happenings in Taos in the year 1905 when he was a boy. He even has written the incidents into an article and has given the article to a local weekly, free-delivery, tabloid-sized paper for publication. The COMMERCIAL printed the article in its July 8th issue.

Here are the facts briefly retold.

John Conway, living in the mining district near Red River, New Mexico whose good reputation had always been unquestioned found it necessary to protect his interests when another man and his son, whose names are unknown, started trouble about Conway's mining claims. Arguments developed into a shooting affray and when the smoke drifted away the father and son were dead and John Conway was alive.

Mr. Conway was arrested, tried for the double killing, and found guilty of first degree murder. He was sentenced to be hanged. The trial had taken place in Taos with a tremendous crowd at each session of court. Interest in the proceedings ran high. It was necessary to take Conway to Santa Fe to the territorial penitentiary for safe keeping as the Taos jail was not adequate for the purpose. The usual postponements, through the efforts of influential friends of Conway, delayed the hanging which was to take place in Taos.

In 1906, Conway was finally returned to the Taos county jail where preparations were being made for the execution. More delays, however, were encountered.

"La Revista de Taos" the Spanish paper of the village published by Mr. Jose Montaner boldly announced through its columns the date of the approaching execution of Mr. Conway. It was later firmly believed that the date was secured, not from the public officials but by arrangements with the merchants of Taos. The result was that the people of Taos County would fill the village on the imaginary date announced and business would flourish. The merchants of Taos found it necessary to employ extra clerks, to handle the excess trade. Of course, the day would pass without a hanging.

"La Revista" would offer an explanation in its next issue, and would announce another date in the not-too-far distance when Conway would swing for sure at the end of a rope. The Taos merchants benefited in this manner on four different occasions.

The day came for John Conway to be executed, but "La Revista" had made no announcement of the date. The rural population being unaware of the event was not present. The local populace turned out but of course the crowd did not compare favorably in size with the four previous gatherings.

It was commonly believed that Conway cheated the gallows on that last day. He had sharpened the handle of a spoon, which he had concealed in his cell, and when he knew that there was no hope of being saved, he attempted suicide by slashing his throat.

Mr. Abran Trujillo, who was the Taos jailer at that time and who still lives in Taos, hurriedly summoned Taos's Dr. Martin. The doctor sewed up Conway's throat in time for the execution. The hanging was held. The law collected its toll but the majority present believed that a corpse was hanged.

The law was not only cheated but that vast throng, which on four occasions had traveled long, tedious miles to witness the law in action, had been robbed of the thrill, in things legal, that it then desired and still craves.

Flechado Pass

by
Lorin W. Brown

"You know," my mother said, "I never reach this point along this road without remembering the story of Charles Kennedy." We had just driven over the top of Flechado Hill, that high grade which separates Taos canyon from the Moreno valley. Some say that this divide gets its name from a party of Taosenos who were set on here by the Indians and their scalped bodies were found later, bristling with arrows.

But it was recollection of another series of murders which was related as we drove along towards Ute Park.

"Here, somewhere near the road, your grandmother used to point out the ruins of Charles Kennedy's cabin. This man was one of many Americans who flocked into this part of the country at the time of the gold boom at Elizabethtown, or E'town as it was then called. This was about the year 1860 and I am going to tell you this as I remember it from my mother and father.

146

"This Kennedy married a near relative of ours, Gregorita Martinez. Your grandmother used to say, when telling me about Gregorita and her husband, 'Tan bonita Gregorita, yet she married this so ugly Americano.' According to her this 'Chales Canada,' as his name was pronounced in Taos, was a great big shambling brute with bulging blue eyes and a mop of coarse red hair.

"Whenever Kennedy and his wife came to Taos he would visit your grandparents. He seemed to be a pleasant enough fellow and thought a great deal of your grandfather. These visits were not very frequent as Kennedy was something of a lone wolf and pretended to be very occupied with his claims. He always seemed to be well supplied with gold in nugget and dust form so that his claims must have been rich ones. The last visits they made to father's, Gregorita very proudly showed him her baby daughter. She was very happy, but your grandmother said that Charles was rather sulky and there were signs of a recent quarrel between the couple. Your grandmother had an instinctive mistrust of El Chales, as she called him, and at that time had a premonition of the terrible thing that was to happen and of the worse happenings which it was to disclose.

"During the years that Kennedy and his wife lived in their cabin by the pass there was much traffic between the mining camps and Taos. Many men from Taos had claims around E'town or Ute Park and were often on the road seeing their families or on some other business. Others were often on the road bent on spending their gold on 'Taos Lightning' or in the gambling or dance halls in Taos. There was much more gold in the ground and what was already in men's pockets was spent freely.

"But men began to disappear someplace along this road. Lone travelers would leave for Taos and never be seen again. Even groups of three or four, traveling together for mutual protection, would never arrive in Taos. Of these, many were strangers over whose disappearance not much fuss was made because there was no one close to be alarmed over their fate. But there were some from Taos and nearby towns whose friends and relatives made efforts to learn their fate—to no avail.

"After this, men went heavily armed and in strong parties and yet some venturesome fellows who would travel this road alone disappeared like the rest. One afternoon a party of eight topped the rise and started to ride down the slope to a favorite camping place. As they were riding by Kennedy's place they were surprised to see Gregorita come running out screaming and calling on them for help. Spurring their horses towards her and surrounding the frantic woman they soon knew what was wrong. It seems that Kennedy in a mad rage had seized their baby and had killed it, throwing the body into the flames of the large fireplace. Then he had turned on his wife and, no doubt, intended to murder her, but she had escaped and, fortunately for her, just as these men were riding by.

"The men after hearing her story rode towards the cabin, leaving one of their number with the weeping woman. As they reached the cabin, Kennedy left through a back door and made a dash for his horse which was tied nearby. A lucky shot in one shoulder made him an easy capture.

"'You fellows think that baby is the only person I have killed?' he asked them. Without any semblance of remorse he boasted of having murdered all of the many who had disappeared on that road. He led the surprised group from grave to grave and in one spot there were four bodies piled in one grave. Altogether he claimed to have killed thirty-one persons. His story was not doubted and next day he was hanged in E'town and his head decorated a pole for many days on the main street of the busy little mining village."

The Raid on the Granary

by
Reyes N. Martinez

During the last half of the nineteenth century the valley of Taos became known as the Granary of New Mexico, exporting large quantities of its surplus grain to the central and southern parts of the then Territory of New Mexico, to Colorado and even parts of Utah. It was in the intermediate period between 1880 and 1890 that year after year bountiful crops were raised by the farmers of the section, causing an accumulation of wheat beyond the local consumption and the export demand. One of the most fertile sections at the time was Arroyo Seco, at the northern end of the valley. Here stocks of grain had accumulated beyond record proportions. Granaries were still filled to capacity even as late as the year 1887, when the sequence of events related in the following narrative took place.

Moving cautiously in the early dawn of a bleak March day, even before the first columns of smoke curled skyward from the chimneys of the earliest risers, a caravan composed of twenty-two men and eighteen wagons was slowly approaching the granary of Don Amador Trujillo, pioneer merchant, extensive farmer and livestock raiser of Arroyo Seco.

Several days previous, an agent for a wholesale concern in Denver, Colorado, had visited the village, offering a substantial price for wheat. An increased demand for grain had developed by the inrush of immigration into the mining regions of the state of Colorado. Having learned of this, the owners of large stocks of wheat had determined to hold their grain pending further offers and higher prices, and the visiting agent had left without substantiating any deals, promising to return at a later date. The news spread rapidly. There was money in wheat. At this time there existed in the Desmonte region, four miles west of Arroyo Seco, a secret gang of thieves. The operations of this gang had attained considerable proportions of late. They had become more bold and no longer concealed their nefarious activities. It was plainly evident that their utter disregard for law was sustained or sanctioned by the authorities in charge. Thus encouraged, this gang had already hatched a plot to rob the granary of the rich merchant, Don Amador Trujillo.

Their scheme was to take the grain into Colorado and realize full value on it, sell the horses and wagons, which they had stolen from different owners in and around Arroyo Seco at the point of a gun, disband and disperse throughout the western settlements, and never return. The leader of the gang was Juan Manuel Velasquez, 33 years old, tall, slim, black-haired, a small, black mustache adorning his upper lip, his ruddy cheeks contrasting with the mischievous glint of his jet black eyes, alert and quick of movement. Dressed in a black flannel shirt, a red bandana handkerchief tied loosely about his neck, black, high-heel boots covering the lower leg of his blue denim overalls, and topped by a wide-brimmed black hat, he rode a buckskin colored horse of spirited gait, truly the rig of the typical desperado of the western country. Up and down the long string of wagons he rode briskly, cautioning and instructing the drivers. The granary was located somewhat back, to the northeast of the residence and store building of Don Amador. As the wagons drove past into the yard in front of the granary, two dogs ran from the house towards the teams, barking at their hind legs. Stationing three men with loaded rifles at the rear end of the row of wagons as guards, Velasquez quickly dismounted and ran towards the granary, and taking a long crowbar from one of the wagons, with the aid of two of the men, he pried open the door.

"Llenen los carros," (load the wagons) he ordered.

Don Amador, awakened by the barking of the dogs, arose from his bed; looking out of the window he took in the situation at once. Dressing hastily he went out through an opposite side door, rushed as fast as he could, notwithstanding his sixty-five years of age, to the house of his compadre, Don Antonio Tircio Gallegos, another wealthy resident of Arroyo Seco, some two hundred yards below. An early riser, Don Antonio answered his excited knock and opened wide the door to let him in.

"Que hay, compadre; que lo trae aqui a esta hora?" (What is the matter, what brings you here at this hour?)

"I have come to ask you to send Pablo to notify the sheriff at Taos that a gang of robbers is loading my wheat at the granary. Send him at once," answered Don Amador.

No time was lost. Pablo was a young orphan boy, thirteen years of age, that Don Antonio had taken into custody, giving him board and lodging for whatever help the boy could give. While the boy dressed, the two men saddled a horse. Pablo galloped away at once, following the bed of an arroyo to keep out of sight of the gang. Arriving at Taos, the county seat, before sunrise, he immediately sought the sheriff and informed him of his mission.

"Ha! So they are raiding old man Amador's granary, eh? Que mal negocio (that is too bad). Toma tu tiempo, muchacho; dejame sacar mis armas y reclutar algunos hombres (take your time, boy, let me take out my guns and recruit some men)," he said. The boy had also been instructed to notify Captain Frederick Muller, officer in charge of a government troop stationed at Taos, and did not tarry with the sheriff, notified the captain and went back immediately. The captain got ready and departed with six of his men for Arroyo Seco.

In the meantime the loading at the granary got into full swing. Don Amador rushed back home from the house of Don Antonio. Advancing toward Velasquez he asked the meaning of their audaciousness. "We are taking this grain that you have stored here, of no benefit to anyone, and are going to sell it for you on commission. You will get your money when we return. You better go back to bed if you value your health, and stay there," answered Velasquez. Not mistaking the intensified glint in the gangster's dark eyes, the old man meekly obeyed and returned to the house to watch from there the proceedings, in the hope that the sheriff would arrive soon.

The wagons were all loaded with wheat and had started to back away from the yard, when a sharp command to "Put them up high!" struck the ears of the raiders. Dumbfounded by the unexpected suddenness of the command, as they never dreamed that the sheriff would betray their trust in him, they reached upward with their hands, while Captain Muller and his men, who had followed the bed of the same Arroyo over which Pablo had traveled, passed through Amador's house from the side opposite the granary, disarmed the guards, and placed all the men under arrest. The whole gang was then marched to the county jail at Taos. The sheriff pretended ignorance of the whole affair, as the eyes of the gangsters looked daggers at him, though he gave an understanding wink at Velasquez as the men were led past to the cells of the jail.

At Arroyo Seco the commotion had attracted the attention of the populace who had gathered in excited groups in the yard of the granary. Soon the wheat was unloaded from the wagons and placed back in the granary.

Three days later a sensational jail break took place. The Velasquez gang had overpowered the jailer and the two extra guards and escaped. Corrupt politics had played its part. Velasquez and his gang disappeared never to be heard of again, and the sheriff, the most notorious political despot that Taos county had ever known, was obliged to resign to save his neck, and left the country for a healthier clime. The boy, Pablo, also was sent back by Don Antonio, fearing for his safety, to his native Chimayo, whence he had come.

This episode is recorded as the most audacious attempt at robbery in the history of Taos County.

Source of Information: Pablo Garduno of Arroyo Hondo who is the boy Pablo in the story and is now a grown man.

A Holdup After Midnight

by
Reyes N. Martinez

It must have been somewhat past one o'clock a.m. one night during the month of August of the year 1870, as the light of the approaching dawn was already noticeable in the eastern sky, when a knock on the door of his home on the northwest corner of the village-square in Arroyo Hondo aroused from his sleep the good priest, Father Lucero.

"Open your door, father; we want you to hear a confession," a man's voice pleaded. "Brother, is this not an improper hour to administer religious service to you? Will you not come after sunrise? I have had very little rest, having stayed up quite late before retiring, and I kindly request that you come later and allow me to obtain a little more needed sleep," he answered. "We are very sorry to inconvenience you at this time of the night, father, but one of our companions has been severely beaten and we fear that he is near death," the voice outside said.

That night a dance had been held at the village dance hall and Father Lucero thought that perhaps the man may have been assaulted at the dance. His sympathetic nature did not permit him to deny the man what, probably, might be the last act of religious charity, so he opened the door and ushered into the room two men supporting a third man whom they laid on the bed of the priest. Bending over him the priest asked: "Is your condition serious?" "Yes, very serious, indeed," answered the man, suddenly sitting up on the bed. "Where is the money that you have been hoarding all these years? We want it and have come for it." Dumfounded at first by the deception worked on him but keeping his presence of mind, Father Lucero offered to deliver the money to them. "Make no commotion," he said, trying to figure a way of escape. "The money is in my trunk," he said, motioning toward a trunk in a corner of the room. "Don't trouble yourself; let me have the key. You sit down here on the bed," said the man who had feigned being injured. Arising from the bed, he made a step toward the priest, who, seeing his chance of escape about to fade, made a dash for the door. The other two men obstructed his passage and seized him, voicing threats to kill the "fraile" (friar).

In the scuffle that followed, the candle that he had lighted fell to the floor and went out. In the darkness friend and foe were alike. Managing for a brief moment to disengage himself from their grasp and remembering a heavy club that he always had behind the door, the priest took it and he swung wildly. He felt sure that he struck one or two of the men, and tried to gain the door, at the same time opening the blade of a knife that he carried in his pocket, just as one of the robbers again grabbed him. Striking at him several times with the knife, the priest and the man rolled out through the door which the priest had luckily managed to open. Over and over they rolled on the ground till the priest felt the hot stream of blood spurting from the man's severed jugular vein, and pushing him away, ran to the house of a neighbor to ask for help. Fearful, the neighbor refused to return with the priest and allowed him to spend the rest of the night at his house.

The next morning the corpse of a man was found by the riverside. The priest identified him as one of his assailants. His companions must have dragged and left him there and fled. The identity of the man was never known. He was buried on the hillside northwest of the village, where a house now stands. The owner of the house says that, on some nights, he hears rapping and knocking from beneath the floor. It is believed that the spirit of the assailant of the good padre still wanders restlessly near the scene of his attempt to rob the holy man.

Years later, when the good Father Lucero died, his rich hoard of money was found buried several feet underground in front of his fireplace, and was carried away by a man named Lavarta, who, old-timers say, fled with it to Old Mexico and was never heard of again.

※※※

In the early part of the 60's of the nineteenth century the archbishop at Santa Fe sent several French priests with orders to replace the Spanish and Mexican priests in several communities in Taos county. Resentful, many of them continued to function independently of the archdiocese at Santa Fe, saying mass and administering the sacraments in their usual manner, and ceasing to pay tributes to the archbishop at Santa Fe. Among these was Father Lucero, stationed at Arroyo Hondo. This good priest was noted for his many acts of kindness to the needy and his ever ready willingness to render service to all. His discontinuance of sending the customary tributes to the archbishop at Santa Fe tended to swell considerably his funds, and it became a well-known fact that he had a large hoard, the whereabouts of which were unknown to anyone else.

Source of Information: Rafael Vigil. Owner of the house over the grave of the assailant of Father Lucero is Guillermo Herrera.

Murder in Mora County Mystery

(Santa Fe New Mexican,
August 12, 1864)

We learn from Theodore S. Whea-
ton, Esq.. U. S. district attorney, the
facts of a most brutal murder committed in ora county. The body of
one Herrera was found in the road
about ten miles from Mora, with
the skull fractured and five bullet
holes through the body.

It was first supposed he had been
killed by the Indians as they had
been seen in the vicinity, but subsequent investigations proved that the
supposition was incorrect. From the
tracks about where the body was
found, it appears that Herrera was
met by someone on the road, that he
alighted from his horse and sat
down by the roadside in conversation with this person, as the marks
on the ground plainly showed, when
in an unguarded moment he was
stunned by a blow from a club, and
then, to complete the tragedy, his
six-shooter was taken from his person, and five shots discharged into
his body.

He was in the possession of about
$200 at the time, and this, it is sup-
posed, was the provocation for the
bloody deed, as it is missing together
with his horse and pistol. It is to be
hoped that the perpetrator of this
foul deed may be brought to justice.

Facsimile: "Murder in Mora County Mystery," *Santa Fe New Mexican*, August 12, 1864, Boothill News, August 29, 1940, NMFWP, WPA #88b, NMSRCA

Pioneer Story: Mrs. Mary E. Burleson

by
Edith L. Crawford

"My husband, Pete Burleson, came to Cimarron, New Mexico in Colfax County in the year of 1876, from the Big Bend country in Texas, which is located in the Davis Mountains. He arrived in Colfax county with about 1500 head of cattle; he settled on a place on the Red river, built a two room log cabin and settled down to raising cattle.

"In 1877, my father, O.K. Chittenden and Clay Allison brought Mr. Burleson down to our house to try and persuade him to run for sheriff of Colfax county, is how I first met him.

"He first said he would not consider making the race at all as he had his cattle and place to look after, and how much better off he would of been if he had only stayed with his first decision as he realized very little out of his ranch and cattle.

"They kept after him until he made the race and was elected by a large majority; this was in November 1877. He took office

January 1, 1878, and one of the first things he did after taking office was to run down a negro man by the name of Jack (is the only name I ever heard him called) who had killed Mr. Maxwell and his twelve year old boy. They had just come to Colfax county from Iowa, and had bought a ranch and were living in a tent; they had this negro Jack hired to cut post for fencing the place; he killed Mr. Maxwell in the tent, took one of his saddle horses and rode down the road and met the boy coming in with a load of posts; he spoke to the boy and rode on by the wagon, turned and shot the boy in the back, watched him until he saw him fall from the wagon.

"The horses with the wagon went on down the road until they came to the gate entering the Maxwell ranch. On passing through the gate one of the front wheels caught on the gate post and held the wagon fast; the team stood there two days without food or water; one of the neighbor ranchers was passing by and saw the team standing at the gate; he stopped by to see what was the matter as the horses seemed to be so restless; he went on up to the tent where he found Mr. Maxwell, dead shot through the head.

"He went back to the horses, unhitched them, fed and watered them, and then started out for help; he had only gone a short distance from the gate when he found the boy face down in the middle of the road.

"He summoned help and started looking for the negro but he was nowhere around the ranch. They knew this negro would know something about the killing, so the hunt for the negro started and they found him at his home in Trinidad, Colorado, where his wife lived.

"Mr. Burleson brought him back to Cimarron, New Mexico to wait trial, but the feeling was so bitter against the negro he was taken to Taos, New Mexico for trial and was sentenced to be hanged at Cimarron, New Mexico. Colfax County citizens still wanted to take the negro out and hang him, but Mr. Burleson appealed to these men as citizens of Colfax County to let the law take its course and hang the negro, and this was the first hanging by law in the Territory of New Mexico. It was in the month of May, 1878. My aunt and I went to see the negro hung but upon seeing him on the gallows and hearing his confession that he did not know why he killed Mr. Maxwell and his son we did not stay to see him hung; but lots of people did as it was a public hanging and the first one in that part of the country. . . ."

Narrator: Mrs. Mary E. Burleson, age 78, Carrizozo, New Mexico.

Red River

by
James A. Burns

Unlike the early days of 'Etown and Cimarron' where to "get his man" was a common saying, there were only one or two killings recorded during the Red River boom. One story is related like this:

Jack Connley, who was associated with Soapy Smith, (and Soapy Smith was just like his name sounds) in the early mining camps of Leadville and Creed, Colo., also of Alaska. Charles Purdy, employed by Connley to work on a placer claim in the vicinity of Questa knew too much, so Connley shot the old man. James Redding, a young boy, appeared on the scene and was also shot by Connley because he was a witness to the first murder. After the shooting, Connley mounted his horse and rode swiftly to Red River, leaving the bodies of the two victims. He reached Red River and hid in his cabin, still known to the present residents as the Connley cabin.

A sheepherder gave the alarm in Questa and the sheriff, also six deputies, were sent to Red River to get Connley. Knowing him to be armed, they took refuge behind rocks and other objects, demanding the prisoner to come out of his hiding place. It was decided that firing on the cabin was the only feasible plan of getting Connley to surrender. When he heard the conversation, he called to Joe Phipps that he would surrender if Phipps would accompany him to Taos. Connley surrendered, Phipps took him to Taos, and the trial was scheduled. The trial found Connley guilty and he was sentenced to be hung. Before the fatal day, a razor was smuggled into the jail and he attempted suicide which was unsuccessful. Later he was hung. . . .

The Capture of the Outlaw Coe

by
W. M. Emery

few miles north of Kenton, Oklahoma, lies the ruins of
the famous "Robber's Roost" of "No Man's Land."

The Neutral Strip or "No Man's Land" as it is most
commonly called, was a piece of land lying between the 100th and
103rd meridian, and north of "36." It was thirty-four miles wide
and one hundred and sixty miles long; it comprised what is now
Cimarron, Texas, and Beaver Counties, Oklahoma. It was claimed
neither by the Texas Republic, nor by the United States, as it had
been missed in all the surveys.[1]

This rough, hilly, isolated country was an ideal place for
fugitives from justice. When one was within its boundaries, the
officers could not go in after them.

In the early '60s, Robber's Roost was built by the notorious
outlaw Coe. Coe—we are told—was the "black-sheep" of a
wealthy, aristocratic, southern family. After some trouble in his

own State he came west and located in "No Man's Land." Here he built a large house, which was headquarters for his gang.

These men made their living by robbing immigrant trains and stealing cattle and horses.

The Government made several attempts to capture Coe. At one time they sent a man disguised as an outlaw to spy upon the bandits. There was a young boy in the camp who had joined the outlaw band just for the excitement which that life furnished him. The spy and the boy became good friends. As the man had collected all the information he wanted and was ready to leave, he persuaded the boy to go with him and return home. He and the boy decided to steal away one night when the gang was camped near Las Vegas, and go to Fort Union. The outlaws had become suspicious of the man and were watching him. He and the boy had not traveled far when they were overtaken and killed by the bandits.

The nearest settlement to "Robber's Roost" was the struggling little village of Madison, New Mexico, which was located about six miles northeast of the present town of Folsom.

Coe and his outlaws were frequent visitors at Madison, where they terrorized the settlers. They caused the people more trouble than the Indians did. They would ride into town, turn their horses loose, demand someone to unsaddle them and feed them, while they either loafed around or went to Mrs. Emery's home and demanded that she feed them.

The settlers had to comply with their demands for they knew the outlaws would kill them if they did not, as the outlaws outnumbered the settlers. Emery's had a large "bunk-house" where these men often slept.

Other frequent visitors at Madison were the United States Cavalry from both Fort Lyons, Colorado, and Fort Union, New Mexico. These men were usually looking for Coe and his men.

After one of his raids on Fort Union where he had stolen some Government mules, (these mules were branded with a big U. S.) Coe was captured and returned to the Fort. He was not there long when he escaped and returned to Robber's Roost.

Some time later he was again captured and taken to Fort Lyons. General Penrose was the Commanding Officer at Fort Lyons at this time.

One day Mrs. Emery saw a ragged, bewhiskered man, who was riding a poor scrawny Indian pony, come toward the house. The man dismounted and came to the door. Mrs. Emery soon recognized him as Coe, the gentleman outlaw.

"Why, Mr. Coe, I didn't know you," she said, "what has happened?"

He told her he had been caught in a hard rainstorm and his horse had gotten away from him. A Mexican sheepherder had loaned him a horse and dry clothes. He never told her he had stolen the sheepherder's clothes and horse and left the poor man stranded on the prairie many miles south of Fort Lyons. Nor did Mrs. Emery tell him that she knew he had escaped from Fort Lyons, and that the Cavalry from Fort Union had just left Madison looking for him.

She gave him his dinner and told him he could go to the bunkhouse and rest because "he looked so tired."

As soon as she knew he was asleep she called her oldest son, Bud, (the late W. F. Sumpter) to her and sent him after the soldiers and his father who was with the soldiers.

Bud rode his little pony in a hard "lope" from Madison to Las Alamos Plaza, which was three miles west of the present town of Folsom, where the soldiers had camped for the night. As soon as they heard his story they mounted their horses and made a hard ride back to Madison.

(It was a delight to Mr. Sumpter to tell of this experience

and how proud he felt as he rode his little pony at the side of the Captain's horse all the way back to Madison.)

The Cavalry surrounded the bunkhouse and ordered Coe to surrender. Coe feigned sleep until the Captain walked into the room and shook him. He surrendered without resistance. As he walked quietly out of the door, he saw Bud's pony grazing a short distance away.

"That pony has had a hard ride," he said.

By this remark the soldiers knew that he was aware of his captor's informant.

Coe was taken to Pueblo and put in jail there to await trial. The soldiers knew that if he ever escaped he would go back to Madison and kill Mrs. Emery and Bud, and possibly every one in the village. One night shortly after his imprisonment the soldiers lynched Coe and without removing the handcuffs or the ball and chain from his ankles, they hung him to a tree on the banks of Fountain Creek.[2]

His disappearance was kept a mystery for many years. A few years ago some men working on the creek banks found a skeleton under a tree, near where—it is rumored—that Coe was buried. The skeleton had a ball and chain on its feet and handcuffs on its wrist.

Sources of Information:

1. This story has been written as it was told to the author by his uncle, W. F. Sumpter, and his aunt, Mrs. Sarah Jane Gleason, of Folsom, New Mexico. Mr. Sumpter was the "Bud" in the story.

2. The ending of the life of Coe was given to the author by A. W. Thompson, of Denver, Colorado, who got his information from Lute Kahill, who was jailor at Pueblo, at the time Coe was a prisoner there.

(Coe was hung in 1868.)

Old Timers Stories: Early Days Folsom: The Killer Thompson

by
W. M. Emery

In the northeastern part of New Mexico the little village of Folsom lies dreamily basking in the summer sun, or snugly protected from winter's howling blasts by the high rocky hills which surround it on all sides. But this little village has not always been so quiet and peaceful as it is now, for in its youth it was the typical cowtown of the western frontier, as wild as the deer in the hills or the steers on the open range. It was also one of the largest towns in Union County and put up such a good fight for the county seat against Clayton, that it held that honor for three days before Clayton won the final decision and became county seat for all times.

About 1895 Folsom boasted two mercantile stores, a post office and three saloons, besides other business establishments usually founds in such towns. The two mercantile stores were operated by Steve Mitchel and John King; the saloons were operated by Sam Watson—proprietor of the "Bucket of Blood"; W. A. Thompson—proprietor of the "Gem"; and Tom Manasker—who operated a saloon for John King.

A short time before the events of this story took place Thompson and King had both been in love with the same woman, although neither man had been lucky enough to win her they had developed a bitter hatred for one another that lasted through the years. It was due to this enmity that King opened the saloon in competition to Thompson.

Thompson, a native of Missouri, had come west after killing a man in his hometown. After coming to Folsom he had served as deputy sheriff for a short time. One day he watched a Mexican go in to the "Bucket of Blood" saloon, which was located across the street from his place of business. This made him angry, and when the Mexican came out on the street drunk, and began to yell and shoot up the town, Thompson walked across the street and killed him; but, being a deputy sheriff, he claimed that he shot in self defense and the case was closed.

Knowing the jealous, envious disposition of Thompson, it delighted King to take men to the Manasker saloon and treat them just to provoke him. This went on until Thompson's anger and hatred knew no bonds.

Early one fall morning, just as the business houses were being opened for business, and the housewives over the town were preparing breakfast for their families, King took a Mexican boy over to the Manasker saloon and gave him a drink. This boy was "flunky" at the Gem saloon. Thompson was waiting for the Mexican as he came down the street. He said a few words to him, then jerked out his gun; the boy ran, with Thompson a short distance behind.

Next door to the Gem saloon was the restaurant and rooming house of Mrs. George Thompson (no relation to W. A.

Thompson). The Mexican dodged around the corner of Mrs. Thompson's house, and running down the side of the house, cut across the back yard between the house and the corral. Just as he started across the yard Thompson fired at him, but the bullet went into Mrs. Thompson's kitchen.

Mrs. Thompson was sitting in front of her kitchen stove when the bullet from W. A. Thompson's gun came through the wall and landed behind the stove near her. She ran out the door as another shot rang out on the still morning air, and saw the Mexican fall to his knees. There stood W. A. Thompson with the smoking gun in his hand, "looking like a thunder cloud."

"What do you mean by shooting into my house?" she demanded.

"Wasn't shooting in your old house," Thompson sulkily replied, as he turned on his heel and went back to his saloon.

The Mexican had taken advantage of his lucky fall—which had prevented his being shot—and this conversation to make a quick getaway.

As Thompson emerged from his saloon he was armed with a rifle. The first person he spied was Billy Thatcher—another bitter enemy and an officer of the law. Thatcher was a block away, coming across the street from the post office. Thompson began shooting at Thatcher, but as he fired his first shot, Jeff Kehl—a married man and father of two children—ran out of King's store and around the corner to see what the shooting was about; he was just in time to receive the bullet in his abdomen. He died that night.

Thatcher and Thompson then began firing at each other as they walked toward one another, Thompson using a rifle and Thatcher a revolver. Strange as it may seem, neither man was able to hit the other although they were drawing nearer and firing with every step. Finally Thatcher succeeded in shooting the barrel of Thompson's rifle, knocking it from his hand.

Thompson then ran to his saloon and barricaded himself in the basement of the building. All day the town men worked to get him out. Public sentiment was running high; had they been able to have gotten him out, Thompson would have been lynched. King was determined to fire the building and burn him out but was prevented from doing this by Steve Mitchel, who insisted that to burn the saloon would mean burning the whole block, including Mitchel's store. This plan was abandoned.

Late in the evening Thompson became so drunk that he gave himself up to the officers. He was taken home and put to bed, and guarded all night. The next day he was taken to Clayton and placed in the county jail. As he was still in danger of being lynched, a change of venue was granted and Thompson was taken to the Springer jail, but was soon released on bond, which had been furnished by friends. While awaiting trial Thompson returned to Folsom and disposed of his business.

After his acquittal (for he was acquitted at the trial) he returned to Clayton. Thompson later went to Trinidad and was there married to the girl from Missouri, whom he had killed his first man over. He then went to Oklahoma where he killed another man, but was again acquitted. He spent his remaining years in that State.

Sources of Information: Mrs. Roxie Emery, Clayton, New Mexico. Mrs. Emery's mother was Mrs. George Thompson of this story. Billy Thatcher, of this story, lives at Trinidad, Colorado, where he is employed in The First National Bank.

When Chris Otto Whipped the Bad Man

by
W. M. Emery

Back in the middle 80's the late Christian Otto and partner, Charley Scheiter, trailed a herd of sheep in from Deer Trail, Colorado and located west of Clayton, New Mexico, in the heart of the cattle range. At that time the cattle companies kept a gunman at fancy wages to fight off sheep men or kill them if necessary.

This bad man, named Cook, was with a winter floating outfit. Cook was ordered to go to the Otto camp and move them on. He found Otto at a water hole alone and rode up and said, "Heinie, you will have to move on with your bla, blas as this is a cattle range, sabe?"

Otto answered, "I don't want to get personal, but if that is what you want you can go straight to hell."

Did he go? No. He crawled off his horse, pulled off his coat and pistol and laid them down and the fight began; it was close, but Otto finally won out. The bad man got up and mounted his horse and looked back over his shoulder and said, "I expect this water hole is yours by right of possession and by being physically able to protect it."

After this fighting man arrived at camp with his eyes blacked, he was asked why he didn't kill Otto.

"Well," he said, "I have an idea. His sheep are poor and will die this winter and he'll be looking for a job. I want to get financed and bet he can whip anybody in the world."

This water hole is still in the name of Christian Otto and Son; Cook, the bad man, is long dead.

Told by Col. Jack Potter in Western Livestock Magazine, Denver.

PIONEER   - -   "Trouble . . "

The County Court House and Jail had been moved from Cimarron to Springer, New Mexico; Springer was proud of the fact that it was county seat town in Colfax County, and the jailor was proud of the fact that he was jailor, as evidenced by the following happenings which started a near riot in Northern New Mexico.

A man--we will call him Hart--had been arrested for some offense and had been placed in the Springer Jail with several other prisoners. (Let us call the jailor--Wheeler). Wheeler got word from three of Hart's friends that they were coming up to get him out of jail. Wheeler decided otherwise.

The jailor had no help, so he took some of the prisoners up into the Court House building and armed them with rifles. When Hart's friends came into the square in front of the jail, it was a small matter for the prisoners to open fire and shoot the three. What was more, they killed them. The prisoners were all returned to their cells--including Mr. Hart.

It can easily be understood that the affair created almost a riot in the city, and it soon spread throughout the county. Word got to Raton, forty two miles to the north, and a group of men formed a posse, decided that the city of Springer whould be entered, and that justice should be done. The greatest delay was in the long ride down to Springer on horses. It proved to be a valuable delay for it gave the local judge time to telegraph to the Governor of the territory. He dispatched soldiers from Ft. Union who arrived in time to preserve order, prevent further trouble and more bloodshed.

                                            C B Thacker - Raton.

Facsimile: "Pioneer, Trouble," Kenneth Fordyce, March 5, 1937, NMFWP, *American Guide*, WPA #188, NMSRCA

A Tough One

by
W. M. Emery

"I guess I've worked with a hundred or more bandits and outlaws," said Albert Easley, "and I found them to be the finest bunch of fellows in the country to work with. They use to come down here to the IOI Ranch and work and rest when the Law was getting too close to them, then all of a sudden they would pack up and leave and go back to their business again.

"But they were a jolly, generous bunch. They'd do anything in the world for you if they liked you. They could take a joke better than lots of men, and were always ready to play some prank on someone. Of course you couldn't ask them too many personal questions, and you didn't want to get serious when you were joking them. Some of them were pretty tough characters, too, but we never had a killing on the IOI Ranch.

"I remember one man, when one of the boys came in and announced a new settler fifteen miles away, jumped up and said,

'I'm leavin'. This country's getting too d—n close for me.' They had their principles, too. Maybe a little less high than a lot of folks, but not broken half as often. They gambled, but not with kids. They drank whiskey, but would not give a kid a drink. Try to find somebody in those businesses now who does that way.

"But the toughest fellow that I ever saw was a boy about twenty-two. I was working for the Pitchfork Ranch up above Folsom, when this kid came in and started to work. He was a pretty good hand, but he was always bragging about how tough he was, but I figured that a fellow who was always bragging about how tough he was couldn't be very tough, because really tough men didn't as a general thing brag about their toughness. But he turned out to be just as tough as he said he was.

"One day he wanted to go to the Cottonwoods to get some whiskey. Mr. Drew was running the store there at that time, and it was just a Mexican Plaza.

"I told him that I couldn't go but if he wanted to go to start out, and if he brought back any whiskey I might help him drink it.

"He was gone a couple of days. When he got back he was just having a big time over the way he had corralled the Mexicans of the Plaza, in the store, and kept them there all the time he was in the Plaza. I never thought much about it at the time, but a few days later I saw Mr. Drew and he told me that the fellow had really done just that, and every time one of them stuck his head out that boy 'knocked sand in his eyes' (he shot so close to the Mexican that he dug up the sand around his feet, and it flew in his eyes).

"After he had worked about six weeks, I had to go to Trinidad for supplies. Rufus (his name was Rufus Rough) wanted to go with me. He rode horseback and I went in the buckboard. As we started up Frijole Hill, we met two Mexicans hauling wood. That boy jerked out his gun and began shooting between the burro's feet.

176

Those two Mexicans were scared to death. They tumbled off of their loads of wood in every direction; I never saw anyone laugh as hard as that boy did.

"When we got to Trinidad he hunted up Dr. Owens and asked for his time. After he had spent most of his money in Trinidad, he went to work for the H Ts, a big outfit over on the Picketwire, below Trinidad.

"A man named Johnson was boss of that outfit, and he and Rufus didn't get along from the start. One day they had a quarrel and Rufus shot Johnson in the hip. The cowboys shot Rufus, and laid him out in the bunkhouse for dead. They put his gun in his bedroll, and went outside.

"But Rufus came to, got his gun out of that bedroll and crawled to the door and began shooting at those boys before they knew what was happening. They surrounded the bunkhouse and recaptured Rufus; then they took him out and hung him to a high tree and shot him full of holes. They made sure he was dead that time.

"That boy was the toughest one person I ever saw."

Told by Albert Easley to the writer.

The Clifton House

by
W. M. Emery

Part 1

Barlow & Sanderson ran the stage line that followed the fork of the old Santa Fe Trail, which came by Bent's Fort, down over the Raton Mountains into the territory of New Mexico, through Willow Springs, where today we find the busy little city of Raton, and six miles on down the Raton creek to Clifton. The passengers rode in stagecoaches which were drawn by four animals, sometimes horses but usually mules.

At the Clifton House, which was the stage station, where fresh horses were hitched to the coach, the passengers could have a good meal, and even stay over night, for it was a hotel as well as a station.

The Clifton House was the headquarters for the entire community. There was a general store and blacksmith shop also. A few dwellings occupied by natives and an Anglo or two completed the settlement.

The Clifton House was started in 1866 and finished in 1870. It was built by Tom Stockton and occupied by the Stocktons for some time after that. The house was a large two-story adobe building with a basement. Broad stone steps led up to the front porch which extended across the front and half way around each side of the building. The hallway, or entry, in the center of the first floor, was where the wash basins were kept for the use of the guests who wished to refresh themselves. From this hall the stairway led to two large bedrooms upstairs. At the back of the hall one entered the large dining room, where several customers could be served at one time. On one side of the front hall was the saloon and the office; on the other side of the hall was the parlor. On both sides of the dining room were two bedrooms large enough to accommodate several guests at one time. The frame structure back of the dining room was the kitchen which had been built-on last. The well was in one corner of the kitchen. There were fire-places in nearly every room. The front rooms of the house had bay windows which were curtained off with drapes. There were several storerooms in the basement.

The trips of the stage coaches were timed so that the coaches arrived at the Clifton House at meal time, or at nightfall, so that the passengers could get a good night's rest at this fine Hotel. The stages, which were to go on immediately, found little delay, for fresh, well-fed animals were harnessed ready to take the places of the tired, hard-driven ones which had just come in off of the trail.

The service at the Clifton House was the one bright spot to travelers in the difficult journey across Northern New Mexico in the 1870's. Rest could be enjoyed there in good beds. Fine foods, some of which were grown locally and other delicacies—which had to be hauled in from the end of the railroad, were to be had at the Clifton House table. Comfort in a modern hostelry was part of life at the Clifton House for it was more like eastern houses, as much of the material for its construction—sawed lumber, glass, and the like—the furniture for the house, and many other things had been hauled in from Leavenworth, Kansas, to which point the railroad had brought them.

Besides the through-travelers who enjoyed the Clifton House, there were the cattle men of the entire Northern New Mexico section who came to the big fall and spring round-ups. The Clifton House was the headquarters for people and happenings in the '70's.

Part 2

Contrary to the belief that the Clifton House was the headquarters for bad-men, and the scene of many robberies and killings in those early days, those who lived there during that time report a very quiet but busy existence with fewer violent crimes than are common in our cities today.

Some would have it believed that the place was literally strewn with the bones of many victims who were robbed, beaten, and killed as they passed through this northern part of the territory. It was once told that the dining room table was placed in front of a curtain and that wealthy guests would be purposely seated so that they could be attacked and killed by husky individuals concealed behind the curtain. But the worst that can be authentically reported is two violent deaths at or near the Clifton House, and the burial of many bad men who were killed in Northern New Mexico and brought to the Cemetery at Clifton for burial.

Both of these killings which were referred to hinge around the well-known Clay Allison and Chunk Colbert. These two were bitter enemies, each waiting an opportunity to get the drop on the other.

The first killing was done by a sheriff from Trinidad; neither Clay nor Chunk were present. Chunk was in trouble in Trinidad; the sheriff wanted him, he had heard that Chunk was at the Clifton House, and he came over after him. The sheriff arrived after bedtime, inquired of the proprietor if his man was there; disregarding the negative answer, he took a candle in one hand and his cocked-gun in the other and started through the house to see for himself. He was nervous; it was a nervous job to go looking for Chunk Colbert at night or anytime. He opened a bedroom door, saw a man in bed, and in his nervousness, fired. He killed one of the waiters, a young man who had come to New Mexico for his health. This was Clifton's first shooting.

Soon after this tragic happening, Allison and Colbert hired a Spanish woman to cook dinner for them. She was to serve it in a small picket cabin at Clifton. She was then supposed to leave them alone. Chunk Colbert took a Mr. Cooper, an educated eastern man, into dinner with him. Allison went in alone. Soon two shots were heard and Allison came hurrying out, carrying his gun in one hand and leading Mr. Cooper with the other. They got on their horses and rode down the river. Colbert was found dead in the cabin. Allison returned to Clifton a few days later, but without Mr. Cooper. When inquiries were made about Cooper, Allison replied that Cooper had "gone south." Mr. Cooper had probably lost his life too. It was known that in the first place Mr. Cooper did not want to dine with the two bad-men, since he knew of their hatred, jealousy and determination to shoot it out, but he dared not incur the wrath of either by refusing to dine when asked.

Everyone evaded Allison more than ever now, but tried

never to do it openly or to hurt his feelings for it was not wise. This accounts for the second and only other killing to take place at Clifton that is known of by those who lived there from the time the House was built in 1866.

✻

Clay Allison figured in another interesting incident which took place at a dance which was held over on the Sugarite some nine or ten miles northeast of Clifton.

Now a dance in those days was about all the social diversion the people had and dances were not very frequent. When one took place, everyone for miles around went; all considered that they were welcome.

Mase Bowman, a blustering but cowardly man of the would-be desperado type, and Clay Allison were at this dance. Deciding that things were entirely too quiet, Allison and Bowman attempted to liven the party up. They drove everyone out of the dancing room, except the fiddler who was made to carry on, placed a stool in the center of the room and each put a cocked six-shooter on the stool. They removed their coats and boots, danced around the stool, each at the same distance from the guns. If one chose to close in on the weapons, the other came nearer also. The rest of the guests, crowded in the other room of the house, expected at any moment to hear trouble start. Fear prompted them to go outside but a blizzard forced them to stay in. One woman more courageous than the rest could tolerate the suspense no longer and went into the room, picked up the guns, and hurried out and hid them in a trunk. She had no more than finished her task when the two men produced two more guns and started the strange dance over again.

Allison and Bowman finally tired of this; they then demanded that every man present, including some who had gone to bed to avoid the fight that they thought inevitable, come in, take off his boots and join the dance. This lasted for hours.

Many men sent their families home and remained themselves, fearing to leave too soon lest they incur the disfavor of one of the bad-men.

✳✳✳

Clay Allison finally became too confident and too domineering. He had a dispute with a man in Southern Colorado and on learning that his antagonist was not willing to yield to his demands, sent word to him that he was coming up to kill him. He attempted to make good his promise but when he arrived at the man's ranch and drove into the yard of the would-be victim, that man stepped out on his porch and filled Allison full of rifle lead.

Since Allison had figured in most of the "wild escapades" at the Clifton House, and since he had been permanently removed, life looked very peaceable for Northern New Mexico and the people who lived at Clifton.

✳✳✳

After the coming of the railroad in '79 and the discontinuance of the stage line the Clifton House was not so important and figured less and less in the life of Colfax County. It soon was vacated, fell into disrepair, and was gradually forgotten. Today it is little more than some ruins with only a few adobe walls to mark the spot which once was so important as a stagecoach hotel along the Santa Fe Trail.

Origin: Alvin Stockton, Stockton Ranch, Raton, New Mexico.

The Fate of a Horse Thief

by
W. M. Emery

There was a time in the West when to steal a horse was a greater crime than to shoot a man. Many a man was lynched because he allowed himself to be tempted by the sight of a good horse, and tried to get the animal without paying for it. But time and again men were shot down practically in cold blood and the murderer was never questioned.

An example of such an affair happened one time in Toll Gate Canyon. A man—whom we shall call Davis—stole several fine horses from a ranch near Trinidad. Two of the men from the ranch trailed him and finally caught him in the Dry Cimarron Canyon, near the Cross-Ell Ranch.

They brought Davis to Mike Devoy, who was then Justice of Peace in that district, and asked him to try the horse thief. Devoy refused on the grounds that the thieving had been done out of his district, and the man should be taken back to the State and district in which the crime had been committed.

"But," he advised, "don't let him get away under any circumstances. Watch him close."

The two men rode away with their charge.

Toll Gate Canyon was only a few miles from Mr. Devoy's ranch, and was the only road leading from Cimarron Canyon north to the Colorado line. It is a beautiful spot. The road running parallel with a deep rocky arroyo—which it crosses in the upper end of the canyon—is walled in on both sides by steep rocky hills, covered with pine, pinion, cedar, and deer brush. The banks of the arroyo are lined with cottonwoods, deer brush, cedar, chokecherry and wild plum trees, and wild grapevines twine in and out over the rocky sides.

In the middle of the canyon there was a steep little hill, with a sharp curve at the top. This hill has been recently cut away and the road widened through the canyon. On the east side the road dropped nearly straight down about fifteen feet to the bottom of the arroyo, but this bank was almost completely hidden by a dense thicket of oak and deer brush.

As the three men neared this spot, the two cowboys dropped far behind. Davis glanced back over his shoulder and saw that his guards were—to all appearances—deeply engrossed in a hot argument. He guided his horse close to the brush-covered bank, then quickly threw himself out of the saddle and rolled down the hill into the thick brush.

It was the opportunity the cowboys had been waiting for. In a flash they had spurred their horses to the spot and began shooting at the rolling figure; one man using a rifle and the other a six-shooter.

When it was over they rode back to Devoy and told him what had happened.

"Well, you killed him, didn't you?" was Devoy's comment,

"now go bury him. I don't want to have anything to do with it."

So the horse thief was buried where he had fallen, and occupies an unknown grave within a few feet of the well traveled road, and the autoists who whisk past the place in their fine cars today, little dream of the tragedy that took place in that beautiful spot less than a half a century ago.

Story told to writer by Levi Tabor, Folsom, New Mexico.

An Unwanted Fugitive

by
W. M. Emery

One of the principal pastimes and sports in the frontier towns of the early west was gambling. Whether in mining town or cow town, this form of entertainment was paramount among the male population. Monte, Faro, and poker games were indulged in and thousands of dollars as well as property changed hands every day through this medium.

This pastime was also responsible for a great deal of enmity which sprang up often between the best of friends and even went as far as gun fights, causing otherwise honest citizens to become fugitives from justice.

So it was with Sam Watson, proprietor of the "Bucket of Blood" saloon in Folsom, in 1897. As the name implies, this saloon was noted for its gunfights and killings.

One day Fred Brown, a professional gambler, engaged Watson in a gambling game which lasted all day, with Watson the constant looser. He knew Brown was cheating but could not catch him, even though Brown chided him every time he lost. Watson—who was a Texan—finally lost his patience and, jerking out his gun, shot Brown in the neck. Brown was dead before a doctor could arrive.

Watson ran to his boarding house where his landlady was even then waiting supper for him. He went to his room and got his coat, then on out the back door without making any explanations. That night he hid himself in the rim rocks of the hills along the Dry Cimarron River.

For two weeks he played hide and seek with the sheriff and his posse. Watson—for the most part—watched the posse drive up and down the canyon, presumably hunting for him; but in reality they were having a grand drinking spree and were racing up and down the road driving good horses to death. They were too drunk even to follow the bloodhounds which they had put on Watson's trail, and which at one time came clear up to Watson.

Watson lived during these two weeks on beeves he killed in the pastures of the cattlemen along the Cimarron. He traveled as far as the McCuistion ranch, about thirty-five or forty miles northeast of Folsom, and killed one beef on this ranch. Often when he killed an animal he was forced to fight a pack of wolves to keep from loosing his own life.

At last he could stand it no longer; the nights were getting colder and winter would soon set in. One night he made his way up Long Canyon and toward the Colorado-New Mexico line. The next evening, he came to the secluded home of "Scotty" McCleod. Scotty was preparing his evening meal when Watson arrived and asked to be allowed to eat supper with him. Scotty welcomed him in and treated him as he would any other guest.

During the meal a loud "Halloo" was heard in the yard. Watson jerked out his gun and covered Scotty.

"Don't let anyone in the house or tell anyone that I'm here, or I'll kill you," ordered Watson, as he hid himself where he could see and hear Watson when he talked to these unknown guests.

Scotty stepped to the door and was confronted by two more outlaws. Fortunately, these men were only seeking information and soon rode on.

After eating a hearty supper—the first real meal in over two weeks—Watson left McCleod's house and was soon in Colorado, and on toward the northwest.

About three years ago the sheriff's office in Clayton received a letter from Sam Watson offering to give himself up if the sheriff would send to Oregon for him, but the case had been forgotten and Watson is today a free man, unwanted by the law.

Source of Information: Mrs. Roxie Emery, Clayton, New Mexico. Mrs. Emery lived near Folsom at the time of this incident. The letter from Watson offering to give himself up was printed in the Clayton News.

DISTRICT TWO: THE TRAGEDY OF PAINT HORSE MESA

"Taking careful aim, the bandits fired one volley at the sleeping boys with deadly effect, and the two boys continued to sleep into eternity."

(from "The Tragedy of Paint Horse Mesa" by Colonel Jack Potter)

The Tragedy of Paint Horse Mesa

By Colonel Jack Potter

by
Carrie L. Hodges

One of the greatest tragedies of the many that unfold in the recollection of pioneer days is that of Paint Horse Mesa, a tragedy which resulted in giving the mesa its name.

It was in the middle eighties that a large cattle company laid claim to the Estancia land grant and, after fighting off the Mexican settlers, stocked the range with 20,000 head of Texas cattle. Jim Stinson was named manager of the huge ranch.

From that time on relations between the cattle companies and the Mexicans were strained indeed, with shootings common and the little cemetery plot near town becoming filled with graves of men who died with their boots on.

Whenever the Mexicans would have a grand baile on their plaza, the punchers would feel it necessary that they be included in the festivities. Almost invariably the affair would end with another funeral processing to "Boot Hill," and the Fort doctor would be kept busy making "repairs." Punchers and Mexicans alike shared in the list of fatalities to which the celebrations gave rise.

It was during these troubled times that a Mexican outlaw gang, under the leadership of Pablo Archuleta, was organized. The primary purpose of the gang was cattle rustling, but picking off a Yankee puncher now and then seemed to be one of their favorite relaxations.

Early one spring morning two punchers from the Estancia decided to return to their homes in Texas, and started out toward Fort Sumner. Each of them had in his pockets a year's wages, and besides their valuable mounts, they also had other belongings of considerable worth.

They were in high spirits, laughing and talking as they rode along to Pinos Wells, where they laid in supplies, filled their water keg and canteens preparatory to the sixty-five miles ride without water to the Zuber sheep ranch on the head of the Yeso.

By the time they had arrived at the watering place on the ranch it was late at night. So, after watering their stock, they rode about one and a half miles north and camped for the night on a mesa. Grass on the mesa, which is nearly a hundred feet high, was fresh and the top was smooth as a floor. It was on this mesa that the two boys spread their blankets and slept—never to awaken again.

Several hours behind the boys rode a Mexican posse from near the Estancia Ranch. When they reached Pinos Well store, members of the posse informed the merchant that they were following the trail of the boys to recover stolen stock.

The Mexicans arrived at the waterhole about four hours behind the two punchers and then waited until daylight before following the trail to the mesa. When the bandits found the trail they dismounted and climbed with drawn guns to the top. The two boys lay sound asleep not more than twenty feet away from the intruders. Taking careful aim, the bandits fired one volley at the sleeping boys with deadly effect, and the two boys continued to sleep into eternity.

After looting the punchers' possessions and taking everything of value—even to part of their clothing—the bandits returned to the water hole, where they rested for several hours before starting back in the direction of the Estancia.

During this time they had been seen by only one person, a Mexican boy, one of Zuber's herders. He was informed of the tragedy and was told by the bandits that they had followed a bunch of horse thieves from the Manzano Mountains, had killed them and were now returning home with the stolen stock. They warned the boy that they were leaving one of their men nearby, and that if he attempted to leave the ranch within two days, he would be killed.

The Mexican lad was in mortal terror of the so-called posse but stood it for only one day. During the night following he started out to the nearest ranch forty miles away. He must have run most of the distance for he had covered the forty miles and was picked up by a line rider in an exhausted condition and taken to the Cedar Canon Ranch where he told the story.

That day a posse was organized and rode into Fort Sumner, twenty-five miles away. The next morning three more men were furnished by the Fort Sumner Ranch with a pack outfit; I was one of the three chosen to go along.

After riding forty miles out on the old Arizona cattle trail, we arrived at the Zuber Ranch and found that the Mexican boy had not exaggerated in telling his story.

A consultation was held and it was decided that it would be useless to follow the bandits, as it was already late in the third day. By now the bandits would have had time to get back to their rendezvous in the Manzano Mountains. So the next morning a double grave was dug on the mesa. The two boys were wrapped in their bloody blankets and lowered into their lonely resting place.

While we were conducting the crude funeral in the best manner we knew, an old paint pack horse came up and looked on. He had belonged to the boys and had been left behind by the bandits because he was too poor and tired to make the long, fast drive to the Manzanos.

For three years after that the old paint stayed near the double grave. It seemed as if he were standing guard over his two dead masters. No one had ever seen him away from that mesa except when he came down to the waterhole to drink. The ranchmen all took a great interest in the old horse, even Zuber, who was reputed to be the stingiest man in the world. He instructed his herders to spare the grass on the mesa.

Twice each year, when the roundup outfits made the place, the old horse would come down and visit with the caballeros for awhile, then go back up the narrow trail to the mesa.

It was during the third year that Old Paint failed to make his visit to the round-up outfit, and old Zuber sent word that the horse had not shown up at the waterhole for several days. A group of punchers from the roundup party followed the narrow trail to the top of the mesa.

While investigating the death of the faithful old mount, one of the boys made the remark that Old Paint had died with his boots on. "He has done his duty and no coyote will ever taste him," the punchers insisted.

When we found him, we dug a shallow grave and covered it with loose rock, giving Old Paint a better burial than had many a man.

Paint Horse Mesa is forty miles west of Fort Sumner, near the headwaters of Yeso (translated gypsum) Creek. At the time of tragedy, it was known as Zuber.

Old Timers Stories:
Mrs. Mabel Luke Madison
(Husband: James Madison)
Interview: June 6, 1936

by
Marie Carter

Mrs. Madison related an exciting episode in her life on the range: "It happened early one morning while we were still in bed," she said. "We heard horses moving around outside, and heard men talking in low but excited voices. Jim got up and went outside. I stayed in bed, straining my ears to hear what the strange men were talking about. Then someone came into my room and by the dim morning light I thought it was my husband. I started to speak when suddenly I felt the cold steel of a gun pressed against my forehead. I started to cry out but ended with a feeble moan. When the man, whoever he was, heard my voice, he backed toward the door saying: 'Oh, I thought you were Tucker.' Just why he said that I don't know. But I think he was so excited that he didn't know just what he was saying."

Mrs. Madison paused, then continued: "I was so scared I didn't know what to do, but finally decided to get up and dress, which I did. Then the door opened, admitting a small figure. It was my son who had been sneaking around outside to see what the men were doing in our corral. He put his finger to his lips and cautioned me to be quiet because Oliver Lee, our old boss, and some of his henchmen were hiding on top of the house. That the sheriff was after them because he heard that they had killed Albert Foundation over at the White Sands. The quick thud of horses' hoofs sent me flying to the window. I looked out—sure enough—the sheriff and his deputies had arrived. The sheriff was Pat Garrett, the same man who had caught and killed Billy the Kid in 1881. Pat and his deputies were starting toward the corral when they saw a red saddle blanket drying on the fence. The sheriff paused, pointed at the blanket, then motioned the men to follow him. My husband, who was outside, told me that they went straight to the corral where Lee's horse was nosing about with several other white horses. The sheriff had no trouble in picking out the horse he wanted, for the saddle blanket, while wet, had faded, leaving great red streaks on the animal's back."

"Shortly after finding Oliver Lee's horse in our corral," Mrs. Madison said, "Pat Garrett, Lincoln County Sheriff, caught sight of the fugitives on top of our house and opened fire. The charge was returned with a volley from the guns on the roof, and we could hear the bullets falling like hail all around us. Just as I grabbed my son and pulled him down beside me on the floor, a bullet crashed through the window, whistled through the room, and buried itself in the wall above the bed. My husband told me that the sheriff went up to bring Lee and his men down, but just as he reached the top of the ladder one of his deputies, who had climbed up on the other side, was shot and rolled off the roof into a wagon just outside the kitchen door. The accident brought the shooting to a sudden stop, for Garrett and his other man went back down to look after their companion. Finding him still alive they decided to take him to the station and when the train came in send him to Alamogordo. So they called my husband and told him to get out a team of horses and hitch up the old wagon. He told them that he hadn't used that wagon for years and didn't have any way to hitch 'em. Then they did the next best thing; they tied a rope to the tongue of the wagon, rode along in front and dragged it after 'em. As they started toward the station they called back to the men on the roof, 'We'll be back to get you fellows by eleven!'

"Be sure ye don't get here before that time, or we might get ye first.' Lee answered.

"The injured man died on his way to Alamogordo, and the sheriff and his deputy were back by eleven o'clock, but Lee and his henchmen were gone."

Mrs. Mabel Madison was born in Montgomery, Alabama, 1870; moved to Temple, Texas with mother, Sofia Luke, 1880; married James Madison in 1886; moved with husband to Marlin, Texas; moved to Rotan, Texas, then to Alamogordo, New Mexico; worked for Oliver Lee three years; moved from Lee's ranch to own ranch, fourteen miles out from Alamogordo. Mrs. Madison has lived in La Mesa, New Mexico for twenty years, where she lives on the family ranch. She is the mother of six children, Zara Madison, Rotan, Texas; Mary Iris Madison, wife of R.F. Hymen, Hebe, New Mexico; Willie Reece Madison, whose wife was the former Opal Chalk of El Paso; Robert Lee Madison, El Paso, Texas; Charley Madison of La Mesa; John James Madison, El Paso, Texas.

Mrs. Belle Kilgore
718 Wallace Street
Clovis, New Mexico
May 10, 1937

200 Words

HIS LAST WISHES

A favorite story among the cowboys published in The Clovis
News July 16, 1909 is as follows:

A young Bostonian came to Fort Sumner and he rapidly caught
the spirit of the country, and as rapidly shook off the semblance
of a tender-foot eastern habit. Rough bearded, leather clad,
sombrero as wide as the widest, a 45-calibre on his hip, he was
as wild as the wildest. Yet within his bosom still burned the
flame of Boston culture and refinement.

One day he was riding with a stranger down the river. Turning his head he saw his companion make a suspicious motion motion toward his hip pocket. Without hesitation he drew his revolver and shot the stranger. The stranger dropped like a log.
The cowboy dismounted and looked at the body of his victim.

"I wonder if he was really going to shoot me," he said to
himself. "'ll see."   Turning the body over he discovered a
flask of whiskey.

"Poop fellow," he said in sorrowful tones, "I've killed an
innocent man and a gentleman at that. He wasn't going to shoot
me, he was going to ask me to have a drink.

m"Well," he said, drawing a sleeve across his mouth, "the
wishes of the dead shall be respected."

Facsimile: "His Last Wishes," Mrs. Belle Kilgore, May 14, 1937, NMFWP,
WPA #153, NMSRCA

200

Battle at Blazer's Mill, Otero County

by
Georgia Redfield

lazer's Mill, in Otero County on the Mescalero Apache Indian Reservation, is eighty-nine miles west of Roswell over US Highway 380 and 70, located in a green valley on the upper Tularosa Creek.

A sawmill was first built on the mill site before the Mexican War, and, it is thought, before settlement of the Rio Grande Valley by the Spanish people.

The buildings were torn down a number of times and rebuilt by different parties. It was not known as "Blazer's Mill" until about 1870. It was used as a sawmill until 1882 when the grist mill was built.

Dr. Joseph Hoy Blazer (born in Pennsylvania in 1828) built the first grist mill, in 1882. Some of the members of the Blazer family who live on the old mill site at the present time are a son, grandson and great-grandson of Dr. Blazer.

A. N. Blazer, the son, was born in Iowa in 1865 before Dr. Blazer moved his family to New Mexico. As a small boy he was a favorite of the Indians. He was taken by them, the only white person, on Indian hunting expeditions. The Blazer family has always been interested in mechanics. He has done research and valuable development work on pumps, water wheels and engines.

Billy the Kid and his outlaw gang, in 1878, made this peaceful beauty spot around the mill the scene of a bloody gun-battle, in which "Buckshot" Bill Roberts and outlaw Dick Brewer were killed and others of the gang seriously wounded.

Twelve outlaws, including Billy the Kid, but led by Dick Brewer (the Captain of the gang at the time), gathered at the George Coe Ranch. With George Coe joining the bunch they started (as they claimed) after horse thieves. They ended their proposed jaunt at Blazer's Mill, arriving just before noon. They were cordially greeted by Dr. Blazer who knew two men of the bunch, Frank and George Coe.

Dr. Blazer asked the bunch to stay for dinner, warning them to keep a look-out for "Buckshot" Roberts, who was after them, as were also the soldiers stationed a mile away on the Indian reservation.

A hundred dollar reward had been offered for each of the gang, dead or alive, who had been with the slayers when sheriff Brady was slain.

Buckshot Roberts (so called because of his bravery under fire) had been a Texas Ranger and an Indian fighter. He, at this time, lived quietly on a little place on the Ruidoso. He offered himself for the dangerous job of bringing in the murderers and was accepted by the officials of the law at Lincoln. He had taken no active part before this in the feuds and war waged around him. While he had not witnessed the killing of Brady, he was determined to avenge his murder.

George Coe and John Middleton were stationed as guards to watch for Roberts, while the other men were eating dinner inside the Blazer home.

In a short while Roberts rode up as expected. As the guards watched alertly he dismounted from his mule and seeing he had placed himself at a disadvantage, he lowered his gun, resting . . . and stood quietly. Recognizing some of the men who had come out from their dinner, he asked to speak with Frank Coe whom he had considered a friend and at whose home he had spent the night before and who knew Roberts's plans for capturing the gang.

Frank Coe promised Roberts that if he would give himself up to the gang he would not be harmed. Roberts replied, "I will give myself up to no gang like Billy the Kid's; they are murderers and I will fight to the last ditch before I surrender to them."

Dick Brewer asked for volunteers to go around the house and take Roberts.

Charlie Bowdre, George Coe and Billy the Kid offered to go. Others said if they were killed they would try their hand.

Bowdre took the lead, George Coe and Billy the Kid were close behind. As soon as Bowdre turned the corner of the house he threw his gun on Roberts, commanding him to throw up his hands.

"Not much Mary Ann," was Roberts' reply. Both his and Bowdre's guns were fired simultaneously. Roberts's bullet glanced off Bowdre's cartridge belt, struck and shattered George Coe's right hand, severing the trigger finger. Bowdre's ball went through Roberts's stomach.

Roberts, mortally wounded, drove his enemies to cover, and fell back into the room. He dragged a feather bed to the door, rolled upon it and resumed his firing. Dick Brewer, concealed behind a log at the old saw mill, fired at the spot where he could dimly see the feather bed, not hitting Roberts; he raised his head to look and take another aim when Roberts shot him between the eyes, killing him instantly.

The outlaws swore revenge. Dr. Blazer quietly suggested that he would go around and see how badly Roberts was injured. He called out, "Roberts, I am Dr. Blazer; may I come in and help you?" Roberts gasped a reply, "No one can help me, I'm killed. It is all over."

Dr. Blazer entered, saw nothing could be done, and told the men there was no use fighting longer, as Roberts would not live an hour.

The soldiers from the Indian Agency appeared in sight. The outlaws ran to the mountains and hid in the timber.

Roberts, brave to the last, died within four hours after he was shot.

The brave man, Roberts, who desired peace at any price, and his foe, an outlaw on whose head a price had been set, lay dead—both victims of the feuds, passion for revenge, and the lust for killing which spread through that part of New Mexico after the coming of Billy the Kid.

Both men lie buried on the Blazer Mill site. The two graves are the only evidence remaining of the fierce battle that took place on that now peaceful spot, nearly sixty years ago.

Sources of Information: A.N. Blazer, son of Dr. Joseph Hoy Blazer, Mescalero, N. M. Lucius Dills, 410 N. Pennsylvania Ave., Roswell, N. M. Autobiography of George W. Coe as told to Nan Hillary Harrison, published 1934. The late W. L. Patterson, "Account of Lincoln County War," 1936.

Mrs. Amelia (Bolton) Church

by
Georgia B. Redfield

Mrs. Amelia (Bolton) Church—daughter of John Bolton, who was head of the Quartermaster Department stationed with army officers at Fort Stanton, New Mexico, for protection of the early settlers from Indians, and wife of the late J. P. Church, a pioneer builder of Roswell—has lived in Southeast New Mexico for sixty-seven years.

Native of Wexford Ireland

Mrs. Church was born in Wexford Ireland July 3, 1862. In 1871 she came from Ireland to America with her mother, Ella (Doyel) Bolton, and a brother and younger sister, who is Mrs. Ella (Bolton) Davidson. Mrs. Bolton and her children, on landing in New York, traveled by train as far as the railroad was built, and then by army ambulance and covered wagons, guarded by an army escort sent from Fort Stanton, by whom they were conducted safely through hostile Indian infested plains to what was to be their new home in the wild newly settled country of New Mexico.

Adobe Home at Fort Stanton

Mr. Bolton had preceded his wife and children in coming to America. After they joined him at Fort Stanton he built for them a new adobe home. Here Mrs. Church lived happily with her parents and brother and sister the three first of her many continuous years of residence in New Mexico.

Old Lincoln Town

In 1873 John Bolton moved his family to the historic old town of Lincoln, New Mexico, where he was made postmaster. Here his daughters, Amelia and Ella, grew to young girlhood, constantly surrounded by danger, not only from Indians, of whom they had lived in terror at Fort Stanton, but from the rough element of settlers of the new town, made up of cattle thieves, gamblers and murderers, and the gun-battles of the two factions of the bloody feudal conflicts, known as the Lincoln County War. The true stories of some of those battles—of which Mrs. Church is one of the few living eyewitnesses—and the traditions of the many historic places of interest in Lincoln County are desired by the Chaves County Archaeological and Historical Society for preservation in the Roswell Museum.

Beginning of Lincoln County War

The killing of John H. Tunstall on February 18, 1878, was

the real beginning of the Lincoln County War. Tunstall, who was a popular young Englishman, had established a ranch on the Rio Feliz and stocked it with cattle and horses. William Bonney, who became known afterwards as "Billy the Kid, and as a blood-thirsty man-killer and outlaw," was employed by Tunstall to assist with the stock on the ranch. They became fast friends. The youthful outlaw made a resolve, while standing over the grave of his friend, that he would never let up until he killed the last man who helped to kill Tunstall. Tunstall was shot down by officials of the law, who were sent to take Tunstall's cattle and property because of his partnership with McSween in the mercantile business in Lincoln. Sheriff Brady was supposed to have been responsible for the attachment issued against Tunstall's property, which resulted in his killing.

Killing of Major Brady

"I knew Major Brady very well," said Mrs. Church during an interview at her home in Roswell in September 1938.

"He was sheriff of Lincoln County when he was killed. I saw him as he and another man, deputy sheriff George Hindman, lay dead in the street, shot down, as they were passing, by Billy the Kid and his gang, who lay hidden behind an adobe wall. Major Brady was killed instantly. George Hindman fell when he was shot, and Ike Stockton who was standing near, on seeing he was still alive, ran to him and gave him water that he brought from a ditch in his hat. However, nothing could revive him for he was mortally wounded and died in a few minutes. The third man, Billy Mathews, who was with Major Brady when the shooting began, made his escape by running into an adobe house nearby."

Old Lincoln County Court House

"Upstairs in the old Court House at Lincoln is the room where Billy the Kid was confined waiting his trial for the killing of Major Brady. There have been many untrue stories told of the Kid's sensational escape after killing his two guards Bell and Ollinger. I remember all the facts in connection with that escape," said Mrs. Church.

"Billy the Kid was playing cards with Bell, while Ollinger, his other guard, was at dinner across the street; he saw his chance and grabbed Bell's gun. Bell darted down the inside stairway, but Billy the Kid was too quick for him, he fired and Bell fell dead at the bottom of the stairs. Billy the Kid then walked calmly to a window and shot Ollinger down as he came running when he heard the shooting. The "Kid" then threw the gun on Ollinger who lay dying and told Goss, the jail cook, to saddle a horse that was feeding in an alfalfa field nearby. The cook helped get the shackles off the Kid's hands but because they were welded on he couldn't get them off his legs; that is why he was thrown from the horse because of having to ride side-wise on account of the shackles. He rode a mile and a half west before they were removed by a Mexican man, who afterwards gave the shackles to George Titsworth, who lived at Capitan, and possessed an interesting collection at that place.

"The old Court House is now in process of reconditioning and strengthening. It is to serve as a memorial to the pioneers after its restoration."

El Torreon—Old Stone Tower

In 1935, Mrs. Church worked untiringly with the Chaves County Archaeological and Historical Society in the securing and restoration of El Torreon, the old round stone tower, built by Mexican settlers around 1840 or 1850, at La Placita—later named Lincoln. The tower was first built to be used as a lookout and protection against Indians. It served in later years as a place of refuge from white outlaws and as a refuge during the Lincoln County War.

"I was interested in saving the old tower that was fast crumbling into ruins," said Mrs. Church, "because we felt safer all through those dangerous years of outlawry just knowing there was always a place of safety to be found behind its protecting walls. It helped keep us brave at times when we needed courage."

"My sister Ella and my mother and I were the only white persons of twenty-seven—the rest were all Mexicans—who spent the night crowded together in El Torreon after we had been warned to seek safety in the tower, for the dreaded Harrell brothers, outlaw murderers, were on their way to wipe out the town. There had been seven of the Harrell brothers. Two had been killed at a baile (dance) after the younger one of the brothers had started a quarrel over a Spanish senorita. This threatened invasion was supposed to be for the purpose of carrying out their threat to kill every man, woman and child in revenge for the shooting of their brothers. We spent the night in fear and trembling, close by the side of our mother, but morning found us quite safe in the old tower. The Horrells had accepted some kind of a truce offered by a friend. They were mollified for the time being and no one at all was harmed."

"I know now," said Mrs. Church, "that our mother who possessed a brave and dauntless spirit and never complained during those dangerous times must have often longed for the peaceful security of her old home in Ireland."

The First Jail Built in Lincoln

Mrs. Church remembers the building of the first jail in Lincoln, the first occupant of which was Billy the Kid.

"I watched the men as they worked on the jail," said Mrs. Church. "They dug a square pit about nine feet deep, then they lowered into it a rough closet-like cell without any doors or windows. On top of the ground, over the cell, they built a two-room adobe house for the jailer. I saw them lower Billy the Kid through a trap door in the top to the cell below. There was a ditch running full of water close by. I was horrified when I heard one of the men who lowered the 'Kid' inside say 'Let's turn the water of that ditch into the cell and drown him like a rat.'"

Knew Billy the Kid and McSweens

While many harrowing experiences and murderings were indelibly impressed upon the young mind of Mrs. Church, she remembers also many pleasant social occasions during the years she lived in Lincoln. There were musicale parties and dancing. She knew Billy the Kid who sang well and was a good dancer. He was a welcome guest at many of the early social affairs of the town. She often visited in the home of Mr. and Mrs. McSween. Mr. McSween, though he never carried a gun, was one of the faction leaders of the Lincoln County War. She remembers Mrs. McSween as being a woman of refinement and culture. She was a good musician and owned a fine piano of which she was very proud. It was burned in her home the night her husband was killed in the final battle that practically ended the Lincoln County War which took place in July 1878. . . .

Mrs. Amelia (Bolton) Church was selected by a Committee of Chaves County Archaeological and Historical Society as one of the Four Outstanding Pioneer Builders of Roswell and Southeast New Mexico.

Alejo Herrera—Patriarch Chihuahua District, Roswell

by
Georgia B. Redfield

Alejo Herrera is dead. There is grief in the Spanish American settlement called "Chihuahua"—in the southeast part of Roswell—and there is a stillness of respect and love in the district, for the fine old Mexican patriarch, who lived a hundred and seventeen years, dying on Sunday, December 27th at the home of Mr. and Mrs. Gus Garcia, 700 East Tilden Street, Chihuahua, Roswell. There was no sickness—not an ache or a pain. It is said he never experienced an illness of any kind during the many years of his life. The cause of his death was only extreme old age.

Alejo Herrera was called "The Methuselah" of the Chihuahua settlement. He was a friend for many years to the Mexican people of that district.

Thrilling adventure, perils and helpfulness are written through the pages of his life's history, as told by himself, his friends, and various records left in reckoning the milestones of his long interesting life.

Apache Indians captured Alejo when he was eleven years old. They took him from his home at Satillo, Mexico, to the Guadalupe mountains and later to the White mountains. He was guarded and watched constantly by his captors. Not once in the nineteen years of his captivity did he find an opportunity for escape. He learned the language of the Apaches, their habits, and customs of living, which clung to him all the days of his life, and he could ride like an Indian.

When Alejo reached thirty years of age, while camped with the Apaches in a deep canyon in the White mountains, a stranger brought "fire water" and gave it freely to the Indians in the camp. This gave him his longed for chance of escape. During the drunken brawl there was fighting among the tribe and the guards and their chief were knocked out. Alejo, realizing this was his chance for escape, caught and saddled a horse, crept back within a few feet of the unconscious guards and took a white girl who had been in captivity with him for three years. Together they rode the one horse and safely made the perilous journey to Santa Fe with the Apache Indians in hot pursuit and others camped on every trail.

Arriving at Santa Fe, Alejo turned the rescued girl over to a man by the name of Johnson who lived on a ranch in the Santa Fe country. He secured work for himself on another ranch as a "bronco buster"—wild horse rider. He rode and broke the horses on many of the first ranches settled in New Mexico.

The Lincoln County War was an interesting experience in Herrera's life. He was a brave fighter, in that war and in several Indian uprisings. His body and hands showed many bullet marks and arrowhead scars. Some of which he received protecting women and helpless children. These he bore proudly to his grave.

After the Lincoln County War, and the Indians had been

subdued and were safely guarded in reservations, Herrera, too old then for bronco riding, was a sheepherder for many years. He worked for Jose Analla, the first sheepman of Lincoln County. Afterwards he was herder for J.P. White (Senior) a well-known sheepman and one of the first stockmen of the Pecos Valley.

Herrera worked for Juan Chaves who had a ranch and the only residence on the land which is now Roswell. At that time provisions for the Chaves Ranch were brought over from Santa Fe by Herrera in a two-wheel "carreta" drawn by two oxen.

"Billy the Kid" had no better friend than Herrera, who concealed him from the sheriff on two different occasions. He rolled the "Kid" up securely in his bedroll at one time, leaving only a small opening at one end for air.

The old Patriarch had no family. He was cared for by his friends, and his word was law in their home. The Garcias cared for him tenderly until the end.

Sources of Information: Notes of Alejo Herrera's own dictation to Ricardo (Dick) Gomez, Carlsbad; J.P. White (deceased) for whom Alejo Herrera once worked as sheepherder. From personal knowledge of writer.

(A note of Gilson Canyon -- quite interesting).

Sometime in the 80's a man named Bill Gilson (Gilson Canyon bares his name) established himself at the head waters spring. Just south of him was a tremendous grove of white oak and walnut trees growing in the largest mescal pits in the entire region.

In the cliff about 400 feet above his dwelling is a cave which had been occupied by the Basket Maker and numerous other prehistoric races.

He was found one morning dead--shot in the back of the head, laying under a small tree from which hung the carcass of a bear which was half skinned, undoubtedly the task in which Gilson was engaged at the time of his death.

No one knows whose hand fired the fatal shot, whether white man or red man, and his grave marked with a crude headstone remains as one of the intrigueing mysteries of the guadalupes.

Facsimile: "Canyons and Caves in the Guadalupe Mountains," Katherine Ragsdale, August 26, 1936, NMFWP, WPA #201, NMSRCA

William H. Bonney ("Billy the Kid"), New Mexico, Courtesy Palace of the Governors (MNM/DCA #128785)

Pioneer Story:
Pedro M. Rodriguez

by
Edith L. Crawford

I was born in Lincoln, Lincoln County, New Mexico, October 10, 1874, and have lived all my life in Lincoln County.

My father, Jesus Rodriguez, was born in El Paso, Old Mexico (which is El Paso, Texas, now). I cannot remember what year he was born in as he was killed when I was about nine years old.

My mother, Francisca Sanchez, daughter of Jose Sanchez, was born in Manzano, New Mexico, I don't know the date of her birth, as she died when I was about twelve years old at Ruidoso, New Mexico.

Father and Mother were married in Lincoln, New Mexico, about the year of 1866, and lived there until my father was killed in 1883; mother then went to Ruidoso, New Mexico, to live with my grandparents Mr. and Mrs. Fernando Herrera.

Father was a Private in Captain William Brady's Company A, First Regiment of Calvary, New Mexico, at Fort Stanton, New

Mexico. He enlisted for one year, October 27, 1864, to October 27, 1865; he was discharged at Fort Sumner, New Mexico. He spent most of his time while in the army fighting the Indians, for in those days the Indians roamed all over Lincoln County.

And they were always killing people and stealing their cattle and horses.

My grandfather, Fernando Herrera, lived on the Ruidoso (where Hollywood is located now). He owned about four hundred head of cattle and he ran them in Turkey Canyon which was in the Mescalero country; the Indians had been killing the cattle for meat, so my grandfather got a posse of men together and started out to gather his cattle and bring them to the Ruidoso, where he could watch them.

In the posse was Billy the Kid, Andres Herrera, Manuel Silva, George Washington and grandfather. They started out early one morning for Turkey Canyon. When they got to Turkey Spring about halfway up the Canyon they met Chief Kamisa and about twenty-five Indians. While the posse was talking to Kamisa the Indians formed a circle around the men and told Kamisa to tell them they were going to kill every one of them. Billy the Kid told the men in Spanish to get off of their horses and tighten up their front cinches, and follow him.

Billy mounted his horse with a six in each hand. He started hollering and shooting as he rode toward the Indians. The rest of the men followed, shooting as they went. They broke through the line and not one of them was hurt.

They gathered a few head of cattle and took them home and put them in a corral.

The next morning, Kamisa and a band of Indians came to my grandfather's house. Kamisa called to grandfather to come out, he wanted to talk to him. Grandfather and Kamisa were always pretty good friends so he went to the door and Kamisa told him if he would butcher three beeves and give them to the Indians, "we do you no more harm." The Indians kept their promise and never stole any more cattle. Grandfather and Kamisa were good friends from then on. I remember Kamisa well. He and I were good friends, I always liked to talk with him. . . .

Pioneer Story:
Francisco Gomez

by
Edith L. Crawford

I can remember when we lived in Manzano that the oxen had big horns and the ropes were fastened to their horns but when we moved to Lincoln they used yokes on the oxen. I had never seen them before. When we planted corn at Lincoln my father drove the team of oxen and I dropped the corn in the furrow. Father would go up in the mountains near our house and cut down trees for wood and would put a chain around the tree and the oxen would snake the tree down the mountain side to the house.

When I was about eighteen years old I went to work for the McSween's. I stayed with them for about two years. I remember that one winter Billy the Kid stayed with the McSween's for about seven months. I guess he boarded with them. He was an awfully nice young fellow with light brown hair, blue eyes, and rather big front teeth. He always dressed very neatly. He used to practice target shooting a lot. He would throw up a can and would twirl his six gun on his finger and he could hit the can six times before it hit the ground. He rode a big roan horse about ten or twelve hands high all that winter and when this horse was out in the pasture Billy would go to the gate and whistle and the horse would come up to the gate to him. That horse would follow Billy and mind him like a dog. He was a very fast horse and could outrun most of the other horses around there. I never went out with Billy but once. Captain Baca was sheriff then and once some tough outlaws came to Lincoln and rode up and down the streets and shot out window lights in the houses and terrorized people. Captain Baca told Billy the Kid to take some men and go after these men. Billy took me and Florencio and Jose Chaves and Santano Maes with him. The outlaws went to the upper Ruidoso and we followed them. We caught up with them and shot it out with them. One of the outlaws was killed and the other ran away. None of us were hurt.

Narrator: Francisco Gomez, Lincoln, New Mexico, aged 84 years.

OFFICE OF

P. F. Garrett,
Sheriff of Lincoln County.

Lincoln,N. M. Oct. 3th. 1881.

County Commissioners

I have in my possession two horses and
one saddle captured from Frank Wheeler also one gun and six
shooter captured of William Bonney,
Which await your orders.

Pat F.Garrett

Report of P.F.Garrett of captured property
Approved & sale ordered
W.W.Paul Ch Co Coms.

Filed Oct 3rd 1881
Ben H.Ellis
County Clerk

Facsimile: "Office of P. F. Garrett, Sheriff of Lincoln County," Edith L.
Crawford, November 10, 1937, NMFWP, WPA #212, NMSRCA

Pioneer Story:
Charles P. Mayer

by
Edith L. Crawford

I have lived in Lincoln County, New Mexico, for fifty-four years. I was born in New York state and grew up in the state of Ohio. I left Ohio when I was twenty-one years old and came by train to Las Vegas, New Mexico, in the latter part of 1883. Soon after arriving in Las Vegas I heard of the White Oaks gold mines so I left Las Vegas for White Oaks. I went by rail from Las Vegas to San Antonio, New Mexico, and from there to White Oaks by freight wagons as there was a train of wagons freighting into White Oaks at that time. These wagons were drawn by mules and horses and it took about a week to make the trip. I arrived in White Oaks in the early part of January 1884, and it was very cold weather. There were not very many buildings in the town at that time and what few there were were built of logs. I opened up a blacksmith shop and did work for the miners and also shod horses, mules and oxen for the freighters and for the farmers in the surrounding country.

I ran my blacksmith shop for twelve years, sold out in 1896 and went into the general merchandise business there in White Oaks. After the mines closed down in White Oaks I moved to Carrizozo and put in a general merchandise and grocery store which I ran until my health failed, and I retired from business in 1929.

When I first came to Lincoln County it was two hundred and fifty miles from east to west and one hundred and fifty miles from north to south, making it one of the largest counties in the state. First Eddy and Chaves counties were cut off from Lincoln County, then Otero and the last one cut off was Torrance, and still Lincoln is a fair sized county.

In the year 1888 I was appointed deputy sheriff for the White Oaks district. My first man hunt as deputy was for a man named George Musgrave, who killed a fellow by the name of George Parker at a roundup camp. Parker and Musgrave had been partners in the cattle business with headquarters about thirty miles east of Roswell. They were caught with some cattle that did not belong to them and Parker went before the grand jury and had Musgrave indicted for illegally branding these cattle. In some way Musgrave was tipped off that the law was looking for him and he skipped out to Arizona. There he met a man called "Black Jack" and the two went into the cattle business in the Hachita mountains in Arizona.

This man Black Jack would never tell where he was from or who his parents were. They told on him that he could offer up a prayer as long as his rifle, and a good prayer too, so he must have been brought up in a Christian home as a boy. After these men had worked together for awhile Musgrave told Black Jack that there was a man in New Mexico that he wanted to go back and kill and asked Black Jack if he wanted to go with him and help do the job. They set out for Lincoln County and came by the stagecoach road. At the head of the Mal Pais they held up and robbed the White Oaks stagecoach.

They went on to Lincoln and inquired if there were any roundups going on in the county. They were informed there was one going on up on the Mesa above Picacho, New Mexico. The two men left at once for the roundup and arrived at the chuck wagon just before dinner. Musgrave knew all the cattlemen and the country real well. When they got to the chuck wagon Musgrave asked the cook if George Parker was with the outfit. The cook replied that he was and would be in for dinner in a short while. Musgrave, Black Jack and several cowboys were eating dinner when one of the cowboys pointed to a rider coming in and said, "There comes Parker now." Musgrave turned to the cowboys and said, "Boys, I have traveled one thousand miles to kill that fellow and I guess I will do it now." Musgrave and Black Jack rose and picked up their rifles. Black Jack said to the cowboys, "Now this is our fight and I will kill the first man that interferes." Musgrave walked out to meet Parker and told him to get off of his horse. Just as Parker hit the ground Musgrave fired and Parker fell, mortally wounded. Parker was riding a brand new saddle and Musgrave took his old saddle off his horse and put Parker's new saddle on it and the two men, Musgrave and Black Jack, rode away toward the Diamond A ranch, near Roswell. Andy Neighbauer was foreman of the Diamond A outfit at that time and these two men stopped there at the ranch and exchanged their tired and worn out horses for two nice fat fresh horses and went on their way. They took the same route back to Arizona that they had traveled coming in to Lincoln county and again robbed the White Oaks stage coach at the head of the Mal Pais, at the very same place as before.

I was in Roswell at the time and as I was the deputy sheriff I was asked by the sheriff, George Curry, to form a posse and follow these two men. I went to White Oaks and picked five good men, Sam Wells, Frank Crumb, Charlie White, Earnest Ooten and a fellow by the name of Zutes. (He was from Kentucky and a brave man. I never knew his first name, we always just called him "Zutes.") We started to follow Musgraves and Black Jack. We crossed the San Andres mountains and came out on the Jornado Flats and on to the Rio Grande river. When we got to the river it was on a rampage and running bank full of muddy water. We stopped and debated as to how we could get across without losing too much time. There were lots of whirlpools in the river and we were afraid of getting into one of these, but finally decided to take off our clothes and put them in a tow sack and tie them on our saddles. I jumped my horse off in the river and caught hold of his tail and swam across safely. I watched each man cross in the same way, then we all put on our clothes and headed due west.

We traveled for two days and when we got to within about one mile of Fairview, New Mexico, we stopped to rest our horses and decide what to do next. We decided that I should go on into Fairview and see what I could find out. I went to the post office and met the postmaster and told him my mission. He said he was also a deputy sheriff and would do anything he could to help me. He pointed to a man leaning against the hitching post and said, "See that man there, he owns a ranch in the Mogollon mountains and it is headquarters for all the cattle and horse thieves and you are going into a very dangerous and rough country for these men." He advised very strongly that we turn back. I went back and talked it over with my posse and it was decided that we would not go on any farther. We came back through the Black Range by way of Magdalena, Socorro, and San Antonio, New Mexico, where the Santa Fe Railroad had built a bridge across the Rio Grande river and we crossed safely on that. We arrived home tired and worn and had failed to get our man. Under the laws of New Mexico we were not entitled to any mileage or fees as we had made no arrests, but Sheriff George Curry went before the County Commissioners and asked them to allow me my actual expenses which was around $80.00, which they did.

On one of the first passenger trains run on the El Paso & Northeastern railroad, a cowboy got on the train at Corona, New Mexico. When the conductor came around and said, "Ticket, please," the cowboy replied, "Hell, I have no ticket, but if you will stop this train I will go back to Corona and get one." The conductor told him that he could not do that but the next stop would be Carrizozo and he could get a ticket there and asked, "Where do you want to go?" The cowboy replied, "To Hell." The conductor smiled and said, "Well, Carrizozo is as near as we can get you," so the cowboy stayed in Carrizozo.

Narrator: Charles P. Mayer, Carrizozo, New Mexico, aged 79 years.

Pioneer Story: Ambrosio Chavez

by
Edith L. Crawford

We were living in Lincoln when Billy the Kid was there but I did not know him very well. When he killed Ollinger and Bell and made his escape I was working on the Henry Farmer ranch near Lincoln. I can remember something that happened once when I was on a visit to my cousin, Martin Chavez in Picacho. Billy the Kid knew Martin well and often stayed with him at his house. Some Texas people were traveling through the country in covered wagons and were camped near Picacho. They had a fast horse that they wanted to race against a mare that my cousin Martin had. The Texas people bet three fat beeves that their horse could outrun Martin's mare. They had the race between the two horses, and Martin's mare won the race so far ahead of the horse that the Texas people had, that they got awful mad about it and would not pay the bet. Soon after the race was run Billy the Kid came by and stopped at Martin's place. Martin told him about the race and that the Texas people would not pay their bet. Billy asked Martin if he wanted those beeves, and of course Martin said that he did. Billy said that he would collect the bet for him then. The women at Martin's ranch just begged Billy not to go to collect the bet as they were afraid that there would be trouble over it and that Billy might get killed, but Billy just laughed at them. He wore two guns and had on two belts of cartridges. He went out to the camp of the Texans and rode into the herd of cattle that they had with them and shot and killed three of their best beeves and told Martin to send after his beef. The Texans were so scared when they found out that he was Billy the Kid that they broke camp and left right away. . . .

Narrator: Ambrosio Chavez, Carrizozo, New Mexico, aged 72 years.

Pioneer Story:
Abran Miller

by
Edith L. Crawford

I was very small for my age when I first went to work for the Murphy, Dolan Company. I got my clothes and board and Mr. Murphy gave forty dollars to my mother, each month. I soon made them a good cowhand and then I got sixty dollars a month.

They sent me with a bunch of cattle to Elk Canyon, in the Mescalero Indian Reservation. These cattle were to be butchered for the Indians as they needed them. A fellow by the name of Lucio Montoya and I were left to watch the cattle and keep the Indians from stealing them. One morning we got up and it was Lucio's time to go and get the horses. We kept a small black mule in the corral to ride after the saddle horses. While Lucio was saddling up the mule I was looking around to see if I could see anything of the horses. All at once I saw an awful dust rising and I told Lucio to hurry up as I feared someone was rounding up either the cattle or the saddle horses. He rode off in a run. I waited for some time and he did not return. I had just about decided that he had been killed, and I went back to the cabin. I was standing in the door of the cabin when about thirty men rode up to the door. The leader was a nice looking young fellow. He said, "Hello kid, do you have anything to eat?"

I said, "Yes, there is coffee, bacon, flour and some canned goods, you are welcome to it, but you will have to cook it yourselves. I have to go and get my horses and see what has become of Lucio."

The leader of this gang was "Billy the Kid." I did not know it at the time as this was just the beginning of the trouble leading up to the "Lincoln County War." This war was between two cattle factions. Murphy and Dolan on one side and McSween and Tunstall on the other.

Billy the Kid saw I was just a kid and was scared and he said: "Kid, don't be afraid for not a man in the crowd will hurt you nor bother anything around here while you are in charge of it." They all got down from their horses and came in. I helped them make some coffee. While we were waiting for the coffee to boil Billy the Kid asked me all about myself, how old I was, where I lived, etc. After they had eaten they all rode off toward the head of Elk Canyon.

I started out afoot to find the horses and soon found them. The mule that Lucio had started after the horses on was with them but I could not find Lucio. I soon saw that a horse of Lucio's was gone and I just decided that he had gotten frightened and left.

I found out later that this gang of men were with the McSween and Tunstall faction but they never bothered me at all.

While my mother was living on the Salado, Billy the Kid came to our house for something to eat. This was after the time he had been to the camp at Elk's Canyon. He recognized me at once and I did him. My mother did not want to feed him because he was not on Murphy's side at that time. I told her how nice he had been to me that time at Elk's Canyon, so she gave him something to eat and let him stay all night. I got up early the next morning and went out to milk the cow. While I was milking the dogs began to bark. I saw several men riding horseback, coming towards the house. I did not have time to warn Billy that someone was coming but he and mother saw them. Mother had a big homemade packing box she used for a trunk and it had a padlock on it. She hid Billy in this box before the men reached the house. (This was after Bernstein had been killed. He was the clerk at the Mescalero Indian Agency, and Billy had been indicted for this killing, and was on the dodge.)

When I reached the house I found that the men were Sheriff Peppin and Florencio Chaves, his deputy, and two other men. (I have forgotten their names.) They were looking for Billy. They searched the house but did not find him. Peppin came out in the yard and asked me who the black horse with the saddle on belonged to. I told him it was my horse. He wanted to know why I kept a horse saddled and staked out. I told him I kept the horse to go round up the other horses. He did not believe me. I know, for he said to one of his men that Billy the Kid should be around there somewhere. When he did not find Billy they rode away. The Kid stayed in our house all that day and when it got dark Mother asked me to let Billy have my black horse and saddle, as she thought that he would return them to me. I did, and sure enough, in about ten days I got up one morning and found my horse, with the saddle on, in the corral. I never did know who brought him back. I was surely glad, for I thought an awful lot of this horse and I was so afraid that Billy would not get him back to me. I had traded with the Apache Indians for this horse. I had given them about ten dollars worth of red flannel, beads and powder for him.

When Billy the Kid and his gang had killed Bernstein, a clerk at the Indian Agency, Mr. L. G. Murphy (of the Murphy, Dolan

Company), sent me to Santa Fe, New Mexico, with the message to the governor. I rode this same black horse. I had to go first to Fort Stanton to see the commanding officer. I got there about three o'clock in the morning. The guard stopped me but when I told him what I wanted to see the commanding officer about, he took me to the officer's house. This officer gave me another message and a fresh horse and I started for Santa Fe. I rode to Pinos Wells, on the north side of the Gallinas Mountains, that night. I knew a fellow there by the name of Merio Payno, and he let me have a fresh horse, and I made it on to Santa Fe on the third day. When I went in to see Governor Axtell and deliver my messages to him he was mad because they had sent such a kid. He asked me why Pat Carillo had not sent his own son, as he was larger and older than I was. He also told me to tell Mr. Murphy to give me three hundred dollars for that trip, and if Mr. Murphy didn't do it, he would. I got my three hundred dollars from Mr. Murphy all right.

That is the only part that I took in the Lincoln County War, although I was working for the Murphy, Dolan Company all during the war. I stayed at the headquarters ranch on the Carrizozo Flats most of the time. . . .

Narrator: Abran Miller, Carrizozo, New Mexico, aged 75 years.

Main Street of Lincoln, New Mexico, showing Watson House, site of burned McSween house and Turnstall Store. Creator: Frasher, Courtesy Palace of the Governors (MNM/DCA #105473)

The Harrell War

by
Edith L. Crawford

The Harrell war, in 1872, takes its name from the principal characters on the American side of the difficulty. The Harrell brothers, with their families, accompanied by others, came from Texas and settled on the Ruidoso, engaging in farming and ranching. A conflict over water rights arose between them and their native neighbors. Irrigation ditches were cut and soon arms were resorted to. One of the Harrell crowd shot and killed one of the neighboring Mexicans while the latter was cutting a ditch. A warrant was issued for the arrest of the slayer, but the officer was resisted and the entire Harrell tribe united and refused to be arrested by a Mexican officer. From that date the feeling between the races grew, and the animosities growing out of that conflict survived long years after the Harrells were driven from the country and the "Tejano" was a favorite term of opprobrium applied by the Mexican population to all Texans for many years.

A large posse of Mexicans from the Bonito and Ruidoso valleys surrounded the Harrells and vigorously attacked them. In the meantime, the Harrells had fortified themselves, and successfully resisted the attacks of their enemies. After a vain attempt to dislodge the Harrells, the attacking party withdrew, seeking reinforcements. While the posse was away the Harrells loaded up their effects, taking their wives and children with them, and started to leave the country. They were followed and a number of fights took place. Finally, the Harrells were attacked in force after they had been traveling and fighting for a number of days, and they were forced to make a stand. They drew up their wagons and equipment in a circle and the battle raged for several hours, in which a number were wounded on both sides and several killed. The attacking party, however, failed to dislodge the Harrells, withdrew and allowed the Harrells to proceed on their way to Texas, which the latter were glad to do.

Joe Haskins and one of the Harrells were killed and several other Texans wounded. Several Mexicans were killed; of the number, however, only five names have been given, viz: Seferino Trujillo, Reymundo and Ceberiano Aguilar, Pablo Romero and Juan Silva. These were killed while the Harrells were being driven from the country, but a number of others were killed by the Harrells during the progress of the strife in the lighter skirmishes that marked this bloody period. The result of this war, as has been stated, was to create a bitter animosity between Mexicans and Texans, which required many years to eradicate, but which now, happily, no longer exists.

Copied from the 1913 Year Book, Lincoln County, New Mexico. Written and edited by John A. Haley.

Story of the Harrell War

by
Edith L. Crawford

The story was told me by my Grandfather, Felipe Maes, who died at the age of 62.

"I was coming from Los Chosos, accompanied by Florencio Morales, who was about seven years old, with a load of corn, driving a team of oxen.

"About two miles below Lincoln we met a man by the name of Philip Buster; after talking to him for a while, he asked if I was going to the dance tonight, and I said, I might. He told me it was much better for me not to go. I asked him why and he only said I was his friend and that was his reason for telling me this. He also told me that there was some men coming on horse-back from the north side of the river and for us to hurry and get to Lincoln as he believed they were the Harrell brothers and that they might kill us.

This man went on down the river and we started on to

Lincoln as fast as we could travel as we were afraid of the Harrell boys.

Philip Buster met the party of horseback riders just a short ways below where we had talked to him. I kept turning my head in that direction to see what they were doing; I noticed one of the men start up the road toward us several times, but each time he went back to talk to these men. After a while Philip Buster overtook us and said to me, 'You can consider yourself lucky that I happened to be here at this time, because that bunch of men wanted to kill you and the boy.'

"That same night I asked my mother for some clean clothes for I wanted to go to the dance. She said there was no clean clothes for me, and for me not to go to the dance. I started to go just as I was. We lived just across the road from the dance hall and the dance was in progress. About the time I got to the middle of the road, I thought of what this man Philip Buster had told me about not going to the dance. So I turned around and went home. As I was getting ready for bed, they started shooting up the dance. They killed several people and wounded three. The next day I was told that the Harrell Brothers did the shooting during the time of the Harrell War.

"They searched everyone who came to the dance and disarmed them, is the reason for the one-sided shooting at this dance."

Informant: H.M. Maes. Lincoln, New Mexico.

Reminiscences of Lincoln County and White Oaks
by Old Sages and Stagers

by
Edith L. Crawford

My Dear Major:

To fulfill my promise I will give you a few lines, and if you see fit you can publish the same.

I left Silver Cliff, Colorado, the day after the Presidential election in '80, and started for White Oaks via Pueblo, La Junta and the A. P. & S. F. R. R. to Las Vegas. About the 10th of November I left Vegas to come on to White Oaks, but "man proposes and God disposes." After being out four days on the road and having beautiful weather, we camped one night this side of the Alkali Wells in the timber, where we turned in. The weather was fine, sky clear, moon shone bright, and everything was lovely and serene. Towards morning I woke up and found myself nearly covered with snow, and it still falling. The wind blew at a great rate, and everything was all but lovely and serene. We decided on stopping where we were until the end of the storm, and we stayed three nights and two days. On the third day we left and got as far as the Greathouse ranch—Greathouse & Cook kept a store and camp house for travelers on the Vegas and White Oaks road. They wanted a man to drive their team and haul water from the Abeel Lake for their ranch. Having heard on the road that times were dull at White Oaks I accepted the situation.

I found at the ranch, besides Greathouse and Cook, some six or seven other men whom I took to be cowboys. Things went on smoothly for a week or more—travelers came and went. I attended to my business of hauling logs for a corral, and water when needed. One day the above-mentioned cowboys went away, but returned about three days afterwards. The next morning, after daylight, I got up, went out to where my team was picketed. And about 300 yards from the house somebody hollered, "Halt!" I naturally turned around to see what was up, when to my great surprise two men had their guns pointed at me. They ordered me to approach them, all the time keeping their guns pointed at me. I went like a little man. When I got to them they got behind me and ordered me to march towards what I supposed was a bunch of fallen timber—and so it was, but there were men behind it, two bold, bad, ferocious looking men, with plenty of guns and ammunition. When I got amongst them one of my captors said: "Captain, we've got one of the S of B's," and I did not resent it even a little bit. They ordered me to lie down with them, and I did so. They wanted to know if Billy the Kid, Billy Wilson or Dave Rudabaugh were in the house. I told them I did not know. They doubted my word and I didn't allow myself to get mad. They gave me a description of the men they were after and I told them that three such looking men were in the house. Then they told me they were a sheriff's posse from White Oaks and would have the notorious trio dead or alive. After a consultation among themselves, more coming from different posts around the house, they decided that perhaps I was not so hard a citizen as I looked, and if I would give 'em my word of honor to come out again I could carry a dispatch into the house telling the boys to surrender, as a posse of 13 men from White Oaks had come during the night, surrounded the house on all sides, and large parties from Lincoln were en route with provisions and everything necessary for a siege, and they had better surrender at once as there was no show for escape.

I took the note in and delivered it to the one I knew to be Billy the Kid. We read the paper to his compadres who all laughed at the idea of surrender. They told me also to rest easy and not be alarmed as no harm would come to me from them. They sent me out with a note demanding to know who the leader of the party was, and invited him into the house to talk things over. Carlyle, the leader of the white Oaks party at first objected, but Greathouse, putting himself as hostage for his safety while he was in there, he took off his arms and walked into the trap. In the meantime I was backward and forward between the two parties carrying dispatches.

Getting hungry about 11 o'clock I went into the house to rustle up a dinner. I found Carlyle getting under the influence of liquor and insisting on going out, while the others insisted on his staying. While I was getting dinner, Mr. Cook, Greathouse's partner, carried dispatches between the camps. For some reason the White Oaks boys became suspicious; things were not as they should be with their leader, and they decided to storm the fort; therefore sent me word by Mr. Cook to come out as war would commence in earnest. I stepped outdoors intending to go to some safe place and witness the bloody conflict. After being out, Cook called me to stop a moment and he would go with me. I stopped and turned when a crash, and a man came through a window, bong bang, the man's dying yell, and poor Carlyle tumbles to the ground with three bullets in him—dead. I started to run away from the house, with Cook behind me and toward a barricade of the White Oaks boys when they commended to shoot at us, and so did all the other boys behind the different barricades. About 60 or 75 shots were fired at us, bullets flying from all directions, and I began to feel decidedly uncomfortable—was afraid some of them might hit me. I thought it was a ground hog case and I had better be the ground hog, so I jumped several feet in the air, threw my hands up over my head and fell flat on my face and lay there. Cook, behind me, thought it a good scheme, so he imitated my example. After 3 or 4 more bullets came very close to my head the firing suddenly stopped. We crawled out amongst the boys when they told us it was all a mistake; they thought we were making a feint to cover the retreat of the desperados.

This is about all there is to the trouble at the Greathouse ranch. Cook and myself went that night to Abeel's ranch, about three miles from there, and returned the next morning. We found poor Carlyle frozen stiff where he fell, tied a blanket around him and made a hole a little toward the east from where he felt, and buried him the best we could. He was afterwards taken up and put in a box by a sheriff's posse.

No more at present. I remain yours truly,
J. Steck.

Written by Joe Steck. Taken from the Lincoln County Leader. Edited at White Oaks, Saturday, December 7, 1889.

Seven Rivers—Lakewood

by
Katherine Ragsdale

*I*t took strong men to withstand the hardships they had to stand here. Such men as Dan Beckett, Dick Turknett, Pete Corn, Lafe McDonald, George Wilcox, Levi Watson, Joe Woods, George Larrimore, Ed Peril, Charlie and Buster Gambel, Pap Jones, John Jones, Will Jones, Sam Jones, John Fanning and Bill Nelson. Some of these men had been Texas Rangers, and all of them were quick with a gun.

It was in the '70s that thirty of these men with their families came in a caravan together from Texas and settled here in Seven Rivers.

In 1877, 4000 head of cattle were stolen from Chisum and Wiley, some of which were sold back to their owners by Indians. These Indians were hired by white men to do rustling for them. It is said that after the death of Bob Edwards, a notorious outlaw, the Indians were not such frequent visitors.

Gradually Siete Rios grew, and in 1878 this old town was established. Captain Sam Samson opened the first store—a saloon and trading post located where Seven Rivers ran into the Pecos River. Carl Gordon and Benton started a store just below Captain Samson; later R.H. Pierce opened a large store where one could get practically anything they wanted; also Mr. R. Semore had a nice store, Fred Sheremyre (now living on top of the Guadalupe Mountains) a boot maker, had a boot shop, and, too, there was a blacksmith shop. Mams Jones opened a restaurant.

At this time there was no doctor in Seven Rivers and Dee Burditt, a registered druggist, acted as their doctor.

Among the people settling here were some criminals—many of which were well educated men but had gotten in trouble in some of the northern, eastern, southern or western states and had come to Seven Rivers to live; many died and were buried under fictitious names. Too there were quite a few "gang" headed by notorious outlaws such as Bob Edwards, Billy the Kid, etc.

This was a "wild and wooly" town of the west, many men were killed over gambling and wild drinking, etc.; things happened in this old town that the old timers refuse to tell.

It is told (by an old timer) that when the sheep men came to this country the cattle men resented their coming in. These sheep men had Mexicans for herders, and when these Mexicans came to town some of the cowboys would shoot them and then bury them in such shallow graves that they would leave the herders' toes sticking out.

Two old timers claim it was such a wild place you could almost read a newspaper at night by the gunfire.

In connection with the store owned by R.H. Pierce was a saloon; Tom Fensey was a bartender; one night he killed the gambler John Northen; after being shot he ran to Pap Jones and hid in the wood box behind the store where he died. Les Dow was the next bartender until he killed Zac Light.

William Doroughty carried the mail in a wagon from upper Denon (now Elk) to Seven Rivers. The stage driver was Jessie J. Rascoe who during a fight had his arm shot off but he continued to drive after this loss. . . .

Wild Cow Mesa

by
Katherine Ragsdale

In the beautiful Guadalupe Mountains, located southwest of Rocky Arroyo, is the beautiful Wild Cow Mesa.

On the way to the mesa one may look from their path on the mountain down on a valley and see in the distance a green elevated table land, a most beautiful sight to behold.

This mesa was at one time (during the wild Seven Rivers days) a meeting and hiding place of the Indians and outlaws.

Working for the outlaws the Indians would come down into Seven Rivers and on up to the Chisum Ranch, down to Lovings Bend, Pierce Canyon and steal cattle and horses and then drive them to this mesa.

Here the white outlaws would pay the Indians for their work and then take over the cattle, sometimes driving them on into Mexico, sometimes selling them.

In driving the cattle to the mesa, often cows would leave

the herd and, becoming lost, would wander over the mesa, living on the grasses growing there. As time went on these cows became wild, thus getting the name Wild Cow Mesa.

Many of these cows were caught and some of the wealthy cattle men of today got their start from these wild cows.

Source of Information: Dave Runyan.

DISTRICT THREE: BAD HOMBRES OF THE EARLY DAYS

"A murder was never a murder, but a 'killing.'
We tried a few murder cases in our court, but I never
knew of a legal hanging. I knew of other hangings—not
legal but probably more effective."

(From "Bad Hombres of the Early Days"
by Elinor Crans)

"Bad Hombres" of the Early Days

by
Elinor Crans

Naturally a new and sparsely settled country is a refuge for criminals and other law breakers, because of the greater chance there of escape from detection and apprehension. "The great and turbulent state of New Mexico," as Kyle Crichton designates it, has perhaps never been meticulously amenable to law and order; and possibly that is one of the features that adds interest to the State's fascinating and dramatic history.

In the old days the wealthy Dons were much of a law unto themselves. It was a reckless age, the law of such a land is generally the Law of Might. Raids into the Indian country for slaves; buffalo hunts to the "staked plains"; *conductas* (caravans) to Old Mexico; even cattle rustling—all these and others were "gentlemen's amusements" as it were.

Later on and through the 1800's the "great state of New Mexico" is still "turbulent." Prominent characters in written history and in tradition include Joe Fowler, ranchman who paid his hired help on pay day with bullets instead of dollars; the Slaughter Boys, reckless cowhands who found pleasure in shooting up the town; Billy Minters, the "well known and highly esteemed" gentlemen gambler; William Bonney, better known as Billy the Kid, youthful reputed Robin Hood of Lincoln county.

"Plenty of bad men in the old days," explains Filipiano, my aged informant. "*Si*, plenty then—plenty now—plenty always."

"Judge Lynch was the most popular judge in my day," says a jurist who came to Old Town to practice law many years ago.

"But," explains Filipiano, "it was not so bad here as in Los Lunas and some of the other towns. There they would hand a suspect over to the lynchers without the semblance of a trial, merely on somebody's say-so, or what seemed to them sufficient evidence. Old Town gave a criminal a trial, or tried to. Sometimes 'Judge Lynch' stepped in and took the man out of jail to hang him on 'Hangman's Tree,' or any other tree that happened to be handy."

Old Town Court House

"The court house," says W. W. H. Davis, visiting Old Town in 1856, "is on the eastern edge of town in a modest looking mud building."

"That," Filipiano points out, "was probably the court house and jail which once stood on Mountain Road, just a little ways down—where that wood yard is now. Just opposite—across the road—was the 'Hangman's Tree.' A house is built now on the spot where it used to be. The courthouse was moved from time to time; there was no regular court house or jail then—just an ordinary house made as secure as possible, where they locked a prisoner. And then"—Filipiano laughed—"they would have to guard the house, for sometimes a prisoner would climb up the chimney and escape. It was a case of guards guarding the jail, instead of the prisoner."

Many tall tales are told of, and by, Elfego Baca, for many years a local attorney and one time sheriff. Now a resident of Albuquerque, Elfego began his career by a spectacular jail break, releasing his own father who as town marshal had killed two cowboys. Baca Sr. was arrested and placed in jail. Elfego and another youth managed to get into a room above the jail, cut a hole in the floor and released Baca Sr. and two other prisoners. The five then hid in the tall grass near the prison all day, escaping at night to Socorro.

Elfego tells of the time that he and Billy the Kid, both about 16 years of age at the time, rode to Old Town from Socorro, "leaving their horses at Isleta where they would be safe," and walking to town—some thirteen miles. They were resting beside a pole in the street when they saw a policeman and companion talking to a third man. They saw the policeman shoot the third party in cold blood, his companion shooting into the air; the two then claimed that the dead man had tried to shoot the policeman. The policeman's word was accepted as was his companion's. But the two visiting youths who witnessed the affair hastened off to Old Town, "wondering at Albuquerque's kind of justice."

There is another side to the shield, however, according to Dick Wooten, an old-time pioneer:

"I think," says he, "the way we used to administer justice in those days had a great deal to do with the remarkable security of property. There was less security for human life, but property was a great deal safer. We always had a judge and jury, and counsel for the prosecution and defense when we tried a man for violation of frontier law."

In "New Mexico's Own Chronicle" we find: "When courts

were few and little legal knowledge existed, the settlers contrived to preserve a certain kind of order, a certain moral standard, in their own way with rough effectiveness."

Emerson Hough, novelist of the Southwest, at that time a young lawyer in southern New Mexico, pays his tribute to the men of the times:

"Much as I detested the practice of law, I loved the creed which actually governed the standards of life in that country. The citizens as a whole were better than the courts and the attorneys. There was something wholly admirable in their code of manhood. To be a citizen meant that the newcomer had to have (or acquire) certain worth-while qualities. A man's word was truly his bond. Theft was unknown; every man carried a discreet tongue in his head, a good gun in his belt, and was supposed to be able to take care of himself. Human life was very cheap. A murder was never a murder, but a "killing." We tried a few murder cases in our court, but I never knew of a legal hanging. I knew of other hangings—not legal but probably more effective.

"And yet," he concludes, "even today the manner of life in that early-day and savage little town seems large as compared with the 'standards of civilization' in which we live at present."

Old Town Albuquerque Chronicles:
Slaves, Serfs, Peones

by
Elinor Crans

"My Uncle Romero had slaves—Indian slaves," says Don Filipiano, "and—vindictively—he made 'em work, too! How did he get them? Oh—raids to the Indian country were common enough; or he could buy them. His hacienda was out in the country where Tingly Park is now. The Romeros were wealthy as a family, so my Uncle too was a very rich man. I've heard him tell how a group of men would get together, and on one pretext or another raid the Navajo country. Since the Navajos were always raiding whites or pueblo Indians, my uncle and his crowd felt their own raids were nothing but reprisals; but sometimes these raids were made just because Old Town settlers wanted help on the ranches, or wanted slave girls for domestic help in the house.

"It wasn't so easy to catch the men, but some of them who couldn't run fast enough to get away on a surprise raid, they'd bring them back. Women were easier to catch, of course; they'd try to go for them when they knew the men were off on a hunt.

"Dangerous? Yes, but exciting! You know the old dons thought the Indians belonged to 'em, anyway, thought they were 'grants' from Spain—just like land grants. Of course the Crown had no right really to grant the lands, and certainly had no right to 'grant' the Indians. But a hundred years ago people did a lot of things they had no right to do.

A Local Slave Trader

"One could buy slaves in the Southwest, at least as late as 1850, when the constitution of New Mexico was adopted, declaring against slavery. Indian and Negro slaves were available. Pedro Chavez, a Cebolitan, used to come to Old Town and other Rio settlements, contracting with wealthy residents to furnish them with domestic help at so-much a head."

Lummis in "A New Mexico David" says: "Pedro Chavez would contract for slaves at five hundred dollars per head. Then he would start out on a campaign, strike a band of hostile Navajos, kill the warriors and bring back the women and children for servants."

"Dangerous business," explained Don Filipiano. "The Navajos could hardly be expected to submit peaceably to capture, and Pedro Chavez's raiders often lost a scalp or two in the melee. Finally, Chavez met a fate in keeping with the horrible business he had been following. Reprisals between whites and Indians continued to stir up a lot of trouble, until they got up a big campaign against the Navajos. A thousand or more New Mexico volunteers, with Don Ramon Luna as their commander. Pedro Chavez joined the troop and went along as captain. The soldiers were on their way back from a not too successful campaign. Close behind them was a band of Navajos who killed the whites whenever possible. The soldiers had orders to stick close together. Pedro Chavez disobeyed orders. He stole away one night with thirty followers, camped that night in San Miguel canyon, and the whole bunch were massacred by a party of several hundred Indians. Not a white was left. Chavez's body was found, my father said, but the Indians had scalped him and even cut off his head!"

Wislizenus, a St. Louis physician passing through the state on his way to Chihuahua, noted the fertile fields and large estates belonging to rich property owners. "These estates," he says, "are apparently a remnant of the old feudal system where large tracts of land—together with Indian inhabitants as serfs—were granted by the Crown to Spanish subjects."

Certainly the old families, including many of the original thirty Old Town settlers and their successors, grew wealthy. But the condition of the common people grew worse. The poorer classes attracted the attention of Josiah Gregg, whose "Commerce of the Prairies" was published in 1844. He says:

"Men's wages range from two to five dollars a month; women received from fifty cents to two dollars a month. In payment they rarely receive actual money, instead thereof they must accept articles of apparel and other necessities at the most exorbitant prices. The consequence is that a servant soon acquires a debt which he is unable to pay, and his wages are often owed for a year or two in advance. According to the usage of the country he is bound to serve his master until his debts are paid."

"It's just about as bad today," says Don Filipiano. "They pay twenty dollars a month for a sheepherder, send him out with the sheep in the mountains. Sometimes he doesn't get back home for a year or more. His work is hard, he has to be on guard night and day, staying right with the sheep. He gets nothing much but beans to eat; no meat unless he kills a sheep—and he isn't supposed to do that. Yet when he gets into debt for his expenses while working for the *patron*, he has to work it out, same as in the old days.

"I don't know what the law is now, but there was a time when anybody could be put in jail for a debt. Once, when Elfego Baca was serving as sheriff, they say he had been away somewhere in the state after a prisoner. While he was gone the sheepmen got a bill passed in legislature, making a debt a jail offense. And when Elfego got back he found his jail just about full of prisoners, all of them serving a sixty-day sentence under this new law. Baca, young or old, was a sort of law himself; he released the prisoners, emptying the jail, and told the men to go back home and pay their debts by working. 'You'll only eat us poor here,' he said, 'just to satisfy a few big sheepmen who had such a fool law passed.'

Baca reported to the district attorney, refusing to hold any other prisoners for debt. And in time the law was repealed. I don't know whether they tried it again or not; anyhow, it wasn't a civilized law. And in times like these—with such a law—there'd be more people in jail than out."

Sources: "Chronology of New Mexico" by E. G. Rich; "A New Mexico David," by Chas Lummis.

Pioneer Story: Interview with Mrs. Pauline Myer A Visit from Outlaws

by
Janet Smith

Soon after she was married in 1875, Pauline Myer traveled from her home in San Francisco to join her husband in New Mexico. He had gone on ahead so that he might investigate the country. He wrote her that it was a rough place, and so, she says, she found it. But her husband had good prospects in the wool business there and she was eager to see a new country. She took the train from San Francisco to Ogden, Utah. After a wait she took another train for Cheyenne, Wyoming. There she had to stay over a day before she could make connections south to Denver. In Denver she changed again for Pueblo which was as far south as the train went.

Her husband, Bernard Myer, met her in Pueblo with an "ambulance," as covered wagons were called in New Mexico. It was a fine ambulance, Mrs. Myer said, with a leather covering. He had a fine pair of horses too. But the journey to Rio Puerco, New

Mexico, she hardly likes to talk about. It was so full of hardships and discomforts. It rained and the adobe roads were inches deep in mud. They changed horses frequently. Usually the change was from bad to worse. The country seemed like a foreign land to her. In the houses where they stopped for the night, the women could not understand her and they had strange ways of cooking. They patted lumps of dough into round thin cake-like objects called "tortillas." When her husband asked for directions, the men seemed too indolent even to point. They pursed their lips and lifted their chins in the general direction they wished to indicate and said "alle" (ah-ee). It was only occasionally that she saw an American face, and then she says she was "tickled."

After a journey of about two weeks, she reached her new home in Rio Puerco, a little Mexican settlement about twenty-five miles southwest of Albuquerque in Bernalillo County. Mr. Myer had a general merchandise store there. He sold the natives sugar and coffee and yards of calico for shirts and dresses, shoes and nails and kerosene oil. When Mr. Myer was away buying sheep, Mrs. Myer had to tend the store. At first she couldn't understand a thing the people said to her, but she soon learned the names of most of the articles in the store and how to use simple greetings, "buenos dias" and "come se va?" Even after she was able to speak their language fairly easily, their brown faces seemed strange to her. "I suppose it would be right in style now," she said, "but in those days I thought I'd never seen anything like those women sitting around the store with cigarettes in their mouths, always laughing and happy."

Mrs. Myer and her husband lived in a big adobe house, the best in town, she said. It was built around a "placita"—a kind of courtyard, she explained, with the building all around it. She rather liked her house for it was always cool in summer, and though it was not always warm in winter, the fireplaces in one corner of almost every room were nice. It was hard for her to get used to the idea of having mud floors, but Nativadad, who came to work for her, knew how to sprinkle them and sweep them with little straw brooms so that they were hard and almost smooth.

In about a year her first baby was born and there was no time to get a doctor from Albuquerque which was 25 miles away. Whenever the baby was sick they had to write to the doctor describing his symptoms and the doctor would send back instructions and medicine. That took a long time and the mail service was unreliable. If the people at the post office felt like it they gave you your letters, and if they didn't they said there weren't any. The safest way was to send somebody on horseback the twenty-five miles to Albuquerque with a note. Once or twice there was an epidemic—smallpox and whooping cough. The time of the smallpox epidemic, Mrs. Myer said that she worried for fear the baby would get it and her husband worried about her and the baby too. "But it stopped at the house on one side of us, passed over our house, and stopped again at the one on the other side." Of course, there was no such thing as quarantine. Mr. Meyer ordered the people to stay out of the store, but they would come in laughing at him for being afraid of them. "They just visited around from one to another and spread the disease. They never seemed to be at all afraid of it, but some of them died just the same. Then there would be a 'velorio,' and we could hear them singing all night long. They would come to the store and buy up lots of food and spend the night praying and eating and singing around the dead one."

There were no amusements and Mrs. Myer was far from her family and friends, but she never had time to be lonely. Later when she and her husband moved to Old Town in Albuquerque, there were occasional "bailes" given by the Mexicans. At first her husband used to take her if he thought the dance would be any way respectable, but it almost always ended in a fight. Usually somebody would shoot the lights out and the women would scream, and her husband would hustle her out the back door as fast as he could. What they fought about she didn't know, some little thing, or maybe nothing. But it was a rare "baile" that ended without a fight, and after awhile her husband decided not to take her. She guessed she wasn't missing much. While she was in Rio Puerco there weren't even "bailes" to go to, but sometimes there was excitement of a little different kind.

Mrs. Myer remembers one bitter cold night when she was awakened by a loud knocking at the gate.

"It was all hours of the night," she said. "It must have been midnight at the least, and I heard a great commotion outside."

She awakened her husband. "Ben, get up, there's someone knocking at the gate."

Ben rolled over. "Let 'em knock."

In a minute she shook him again. "Ben, they're still knocking. Who could it be at this time of the night?"

"Whoever it is, I'm not moving on a bitter cold night like this. They can go on."

But they heard people scrambling over the high wall, and in a minute the knocks began again at the door of the house.

"Who's there?" Mr. Myer called out.

"Open the door," was the answer.

"Not until I know who's there," her husband called back.

"You open that door, if you know what's good for you," was the reply.

Mr. Myer got out of his warm bed then and opened the door. Three tough looking men came in with the blast of cold air. Mrs. Myer said they were as frightful a looking set of men as you could want to see, armed to the teeth with guns and knives—"a regular artillery."

One of them spoke very good English. He demanded food and hot coffee and a warm bed to sleep in.

There was nothing for Mrs. Myer to do but get up too and fix them a meal. There was only one bed in the house besides the baby's cradle, so she and her husband were forced to go to the store for a new mattress and some blankets which they put on the dining room floor, and the three men went to sleep in their warm bed. They demanded to be called early in the morning and ordered a warm breakfast.

Mrs. Meyer said her husband woke her before daybreak and she hurried to prepare breakfast as they were both anxious to get the men out of the house. The three men ate in a hurry.

Before riding away, they stopped at the store. Mr. Myer had a new saddle. He had paid sixty dollars for it and was very proud of it. One of the men wanted it.

"Not that saddle," Mr. Myer said. "You can have anything else, but not that saddle."

However, as Mrs. Myer said, there was no use arguing with that kind of people. They rode away with the saddle.

Both Mrs. Myer and her husband were glad to see them go. An hour or two later Mrs. Myer looked out the window and saw a cloud of dust coming down the road. She knew that meant more men on horseback. She ran to the store to warn her husband, but he was already standing in the doorway watching it.

As the cloud came nearer they could distinguish one man riding in the lead and ten or so behind. In another minute they saw that it was the sheriff with a posse. They were heavily armed and pulled up their horses to ask Mr. Myer if he had seen three men on horseback. He told them of the story of the previous night and pointed to the northwest which was the direction the men had taken.

Several days later Mrs. Myer and her husband heard that

the sheriff and his men had overtaken the three men and had taken them to Bernalillo by another route. There they hanged all three at once from the same huge cottonwood tree. Their names she couldn't remember but she knew they had robbed and killed before coming to her house.

Vernon Smithson

JUL 1 7 1937
el. 300

SHACK STEALING

The early day settlers built little shacks on their
claims. These shacks were very light and usually built
something like a box-car. These could be put on a wagon
and hauled away, and a gang of "shack-stealers" found
the stealing of these shacks a very profitable business
for building materials were very scarce in the early days.

Many a homesteader who had stayed on his claim for
the alloted time each year, then went somewhere else,
either to work or visit, returned to find his claim bare
of any buildings.

Sometimes these shack-stealers were surprised at
their work and many amusing incidents were told of these
encounters between the claim-holders and the theives.

One cagy claimholder went to town and let it be known
that he was leaving for a visit in the east, then slipped
back to his claim and loaded his shotgun and waited for
the theives in the darkness. Soon he heard them coming
and he kept quite while they loaded the light shack on
their wagon. Seeing that the theives were moving his
shack over to another corner of his claim where he had been
contemplating moving his shanty, he waited until they were
near the locality where he wanted to move to, then he stepped to the door and let out a whoop and fired his shotgun.
Needless to say, the theives left out, not even waiting to
unhitch their horses. The claimholder got the plunging
horses under control and unhooked them. The next morning
he unloaded his shack an d found himself the owner of a
fine pair of horses and a wagon and his home moved too.

Facsimile: "Shack Stealing," Vernon Smithson, July 17, 1937, NMFWP, WPA
#153b, NMSRCA

Wild Times in Santa Fe

by
N. Howard Thorp

On the night of February the fifth, 1891, someone on horseback fired a charge from a shotgun loaded with buckshot through the window of Thomas B. Catron's law office in an attempt to assassinate Mr. Catron and his partner, Mr. J.A. Ancheta, both very prominent Attorneys.

The office was situated in the Griffin block at the intersection of Washington Street and Palace Avenue. At the time there was being held a very important political meeting, and also present were a number of members of the State Legislature, who barely escaped with their lives.

Mr. Ancheta was shot in the neck and shoulder. At the time, he was standing in front of one of the windows of the Catron Office. A shot from a rifle was also fired through the window, passing by a narrow margin the head of one of the Senators present. Mr. Catron was standing near a desk, almost in front of Mr. Ancheta and a window. There was a large pile of legal papers on the desk, and the buckshot striking these papers probably saved Mr. Catron's life. The reason for the attempt upon Ancheta's life was never known, but it was believed at the time the intention was to kill Mr. Catron.

The State Legislature offered a reward of twenty thousand dollars for the arrest of the would-be murderers, and a great deal of money was expended in employing detectives in an endeavor to find and arrest the would-be assassins. Mr. Ancheta eventually recovered from his wounds and died at Silver City New Mexico some seven years later.

Several years afterwards, Jose Amado Martinez—a friend and confidant of the conspirators—stated under oath that it was intended to kill Mr. Catron, and not Mr. Ancheta. At this time the city was so corrupt politically that no attempt was made to capture the would-be killers, at least by the duly authorized officers of the law.

At this time Romolo Martinez was U.S. Marshall and Francisco Chavez was made Sheriff of the county and became the most powerful man politically in the City. Among his strong political adherents were Silvestre Gallegos and Francisco Gonzales y Borrego. In the election of 1890, Borrego was elected Coroner, and also Chief of Police of the City of Santa Fe.

As the town at this time became incorporated, the office of Coroner became of no value and the duties of Chief of Police were taken over by an appointee of the Mayor of the City. Gonzales y Borrego felt he had been imposed upon, and sent in his resignation to the board of county Commissioners, which they accepted, and appointed Silvestre Gallegos in his place. Bitter political differences resulted.

At a baile given at a dance hall at the intersection of San Francisco and Galisteo streets in the capitol, hot words occurred between Gallegos and Borrego. Gallegos invited Borrego into the street to fight the matter out. The challenge was accepted, and a large crowd followed the principals out. In this fight Gallegos was killed. This affair was the beginning of a series of murders and tragedies as bad as any happening in the annals of the Territory of New Mexico.

After the killing of Gallegos, Gonzales y Borrego was taken to the county jail, where he was placed in irons. Sheriff Chavez, who had been out of the city at the time of the killing, went to the jail and was so mad he proceeded to give Gonzales y Borrego a whipping. At his trial before the Justice of the Peace—being on the right side of the fence politically—he was acquitted. Among other witnesses relied upon by Borrego, in his plea of self-defense, was Faustin Ortiz. Some time afterwards Ortiz mysteriously disappeared.

In those days most of the male population—and often teams of women and girls—in all the towns of New Mexico played a game they called Chueco, or shinney. Starting their days with early mass the people would attend to their irrigating and other duties; and as the sun got high they would take their siestas in the shade of the buildings. In the cool of the evening, and especially holidays, armed with shinney sticks they would assemble in the different streets, roads or smooth arroyos and play until dark. Although the game of Chueco has almost entirely disappeared, in days past it was the most popular pastime in the State. The sticks were cut from the pinion trees so cost nothing, while the ball was made of a stone covered with green rawhide. The game of golf with its elaborate equipment has now supplanted it.

One day while the game was in full progress in the arroyo Mascarena—above where the railroad track is now located—a boy, in whacking the ball, struck something which was protruding from the sand; it was a human foot. Attached to the foot was the body of Faustin Ortiz, who had so mysteriously disappeared, like many of those who had been put out of the way by the Goras Blancas or "white caps."

Ortiz, after his disappearance, had been reported as seen in Mexico, California, and other distant points. It was generally supposed that Ortiz had been murdered on account of his having stuck up for the cause of Borrego. The following facts concerning the murder of Ortiz were told under oath by Jose Amado Martinez. Ortiz on some pretext was induced to visit the office of the Justice of the Peace in the county jail building and while there was attacked and murdered by Juan Ortiz—the Justice of the Peace—Eustaquio Padilla and several others, all bearing commissions of deputy Sheriffs. At night the body was removed and buried in the arroyo Mascarena.

Coming to trial before Justice T. Smith, Eustaquio Padilla was charged with the murder of Ortiz, but was acquitted. Presently the Grand Jury returned indictments against a great many prominent people including Sheriff Chavez, all charged with Ortiz's murder, though eventually these indictments were all quashed.

In May in 1892, while going from the city to his residence across the Rio Santa Fe, and in front of the Guadalupe church, Francisco Chavez, who had resigned as Sheriff, was assassinated.

The assassination of Francisco Chavez created a great sensation in Santa Fe and over the state by reason of his popularity. He was very generous, and had hosts of friends who mourned his passing.

Next, in front of the residence of the Archbishop, Juan Pablo Gallegos, who had been a deputy under Sheriff Chavez, was shot and killed by Francisco Gonzales y Borrego while in the company of Lauriano Alarid, Antonio Gonzales y Borrego, and another man. Gallegos, it was claimed, was laying in wait for Gonzales y Borrego, and at the time of his death was trying to fire his pistol, but it misfired; a knife and a billy were found on his person, but they may have been planted there.

Gonzales y Borrego was tried for this killing, and acquitted.

The prominence of the murdered Sheriff Francisco Chavez started an investigation during the administration of Governor Thornton, who succeeded L. Bradford Prince, and which led to the arrest of Francisco Gonzales y Borrego, his brother Antonio Gonzales y Borrego, Lauriano Alarid, Hipolito Vigil, and Patricio Valencio. At the time of the arrests Vigil was killed while resisting Sheriff Cunningham. At the June term 1894 of the Santa Fe District Court these men were indicted for the murder of Francisco Chavez. In April in 1895 the five accused men came to trial, and under Judge Hamilton each were found guilty.

Then an appeal was taken to the Supreme Court, but with no results; next, efforts were made with the President of the United States to secure a commutation of sentence. They were unavailing. The principal counsel for the accused was Thomas B. Catron, who on account of the vigorous way in which he conducted the defense, the money which necessarily had been expended and the malicious statements and insinuations of political rivals and enemies, was charged with having more than a professional interest in the outcome of the case. Finally the defendants were hanged. Prior to their execution they confessed their guilt, but denied that Mr. Catron or any other outsider of those who had been charged with the crime had been connected with the murder in any way. Revenge was undoubtedly the controlling factor in the crime. The mother of Faustin Ortiz, at whose home these men were accustomed to meet, had a strong influence over them on account of the murder of her son, and may have helped in their taking revenge.

Politics undoubtedly was at the bottom of most of the crimes which were committed at that time, although when Francisco Chavez was assassinated he had resigned the Office of Sheriff and consequently had ceased to be a factor in the political situation.

The End

Grant Wheeler and Joe George New Mexico Train Robbers

by
N. Howard Thorp

In January in 1895, two cowboys, Grant Wheeler and Joe George, held up a Southern Pacific train, some five miles west of Wilcox, Arizona. George was practically raised in the Sacramento Mountains of New Mexico while Wheeler was a tramp cowpuncher who had drifted into New Mexico and was at this time living in the Chiricahua Mountains of Arizona. Both at one time had worked for the Diamond A, and the three C.C.C. cattle company. However, thirty dollars a month fighting cattle failed to appeal to them, and seeing so many others riding silver mounted outfits, who were no better cowhands than themselves, induced them to try their hands at the easiest way to riches, so they decided to hold up a train.

Now, according to the best authorities, there should be not less than five men to make a successful train hold up: one man to hold the horses, one on either side of the train to shoot shots of warning at anyone on the train who might be foolhardy enough to interfere, and the other two men covering the Engineer and fireman to make them do their bidding.

The above is the ideal setting and in accordance with the rules as laid down by the best authorities.

Although both Grant Wheeler and Joe George had been mixed up in many minor criminal affairs, this was their first attempt at the man-size job of train robbery. As these two figured it, the smaller number of men on the job the greater the profits, so at it they went.

Mounted on good horses they rode into the town of Wilcox, and bought a supply of fuse, caps and gunpowder, telling the store clerk they were doing some mining in the mountains to the south.

Going to where they expected to rob the train, they cached their powder, tied their horses in a cedar thicket, walked back to Wilcox and got aboard the train they intended to rob.

Climbing between the tender and the first car, as soon as the train got well under way they went over to the coal in the tender, and covered the Engineer and fireman with their six-shooters, ordering them to stop the train about three miles from town. They made the fireman get down and cut off the mail and express car from the rest of the train. And they had the Engineer move the cars ahead about two miles to where they had left their horses and giant powder.

The Express Messenger, realizing it was a hold-up, took what valuables he could carry, and as the train slowed down jumped from the side door and ran back to the passenger cars, which had been left two miles or so behind.

The outlaws broke open the express car door and found the messenger gone. There were ten sacks of Mexican silver dollars on the floor of the car, about a thousand dollars in each sack. The hold-ups placed giant powder on top of the safe and sacks of Mexican money above it, so the force of the giant powder exploding would be exerted against the top of the safe. Several attempts were made before they blew the safe open, and the explosions scattered Mexican dollars over the ground for some three hundred feet distance. The hold-ups got little from the safe, but gathering up what money and jewelry they could find, left on their horses headed south towards the Chiricahua mountains.

The Mexicans who lived along the railroad were busy for weeks raking the ground and gathering silver dollars.

As the hold-ups wore masks, it was not for some time fully established who they were. Deputy U.S. Marshall Breckenridge, who was soon on the scene, found a quirt and a pair of spurs at the point where the hold-ups had tied their horses. These were soon identified by some cowboys as belonging to Wheeler and George; thus their identity was uncovered.

On February 26, 1895 these men came out of their hiding place in the mountains and again held up the same express train at Steins Pass in New Mexico. They recognized the Engineer and fireman with a cheery greeting of "Well, here we are again." In the excitement they made a blunder and only cut off the mail car, leaving the express car attached to the train. When the train got to the place where their horses were they found their mistake. They did not molest the mail car but told the Engineer to go back to the train, and soon after he left them he heard an explosion. The men had evidently exploded their giant powder and given it up as a bad job. Getting on their horses they headed east intending to leave the country.

About three weeks later, Officers got a clue which led them to Durango, Colorado. From Durango the trail now led to Farmington, New Mexico on the San Juan river. They learned that Wheeler was at the ranch of a fugitive from Justice named Short, who had come from Texas. The Officers went to a ranch near Short's and learned Wheeler had taken a trail to Hidden Springs, a great resort for cattle thieves, and on the way to Cortez, Colorado, the county seat.

Next day the Officers followed his trail to Cortez, but missed him. Cortez is close to the Blue Mountains in Utah, which is a great resort for outlaws in hiding. The Officers now left for the town of Mancos, which they reached after dark; a liveryman of that place being questioned stated Wheeler was camped in a pasture about a quarter of a mile from town.

The Officers consulted with two deputy Sheriffs who lived there, and one of them rode through the pasture presumably hunting a stray horse, and saw Wheeler on top of a haystack where he had been sleeping. They passed the time of day, and Wheeler said he would be down town directly, and, as he had to get his horses up, he would bring the stray with him if he found it.

The deputy Marshall Breckenridge, who had constantly been on his trail—from a hotel window—saw Wheeler put a pack saddle on one of his horses, and his saddle on another, but he did not as he expected head towards town, but rode down into a gulch and disappeared from sight. It looked as though Wheeler had gotten a scare and was making his get-a-way. Breckenridge jumped his horse and followed him, and as he got near the gulch, Wheeler came up the bank in plain sight.

The Marshall called to him to throw up his hands. Wheeler replied he had not done anything, and would not do it, and started back for the gulch. Deputy Breckenridge fired at him as he disappeared from view. Almost immediately a shot was heard but no one knew what had happened. The deputy ran his horse past the mouth of the gulch. He saw Wheeler lying with his head almost in a fire he had built to cook his breakfast. He found he had placed his pistol in his mouth and shot himself through the head.

At the Coroner's inquest it appeared he'd told a cowboy friend the day before that the Officers were after him, that he did not want to do any more killing, but would kill himself before surrendering. Wheeler had told Short about the train robberies, and that he and George separated while on the Blue River; and that he had started for relatives who lived at Salida, Colorado, while George headed for Socorro or the Sacramento Mountains in New Mexico where he had friends and relatives. George, after he crossed the Blue River, must have ridden off into space, as he has never again been heard of.

The End

Broncho Bill, "Train Robber"

by
N. Howard Thorp

roncho Bill, "Alias William Walters" whose right name
was Walter Brown, was sentenced to the Territorial
Penitentiary at Santa Fe, New Mexico, May 23rd, 1899
from Socorro County, New Mexico for the crime of murder, to
serve life. Pardoned April 17th, 1917. Afterwards killed in fall
from windmill tower, on a ranch in the southern part of the State.

After Broncho Bill's release from the Penitentiary in 1917,
he went back to his old home in Brown County, Texas, but his
record had been so bad he did not stay long, as his relatives would
have nothing further to do with him; so after his return he went to
work on a ranch in the southern part of the State.

An old ex-outlaw now living near here, and who formerly
knew him well, recently told me that Broncho Bill brooded so over
what he considered an injustice by his relatives that he jumped off
the windmill to end it all; this is probably true.

Broncho Bill was born and raised in Brown County, Texas, which was named after his father who was Sheriff of the County for twelve years.

Walter Brown early in life got into a shooting scrape and mounting a good horse hurriedly left for New Mexico, where after being mixed up in various cattle stealing operations, he threw in with Tom and Sam Ketchum, and pulled off—what was well known as—the Steins Pass train hold-up, which netted some ten thousand dollars. This, at the time it was committed, was laid to three other men, who on circumstantial evidence were convicted and placed in the Santa Fe Penitentiary.

Just before Tom Ketchum was hung at Clayton, he made a confession implicating himself, his brother Sam, and Broncho Bill as the three who actually did the job. This confession eventually freed the three men who had been wrongly convicted. This was one of the few decent deeds which may be placed to Tom Ketchum's credit.

The next hold-up with which Broncho Bill was connected was that of an A.T. and S.F. train between Swanee and Grants, New Mexico, with Broncho Bill was Red Pitkin and Billy Johnson, son of old Abe Johnson. These men made camp and hobbled out their horses. They successfully held up the train, in the usual manner, getting from six to ten thousand dollars, about half of which was in gold coin; they then lay down and went to sleep. Sheriff Virgil, in some way becoming wise to the hold-up, formed a posse and went in pursuit, taking along three Indian trailers. The posse rode up at night close to the camp, and found the hold-ups asleep.

The Indians found the outlaws' horses, which they unhobbled and quietly drove off; then told Sheriff Vigil they would go—if he said so—and grab and tie the three sleeping men. The Sheriff, who had no previous experience with outlaws, replied, Wait until they wake up, and I will read the warrant for their arrest to them, and we will take them to jail. Unfortunately for the Sheriff's plan, when the outlaws awoke, they rose up shooting, killing the Sheriff and chasing the Indians and deputy away. As the outlaws were now without horses, they buried most of the money and made their way a-foot to the Block Bar ranch, where for three hundred dollars they bought three horses and saddles to make their getaway.

The three bandits were now on the dodge. With most of their money buried, and afraid to return and dig it up, they took to the mountains and many hide-out places known to bad men.

Finally George Scarboro, noted Peace Officer—who afterwards killed John Selman in El Paso Texas, and was himself killed by an outlaw in Arizona—took up the trail of the three hold-ups.

In the fight which followed when overtaken, Billy Johnson was shot off his horse and Red Pitkin and Broncho Bill were wounded and arrested and taken to the Socorro County Jail, where after their trial and conviction they were sentenced to the Penitentiary for life.

Some time after Broncho Bill's arrival in Santa Fe, owing to good behavior, he was made a Trustee, and a sort of flunky in the hospital.

Bob Ormsby, who was deputy State Treasurer and chief clerk at the Penitentiary at the time, relates the following concerning Broncho Bill. Broncho Bill, one of Black Jack's gang, was a tough egg, not only outside the Pen but in it. Bob Ormsby recalls as follows. "Broncho Bill met a tougher egg while here than himself, which nearly cost him his life." Ormsby continues. "Years ago a typical east side New York Bowery tough was an inmate of the Prison, and through good behavior he had become an outside trustee."

One day Ormsby gave him a package to take over to one of the guardhouses, the package being a tightly nailed box.

276

King, the Bowery tough, sensed that the package contained liquor; he opened it and found a full quart of bonded whiskey and drank a pint. A few minutes after, reports began coming into Ormsby that a man was running wild outside, and refused to go inside the walls for the regular daily count. Ormsby girded up his loins—so to speak—and went outside to investigate. He found King carrying two scuttles of coal up a ladder in the main tower. Ormsby called to King to come down, but instead of coming down he dropped both scuttles of coal on Ormsby's head. Assistance was called, and King was put inside the walls and lodged in the hospital to prevent his creating a disturbance among the other prisoners. Now the hospital was ruled over by Broncho Bill, who had but one good arm, for like most of the Black Jack gang, he was shot before he was captured, and one of his arms was rendered useless.

When King got warmed up and the liquor began to take good effect, he created such a disturbance as Broncho Bill could not allow in his hospital. The two men came to grips. The Broncho was decidedly at a disadvantage, as King was a burly customer in good health and pepped up with a pint of good liquor inside of him. Broncho Bill had no weapon, while King was armed with a pocketknife he had obtained somewhere. Spying a Morris chair, the Broncho wrenched a brass rod from its back and literally wrapped it around King's neck, but the Bowery tough only smiled, and came in for more. A few minutes later Ormsby got a telephone call. This is from Broncho Bill, the voice said, and you had better send up a Doctor, I'm pretty badly cut up. When the Doctor came, he found that Broncho Bill had eleven long gashes in his back, just as deep as King's knife blade was long. One of them had pierced his abdominal wall, and peritonitis set in. Any ordinary man would have died, but Broncho Bill pulled through. After he got well, Ormsby recalled, Broncho Bill always insisted that had the rod in the Morris chair been of heavier stuff, he would have won the decision.

'Tis a curious fact that most all the hold-ups have been crippled in one arm. Sam Ketchum died from a shot in one arm, blood poisoning having set in, Tom Ketchum "Black Jack" was shot in the arm and had to have it amputated, Broncho Bill lost an arm by having it almost shot off, and the outlaw who told me the first part of this story also has a crippled arm caused by a bullet.

The money from the Broncho, Johnson, and Pitkin train hold-up was very hurriedly buried, and I believe still remains where deposited. Many searching parties have looked in vain, but each year finds its new crop of prospectors.

The End

New Mexico Rustlers, Courtesy Palace of the Governors (MNM/DCA), #014264

Bob Lewis, "Peace Officer"

by
N. Howard Thorp

For more than forty years, Bob Lewis has—in one capacity or another—served in New Mexico as a Peace Officer. He now is Marshall of the town of Magdalena.

A man with a splendid personality, which has often pulled himself and others out of difficult positions.

Absolutely afraid of nothing that rides or walks, he has brought order out of many rough houses, and ended numerous fights with the principals, afterwards becoming his friends.

Coming from Texas as a boy, he found New Mexico to his liking, for to all young cowboys the wilder the country was, the greater its appeal.

At the time of Bob Lewis's arrival, the country was overrun with cow and horse thieves and other desperate characters, who for good and sufficient reasons had to leave the states to the east and seek oblivion in the wild—and then little known—mountains of New Mexico.

Knowing New Mexico thoroughly, Bob has been with many a posse ferreting out those in hiding and wanted by the law, and while lone-wolfing he has the reputation of always having brought in his man.

During the hard days in Socorro, Bob was either acting Sheriff or deputy, and a volume could be written concerning his duties as a member of the New Mexico mounted Police. I doubt if the State will ever see another body of peace officers as efficient. When the N.M.M.P. were in existence, there were but few roads and no highways, ranches and waterings were far apart and only connected by rough trails, and—excepting between the larger towns—no telephone connection. Radios were unknown, so consequently no wide-cast alarms and descriptions of those wanted could be broadcasted.

A bank would be held up, for instance; the robbers on good horses would make a dash for the mountains or brush country. The Sheriff with a quickly formed posse would take the trail of their saddle horses which, if the bandits did not split up, was fairly easy to follow; but when the bandits took to the roughs, the trailing was slow work, and the pursued would make two miles to the pursuer's one.

Bob Lewis tells of one time—while out lone-wolfing after an outlaw whom he had been following for five days solely by his horse's shod tracks—when if it had not been for the rabbit's foot he carried in his pocket warning him, he would have been killed. The man he was following was an escaped convict with several charges of murder against him, a man who could not take any chances of recapture.

Bob had been warned to be cautious, as the man would fight for his life, knowing if re-taken it would be a life sentence or worse. From where Bob Lewis first struck his trail the man—well mounted—followed no established trail but headed north and west, crossing high ridges, running from the Sangre de Cristo range of mountains. Water in springs and small creeks was plentiful, but never once did the outlaw go near a ranch. From the trail Bob was following—although he had been told the man was from another state—he evidently knew the country, for if he followed the direction in which he was headed he would eventually cross the state line and enter the rough country along the San Juan river in Utah.

The little grain Bob had started with for his horse had all been used, also his little snack of tortillas and bacon and coffee. On the fifth night a little after sundown he saw a campfire some distance off and to the south.

As it was getting too dark to longer follow the fugitive's trail, Bob took his bearings as to relative positions of where he quit the trail and the campfire he saw in the distance; he headed for the light. Apprehensive it might be a fire built by the convict, he proceeded with caution, but soon had his fears allayed by the smell of sheep, and presently came to a flock bedded down for the night; while close by was the camp of the herder and burro boy.

To his hail someone replied, and Bob riding up to the camp got a square meal of stewed mutton, chile, coffee, and frijoles. Bob said he has eaten in most all the fine hotels in the west, but that meal at the sheep camp he believed was the best. Watering and hobbling out his horse, he borrowed some sheepskins and together with his saddle blankets made a bed, and slept until sun up. As Bob well realized in sleeping near a campfire, he was taking a lot of chances, for from the fresh looks of the horse tracks he had been following, the fugitive could not have been far ahead, and had he seen the camp fire in passing could later have returned and killed those sitting around it. However, dead tired as he was after five days' continuous trailing, one will take a chance.

This herd of sheep was on the trail coming from the west

and headed for the Pecos river some hundred and fifty miles to the east to lamb. The herder told Bob that three days previously two men "Americanos" had come to their camp, had supper and stayed all night. Upon inquiry Bob learned they were tall, dark haired and riding two bay horses which seemed almost exactly alike. From the questions these men asked about ranches and watering to the west, they were evidently strangers to the country, though they told the sheepherder they were hunting lost horses. From this information Bob inferred they were the other two men who had broken from the Penitentiary at the same time as the fugitive he was following; they had been suspected of having gone east to their old stamping ground in Oklahoma. These two men from their description were undoubtedly the other men wanted, especially as it was reported that they had stolen a very fine bay buggy team and saddles belonging to the Chief of Police at Santa Fe. Undoubtedly these two men mounted on the bay horses had made an agreement to meet the third man Bob had been following, and were awaiting at some designated spot his coming.

After breakfast, and taking some tortillas and jerky in a sack, Bob returned to where he had quit the trail the night before. He realized that he now had three men to deal with, and must try to overtake the fugitive he had been following before he joined the two reported by the sheepherder to be ahead. Taking up the trail, he soon came to where the fugitive's horse had been picketed out and the man had slept, a small bed of coals underneath a bush indicating where he had cooked a meal.

Jogging slowly along with his eyes on the ground, he followed the fresh hoof prints of the outlaw's horse.

He had not gone over a couple of miles when he saw a horse with his reins hanging down standing crosswise in the trail.

This looked to Bob like an ambush—for it is an old trick of outlaws when followed to leave their horses in the trail inviting approach of anyone following—and with their gun walk back a few hundred feet, conceal themselves beside the trail, and kill any pursuer.

Fully alive to the possibilities, Bob left the trail and tied his horse in the heavy timber; then afoot made a wide circle, and creeping up behind the man covered him.

So intent was the outlaw in watching the back-trail, that Bob's call of hands up was the first intimation he had that anyone was near. Disarming him, Bob slipped the handcuffs on and told him to mount his horse and come on. Bob made a bee-line back to the sheepcamp and told the herder not to move camp until he returned. Lewis deputized the camp cook to look after the prisoner, whom he chained to a tree. Returning to where he had found the prisoner, he again took up the trail. As the general direction which the herder had given him as to where the two other men were camped was almost straight west, he lined up a mountain he saw in the distance and headed for it in a trot.

Along in the afternoon he came to a small creek, and getting down from his horse loosened the cinch so he could more comfortably drink. Laying down, Bob himself drank long and heartily; when raising his head, he thought he heard voices. Keeping perfectly still he listened intently and at last located positively the direction from which he had heard the voices. Tying his horse in a thicket, he cut into the grain sack he had been carrying and wrapped his feet so as to avoid making any noise while approaching their camp.

In less than a quarter of a mile, he ran on to two bay horses hobbled and sat down to wait, knowing that sooner or later their riders would be after them.

Just before sundown the escaped men, unarmed, appeared, each with a rope in his hand, evidently intending to lead their mounts to water.

Bob waited until stooped over, engaged in taking off their horses' hobbles, when he threw down on them. Necking their horses together, and with handcuffs on the men, he drove them before him to the sheep camp, where he added the first convict to his catch. On reaching the railroad Bob turned over his men, and was well rewarded for the capture of the three convicts, and paid a handsome reward for the return of the three stolen horses and saddles.

The End

Albuquerque, Marino Leyba (Outlaw)

As told to me by Mr. Skinner, of Old Town, Albuquerque, New Mexico

by
N. Howard Thorp

I n the summer of the year 1880, a man of military bearing, mounted on a handsome bay horse, who carried a regulation army saddle rode into Albuquerque, evidently coming from the west. The rider clothed in grey, with a large black sombrero, was a striking looking man. He spent the night at one of the leading hotels and the following morning left, heading towards the east.

That night he rode up to the house of a man well known in the Manzano Mountains, Mr. Carpenter of Tijeras. The man on horseback, after showing his letter of introduction, was greeted as Colonel Potter. Colonel Potter explained he was on his way to Santa Fe, and as the roads on the Rio Grande bottom—owing to recent high water—were impassable, he had been advised to take the eastern, or Mountain road.

In the morning, when Colonel Potter left, Carpenter advised him that there were only two men on his proposed route who could speak English. When Potter came to where the trail forked about twenty miles north he learned that the left hand trail went to San Antonito, near which settlement Mr. Skinner had a sawmill. The right hand trail led to the little settlement of La Madera, where a character named California Joe ran a saloon, and often put up and fed people, if belated or caught in storms. This later route, Carpenter had explained, was the more direct route to Galisteo and Santa Fe, the latter being Colonel Potter's objective. As his horse had cast a shoe and become foot-sore, Colonel Potter decided on the shorter route, but it was sundown when he rode up to California Joe's place.

Inside, standing at the bar, were a few loiterers, and as was the custom of the times, Colonel Potter invited every one to have a drink, in settlement for which he laid a twenty dollar gold piece on the bar. In those days, especially among a gathering of small ranchmen, one possessing twenty dollar gold pieces and also a gold watch and chain and two handsome rings, was classed as rich.

A short talk with California Joe, and arrangements were made for the accommodations of the Colonel and his horse, the proprietor also agreeing to send a guide with him to put him on the Galisteo and Santa Fe road.

Although Colonel Potter did not know it, the outlaw Marino Leyba was one of those in the barroom, whom Colonel Potter had invited to have a drink. It seems that after Colonel Potter had retired, California Joe called Marino into a back room, and said, "Well, Marino, it looks as if we have a fat chicken to pluck who has probably got lots of money, and it's up to you to do the plucking." The following morning, with a man named Miguel Barbero in the lead, and riding a burro, Colonel Potter left the Dead-fall of California Joe.

Presently the wood road they were following made a steep dip into a canyon and turned to the left, at which point a trail led to the right. When this point was reached, the man on the burro insisted on taking the right hand trail, as he said it would be a big saving in distance. Although Colonel Potter was against leaving the wood road, the man on the burro insisted it was best.

They had no sooner reached the bottom of the canyon, when a man on horse-back appeared some hundred feet ahead and opened fire on the Colonel. Jerking his pistol the Colonel returned the fire, his bullet entering the bandit's right shoulder and breaking it; this man afterwards proved to be Marino Leyba. The two men who accompanied him, Faustin and Escolastico, now opened fire on the Colonel, who fell from his horse dead.

The outlaws then stripped the horse of his saddle and bridle, the Colonel of his clothes, rings, watch, chain and money. They then built a big fire of brush, which almost completely consumed the body.

A small boy who was herding goats on a neighboring hillside—after the bandits had left—went to investigate. Looking closely the boy saw a hand sticking out of the dead embers, and on the charred finger was a smooth gold ring, which undoubtedly the robbers had overlooked. Inside the ring was some writing, which the little boy could not read.

After putting the goats in a corral, the boy saddled his pony and rode to Bernalillo to tell his patron, Don Jose Perea, at that time the richest and most influential man in the county.

After showing his patron the ring, and naming who he saw commit the crime, Don Jose took from the wall a crucifix, and making the boy kneel down, told him to swear he would tell no one until such time as his patron told him to. This boy's name was Vidal Mora.

On Christmas Eve 1881, six months after the above happenings, an army ambulance drawn by four mules stopped at Skinner's sawmill at San Antonito, a short distance from where the crime had been committed. As it was snowing hard, one of the two Officers in charge asked Mr. Skinner if he would furnish a room so that his party could get out of the storm. The party was composed of two Officers, four privates, and a negro cook. They were all armed, and had brought plenty of fodder and provisions. The Officers did not mention their business, though they stayed a month, every day prowling the hills, evidently in search of something.

The Soldiers were armed with old-fashioned guns, which had iron ramrods attached; these the Soldiers carried in their hands, at times prodding into the earth.

At the end of the month, the head Officer called Mr. Skinner into the house and showing him a picture of Colonel Potter asked if he had ever seen such a party. Mr. Skinner truthfully answered no; but stated that if the Officers would wait a day he would make inquiries. Mr. Skinner immediately got the neighbors together and questioned them, but they knew nothing. Then someone suggested sending for another neighbor, who was known to have a very retentive memory. When asked, he replied, on a certain evening, giving the date of the month, his dad had seen a man dressed in grey, wearing a black hat, and mounted on a bay horse upon which was an army saddle, stop at California Joe's place and upon being shown the photograph, identified it as the man he had seen. The following morning the ambulance and party of Soldiers left. Some days later, Perfecto Armijo, the Sheriff of Bernalillo County and his deputy arrested California Joe, Faustin, Escolastico, and Miguel Barbero the guide, who rode the burro, and who was a party to the killing, but Marino Leyba they could not find. These prisoners were taken for safe keeping to the jail in old Albuquerque, but a mob took them out shortly afterwards and decorated the cottonwood trees surrounding the old Plaza with their bodies. Learning that Marino Leyba had been seen far to the east in Canyon Blanco, Sheriff Perfecto Armijo and deputy left to try and make their arrest. Neither Sheriff Armijo nor his deputy knew Marino by sight, nor had Marino ever seen Sheriff Armijo.

Arriving at a small ranch in Canyon Blanco, they rode into the corral to water their horses, when suddenly three Tejanos "Texans" stepped out of the house with Winchesters in their hands and wanted to know who the blankety blank had given them permission to water their horses. One word brought on another, and in no way could Sheriff Armijo pacify the ranchmen. Just as the argument got to the shooting stage, a young fellow on a white horse dashed by the end of the house, jerked his horse to a halt, and with a six-shooter covered the nearest Texan and made him drop his gun, telling the others if they didn't put up their hands he would kill the one he had disarmed. Undoubtedly, if he had not acted as he did the Texans would have killed both Armijo and his deputy, as these men were on the dodge.

Inviting Armijo and his deputy to follow, Marino took them to his ranch where they spent the night. Before leaving, the Sheriff asked Marino his name; he promptly replied Marino Leyba. Sheriff Armijo then introduced himself and deputy, telling Marino he had a warrant for his arrest, but in view of his having saved their lives, he would not serve it, as if taken to Albuquerque he would undoubtedly be hung by a mob; therefore, if he would promise to surrender to the Sheriff of San Miguel County of Las Vegas, he would put him on parole, and trust him to do so. Marino left immediately, and when he arrived at San Geronimo, a few miles from Las Vegas, sent the Sheriff word he was waiting there to surrender. The Sheriff happened to be away, and his Chief deputy, who sometime before had had a quarrel with Marino, immediately got together a posse and galloped off to make the arrest. Marino saw them coming, and getting behind a big pine tree, shot the right stirrup off the deputy's saddle and kept up such a fusillade they were glad to retreat. Upon the Sheriff's return Marino surrendered. As all the witnesses to the late crime but the goat herder had been hanged by the mob in Albuquerque, Marino got off with a light sentence. Upon his release he went to work for Mr. Skinner at the sawmill at San Antonito; living with his family, he was leading an industrious life.

One day two men, Polito Montoya, and Carlos Jacoma, rode into San Antonito from Santa Fe, and meeting Marino stopped—apparently in a friendly way—to talk. Upon parting, Polito Montoya extended his hand, and while holding Marino's hand in his grip, Carlos Jacoma shot Marino through the head.

This was supposed to have been done over some division of loot from a robbery they had all been mixed up in at Puerta de Luna some years before, and also to gain an old reward offered for Marino dead or alive.

The End

As told to me by Mr. Skinner of Old Town Albuquerque, New Mexico.

Alameda

by
N. Howard Thorp

According to Vetancur, Alameda in the year 1680 was a flourishing Indian Pueblo, was eight leagues north of Isleta, had a population of three hundred, was the seat of the Mission called Santa Ana and was named for the poplar or cottonwood grove, which shaded the road for a distance of four leagues. At this time the Rio Grande flowed on the east side of the valley, leaving Alameda on the west side of the river, but some time after the Indian revolt the river changed its course and cut a new channel to the west of the Pueblo. Some years after its abandonment by the Indians on account of floods, the Spanish people—being induced by the fertile lands—settled on the site of and around the old Pueblo, whose rights extended as far south as the Ranchos de Albuquerque.

Some of the descendants of the families who obtained lands in the Grant and settlement of Alameda from 1710 to 1820, live now at the new Alameda, ten miles north of Albuquerque on fourth street. To be a little more definite regarding the location of the old Pueblo, will say it was about a mile west of the present town and church of Alameda, or La Natividad. The old Church which was washed away in the big flood of some thirty-five years ago, and whose foundations may still be seen, was a little north and east of the bridge which crosses the Rio Grande on one's way to Corrales. Many of the ruins of houses which surrounded the Church may still be seen, though the bottomlands where they stood have grown up into bosque, some of the trees being a foot and some of the trees being a foot and half in thickness. The names of a few of the Spanish families who took possession of the lands and built houses and homes I will mention.

Juan Gurule and family

Jose Benito Griego and family

Luis Baca and family

Tomas Baca and family

Juan Pacheco and family

Jose Miguel Lucero and family

Jose Domingo Gurule.

Then there was a Spaniard named Antonio Lerma, who owned the general store and Geronimo Pacheco Hermano mayor of the Penitentes. After the last flood, these families moved further east to higher ground and two Penitente Moradas—still in use—are all that remains to mark the site of the former settlement. Many of the Ornaments of gold, which decorated the Altar of this old Pueblo Church, are said to have been fabricated from the metal found in the old Montezuma mine some twenty miles to the north and east. What became of these Church ornaments, there seems to be no record.

Regarding the extent of the flood which drove the last settlers out, the waters must have covered the entire bottom. There is an enormous old cottonwood tree standing by an acequia, which passed through the Pueblo, that some of the old settlers say, after the flood passed, there was found on a limb of this tree—some ten feet from the ground—the body of a sheep which the water had carried there.

An event happened while this Colony was living at Alameda Viejo, which seems well worth relating, time about fifty-five years ago.

As I have above stated, a Spaniard by the name of Antonio Lerma ran the general store at that point, in a flat roofed adobe house typical of that period. Returning with his family from Albuquerque, Lerma found the front door of his store building open; as he struck a match to see what was the matter, a shot rang out and he fell dead in the doorway; the sound of a galloping horse in the darkness indicated evidently the departure of the killer. His cash drawer had been rifled as it afterwards proved and many other things of value were missing.

This door had no lock, only a catch on it, a heavy wooden bar inside holding it: this bar had been removed. As the windows all had iron bars on them and the store had but one door opening outside, how had the thief entered? The only solution was, he had come down the chimney. The chimneys in these old houses were fogons de campana, and very large. When daylight came, a search disclosed boot marks on the roof, but of only one man, and by the side of the chimney lay a man's hat with a silver cord around it, evidently knocked off as the thief entered the chimney. Numerous robberies were happening about this time, but the thief could not be located. Antonio Lerma's widow hung the hat in the store, and hoped the owner would come and claim it. Although several people said they had seen Pantaleon Mera wearing a similar one, but as at that time Pantaleon was supposed to be one of the gente fina "fine people," the idea that he could have robbed the store was ridiculed.

Some years before this robbery when there were many freighting wagons going westward towards the Pacific coast, many of the men who started with them never were heard from again. Relatives of those missing in many instances traced the missing men to a small town known as Algodones in Sandoval County, a few miles north of Bernalillo. Two strangers appeared in Bernalillo, rumor stated they were Detectives, and so they proved to be.

It soon became known that Don Pantaleon Mera was the head of a gang of outlaws who made a business of enticing strangers into a house at Algodones, and after killing and robbing them, buried their bodies in a pit underneath the building. Suddenly Pantaleon disappeared.

A year or so passed; Mrs. Mera received word her husband had reached California. He vowed he had reformed, and was now a respected Citizen, but was homesick for home and wife and begged to be forgiven and allowed to return home. This state of affairs existed for some years, but as time passes people forget, hearts relent, and soften, and finally after many vows and promises, mingled with the tears and prayers of his family, the good people of Bernalillo relented and Pantaleon Mera came home.

One day a stranger, superbly mounted, rode into Bernalillo. He had a full-rigged California saddle, was dressed in tight Mexican clothes and at his belt wore a pair of Colt's forty-five pistols. He inquired where he could get a guide to take him to a small town in the mountains some fifty miles east of Bernalillo. A young man named Marino Leyba was recommended as one who knew the country, and after arrangements were made, the next morning they started out. Several months elapsed and various strangers came to town, made inquiries about sundry matters and left. Later another man appeared and showing his credentials that he was a U.S. secret service man, told the Sheriff that a government official on special business in that section had disappeared some months previously. He had been traced to Bernalillo, where his trail seemed to stop. The Sheriff asked for a description of the missing man, and the Detective handed him a photograph which he at once recognized as the man who had engaged Marino as a guide. Now the law started to hunt Marino, but the Mexican, it was learned, had not been seen in Bernalillo for many weeks.

In a pawnshop in Albuquerque, the Detective found a gold watch and chain that belonged to the man who had disappeared. Taking Marino's trail, a posse found that he had led the Detective into an ambush where he was murdered. After taking his valuables, the killers had burned him; everything was reduced to ashes except a few Military buttons that were on his vest; these and other clues resulted in tracing the crime to an organized gang, and to everyone's astonishment Pantaleon Mera was the leader.

The discovery of this last crime created much excitement in Bernalillo. Pantaleon and one of his men—in size almost a Dwarf—had been thrown into the Calaboose, back of the Sheriff's and Alcalde's office. The word was passed around to assemble that night at a warehouse near the railroad depot. After a discussion, those assembled went to the jail. In front of the Alcalde's house was a big cottonwood tree with branches some twenty feet above the ground. A dry goods box was placed on each side of the tree, and two lariats were suspended from the limbs and placed around the two men's necks. The Dwarf pleaded for his life; "not Pantaleon": he sneered at the other's pleadings and like an Indian sang a death song, while boasting that he had killed in his life over two hundred Americans and was proud of the fact. The boxes were kicked away and his song silenced forever. Of the seven men in Pantaleon's band, including himself, four of them were captured by Don Perfecto Armijo, Sheriff of Bernalillo county and stationed at Albuquerque. These men were locked up there and later taken out of the jail and given the same punishment as the Dwarf and Pantaleon had received.

The seventh man was the Marino Leyba I have before referred to. He kept on the dodge and avoided all traps laid for him. Although many people claim at different times to have seen and even talked to him, I personally—if he is not dead from old age—believe him to be still at large.

Rosario O. Hinjos

In the year 1893 I don't recollect the exact date-
Tomas Martinez, a brother of Pablo Martinez, a merchant of Abiquiu,
lived on his ranch, not very far from this town, he was herding his
cattle and sheep, with him was his big yellow dog; about dusk one
evening a man came to ask for a bite to eat; Tomas killed a lamb,
roasted part of it, made some coffee, and gave him of the best he
had there. On the following day, a man living on a ranch, a few miles
distant saw a large yellow dog coming towards him, panting and
tired, but, on seeing the man, he began to bark and howl, and taking
hold of his trousers, would pull at them, then run a little distance
towards the same direction from whence he came and seeing the man
did not follow he would come back, and go through the same performance,
until the man recognized the dog and realized that the dog was trying
the best way he could, to tell him something; so he followed the
dog, who kept running ahead and looking back to see if the man was
following until they arrived at Tomas' ranch, then the dog led him
to a pile of embers and ashes; and there sticking out from the coals
and ashes was a human foot, and the charred remains of what he
thought was Tomas; he went to his ranch saddled his horse, as Tomas'
horse had been taken and came into town to notify his relatives and
friends, relatives and friends went there and recognized the boat
and sack as belonging to Tomas; after two men Jesus Villalpando and
Donaciano Chavez, cattle thieves, on whom the deceased had come upon,
as they were killing and roasting one of his steers and on this
ashes they found the remains of Tomas; and the real murderers were
aprehended, tried, convicted and hung, on a little hill on the north
side of town, and the man whom he had fed and whom all suspected as
the culprit, although they never knew who he was, was cleared.

Facsimile: "In the year 1893," Rosario O. Hinjos, no date, NMFWP, WPA #233b, NMSRCA

Original Narrative on San Juan County

by
Mrs. Helen Simpson

The activities of Tom Nance in and around Durango were such that the Eskridge gang found that they could not carry on their nefarious work with impunity. They therefore planned to put Nance out of the way. He rode frequently into town and visited saloons and was about generally. So they made up a bunch of their most daring gunmen and one evening followed him out of town and up Wildcat Canyon on his road south. He was too wary for them, expected just such a thing and kept watch on all their movements. He discovered their pursuit and let them get near enough to show their hand. He knew the importance of a good horse and a long-range rifle and he had both better than his enemies. When they got near in range they opened fire; he answered and having a longer range and higher powered rifle and long experience of that kind of warfare on the Texas plains, he made it too hot for them, so they had either to retreat or take cover. This was continued all up the canyon to the Ft. Lewis Mesa, where he had the advantage of cover and compelled them to retreat.

While the Eskridges were making havoc among the cattle near Durango, Port Stockton was being accused of stealing and butchering cattle down in New Mexico. It was said that he made his living that way. He did no work on the ranch and rode around his neighborhood and at times drove away, presumably to Durango, to replenish his stock of whiskey which he had to have daily. It was also said of him that he was in collusion with the cattle thieves in Durango, and helped them in every way he could. However that may be, he had made such a reputation that people generally believed all the stories that were told. When he heard them and found any clue to the makers he threatened to kill them on sight. The cattlemen of this New Mexico section goaded to action by their losses and seeing no help for it called a meeting to be held at Farmington, to take united action against these unlawful proceedings. It was largely attended by the owners of the range cattle in the lower San Juan who were the ones most nearly affected by these depredations. The situation was gone into thoroughly.

It was plain to all that in the present condition of law and order in this country no efficient help could be had from courts or court officers and it came to the conclusion that force must be met with force, and violence with violence. No special form of attack or defense was agreed upon at this meeting and it adjourned without any future plans, except that there must be armed resistance to curb this lawless outbreak. The case of Port Stockton was brought up, but nothing determined. It was said that he was "Hellbent on dying with his boots on" and confidently predicted that he would meet with that fate sooner or later.

There were several of these men who lived on the upper

Animas, and on their way home had to cross the river near the Port Stockton cabin, which they must pass. It was a cold windy day: a sand storm was blowing and there was bloom everywhere, and one's nerves were irritable with these unwholesome conditions. When this group of men came to the Stockton cabin he came to the door and called to Alf Graves, who represented the Cox interest, and whom he had threatened because of some story about his stealing cattle that he said Graves had told. He called Graves and said he wished to talk with him, and for him to come up to the cabin. Tom Nance, who was one of the party, said, "Don't go Alf, he is ready to kill you." Graves did not seem to think so. He turned his horse and rode up to the cabin door, where Port stood. Stockton opened up with all kinds of offensive language and pulled his gun. Graves had on an overcoat, tightly buttoned to his throat, and his gun was under this, he could not get it out quick enough, and it seemed death for him right there. Nance, when he saw Graves would go, realizing what would happen, dismounted, laid his Winchester across his saddle and drew his sight on Stockton, and just as Stockton pulled his gun to shoot, Nance fired and Stockton fell, his shot going wild.

Mrs. Stockton then came out armed with a Winchester and began to shoot into the group of men around Nance. One of these with his Winchester, seeing that she was about to kill some of them, tried to a shoot the gun out of her hand. He succeeded, but also splintered the gunstock fragments which wounded her in the arm, though not seriously. The story of this affray spread all over the country, east and west, and was exaggerated to suit everybody. Ike Stockton, the brother of Port, who was then living at Durango and accused of being one of the Eskridge gang, came out in the Durango newspaper and denounced all of the lower country and swore to avenge his brother's murder, as he called it. He at once took part with the Eskridge gang and began a series of raids on the

New Mexico people that was kept up all of the spring of 1881.

The New Mexico cattlemen at once organized a body of armed men and prepared to defend their stock. These ranchmen who had no stock and had taken no part in these cattle wars were also called on to defend themselves, as reports and rumors were rife all over the country that the Stockton-Eskridge gang were waging war on women and children, in revenge for the injury to Mrs. Stockton. Just at this period there was a Reign of Terror all over the lower San Juan Country. The men only ventured out in groups armed with Winchesters and pistols and ready to repel these raiders. It was so wide a battlefield that with their limited numbers they could not cover but a small part of the country invaded. There were two places on the Animas river that had been built for refuge for women and children when an Indian scare had come several years before and these were used now at night, especially when most of the men were absent. One of these was on the Riley Williams ranch. This was a large cellar built with heavy cottonwood logs and covered with dirt so as to make it fireproof and with portholes to fire through at the enemy. It was near a cabin, and access was had to this underground fort through a hatch door in this cabin and by an underground passage. Here women and children found refuge when the men were out on the warpath, or when it was thought that a raid would be made. All ranch work and business was at an end and nothing was talked about or thought of except the Stockton War.

Some of the older and wiser as well as more peace loving men went to the commander of the United States soldiers at Ft. Lewis and asked him for protection, but he told them that though he sympathized with their plight he could not move in the matter without orders from headquarters at Washington. That, in case of an Indian outbreak, he could interfere; in the case of the white settlers, they were supposed to have their local government and officers to cope with this situation, and the federal government could not interfere except under a state of civil war, and then only when all other means had failed. So there was no help there and the local government just then could not function by reason of their distance from headquarters. So these men were compelled to fight their battle alone and with their backs to the wall. It was a trying time and men were perplexed to know what was best to do to save their lives and property and to protect their women and children. . . .

Narrative by Mr. Kello, July 20, 1936.

An Incident of Farmington, In the Fall of 1895:

Personal interview with Mr. W. A. Hunter, retired merchant of Farmington, New Mexico

Recorded by Mrs. R. T. F. Simpson

In 1895, "Uncle Alex" and "Judge" Bowman were the owners of Bowman Brothers Drug Store, which was held up one day. I was most unexpectedly included in the affair. I had left the Post Office, which was in a two-story brick building in the block where the Farmington Drug now is, and was crossing the street, diagonally, when "Uncle" called to me and I went back to talk to him. We stood at the window west of the entrance to the drug store, each one of us leaning against one of the shutters of the window. A tall man wearing a big hat with a tall peaked crown stopped and asked us where he could get some peaches. We directed him to a certain ranch. He thanked us and went on into the drug store, but soon came out and went around the building, and then circled it the other way, this time facing us as he rounded the corner with a six-shooter in his hand pointed directly at us and held on a level with his eye. He marched us into the building and down to the center of the store, till we came to the "Judge" and "Old Man Jarvis" sitting not far from the safe, and he ordered them to join us. Judge was inclined to argue a bit, and old man Jarvis just laughed. (He was called "Laughing Jarvis") and did not heed what he was told, so the hold up man in the peaked hat stepped up and gave him a good swift kick in the shins which brought them both to their feet with their hands in the air like the rest of us.

We were marched to the right-hand corner of the room, and as we passed the safe and the partition across that part of the store, we realized that there was another man standing there with his gun leveled on us. He was shorter than the first one. After we were all herded into the corner, Judge Bowman was ordered to walk back to the safe and to open it. Again, he was inclined to parley about it though his brother urged him, in a deep voice, "Open it, open it."

Really, he could do nothing else, so back he marched, still under the guns, and as he was opening it, a man named Friend entered the store and walked up to the "Water Pail" and took a drink of ice-water. Whereupon, the holdup ordered him to join the judge in his march back to the corner, where we all stood with elevated hands while the tall one rifled the safe, the short one still covering us with his gun.

During the rifling of the safe, a man named Gambol, the village blacksmith, by the way, and slower than time, stood outside looking in through the screen-door, his nose flattened against the screen as he peered in trying to decide what was going on inside. He said afterwards he thought at first it might be a secret society holding a meeting back there, then realizing it was a holdup, he ran for help to Pierce's store across the street. It was closed, so he ran into the grocery of Cooper and Williams, but they had no firearms in the place, so he ran to the next place which was the "White House Saloon" owned and operated by Ed Hill, which was where he should have gone in the first place where he was sure of finding help. The alarm was given to the men assembled there, but by this time the bandits were on their horses, which were tethered nearby, and far away.

As the men ran out of the saloon, excitedly, they saw across the street a group of men squatting in cowboy fashion, swapping stories. They shouted to them asking if they had seen a couple of horsemen pass, and one man named Boon Black said yes he had and they had gone toward the west end of town. So they all mounted and rode off in the direction indicated, but returned without finding the trail of the holdups, a disappointed lot.

Ed Hill insisted on keeping up the search and, with a few other men, went to the old Blake ranch south of town which was managed by Dillon and Sizer, where lived a tall and a short man who were working on the ranch. Mr. Dillon and Mr. Sizer both said both the tall and the short man had been at home all the evening, and had just gone to bed. Hill, regardless, routed them both out, holding a gun over them, took them to town for identification by the men who were in the holdup, but all denied that they were.

No one had been hurt in the holdup and the bandits got away with everything in the safe which included funds of the Bowman Brothers, $300.00 belonging to Ed Hill, money and papers belonging to the Post Office, and some diamonds owned by a man named Jim Howe from Louisville, Kentucky, valued at about $1,500.00 and some valuable papers which were not negotiable, belonging to Jarvis and others. . . .

The short man inside the drug store who greeted us with a leveled six-shooter was a man named Frank Mayer, from Durango, who had been a guest at my house in Farmington, along with Arthur Cornforth, who later became Lt. Governor of Colorado. The tall man I saw and recognized in Mancos a few days later, and the man named Brown was also an accomplice who was holding the attention of the group of men squatting in a circle, by telling tall stories while the holdup was in progress and by misdirecting the men who tried to trail the holdups.

Though the Bowman Brothers were reliably informed as to the identity of the men who robbed them, they steadfastly refused to do anything about it.

Why, no one ever knew. Possibly because no one was hurt, nor was the cash drawer robbed, nor the pockets of the men standing in the corner, some of which held considerable cash.

But strangest of all, these men were considerate enough to return, through the mails, all the nonnegotiable papers taken by them. Sometime later, these papers were mailed to Farmington from San Angelo, Texas.

Pioneer Story: Interview with Ella May Chavez

by
Janet Smith

A gentleman from Buffalo was reading a newspaper on the portal of old La Fonda in Santa Fe. It was with especial interest that he read his morning paper for the news of the assassination of McKinley was headlined on the front page. Several other guests of the hotel sat in the rocking chairs, reading and talking. At one end of the portal two little girls in high-necked plaid dresses were playing with jacks and a ball. Groups of people straggled by the hotel on the way to church at the end of San Francisco street. As the stagecoach pulled out for Taos, the gentleman from Buffalo turned a page of his paper, and continued to read with the paper held directly in front of his face so that he could not see the street.

A young man walked briskly but quietly up the walk to the portal, his hand in his pocket. Suddenly a bullet sped through the newspaper into the heart of the man from Buffalo.

The young man who fired the shot was Jean Lamy, nephew of the famous archbishop. He explained quietly and succinctly that he had not liked the manner in which the man from Buffalo looked at his wife. Guests of the hotel remembered that the evening before a young Spanish woman had played old songs on the piano in the hotel parlor. A stranger from the East, from Buffalo, had stood beside her, turning the pages of her music. Young Lamy had resented the expression in the stranger's eyes.

Of course the shooting caused a furor in Santa Fe. Some even went so far as to ask Lamy why he had not given the man a fair warning. Lamy replied that he *had* warned him to stay away from his wife. Nothing was ever done about the affair. No jury could be found to sit in trial of the archbishop's nephew.

This story was told to Mrs. Chavez by her mother who first arrived in Santa Fe on the day of the murder. Although born in New York, Mrs. Chavez is an old resident of New Mexico. She spent much of her life in Santa Fe where her father, William Berger, was a well-known lawyer.

I asked Mrs. Chavez if she could tell me stories of Archbishop Lamy. She replied that she could tell me plenty of stories, "not at all to his credit." She thought awhile and decided to save her stories, as some of the Archbishop's relatives are still living and "one doesn't like to hurt people."

Even as late as 1889 little resentments were apt to be settled with a gun in New Mexico. In that year the legislature was debating whether or not to have public schools in Santa Fe. Up to that time the only schools in the territory had been parochial. Again and again the bill for schools to be supported from public funds had been presented to the legislature and defeated. The Catholic priests especially were against it, and their influence was strong. At this session of the legislature, however, the contest was close. The deciding vote, cast by one Archuleta, passed the bill in favor of public schools. The next morning Archuleta was found shot. No one ever knew who shot him. No one ever tried very hard to find out. . . .

Interview with Ella May Chavez.

DISTRICT FOUR:
WHEN VILLA
RAIDED THE TOWN
OF COLUMBUS

"Every time there was a lull in the shooting they could hear a Mexican somewhere nearby playing a violin."

(From "When Villa Raided the Town of Columbus"
by Betty Reich)

Old Days in the Territory of New Mexico

Desperado Milton Yarberry, the Kinney Gang, Major Fountain

by
N. Howard Thorp

During the year of 1880 the Territory of New Mexico was overrun with desperados of all kinds.

Stage, and later train-robbers, hold-ups, cattle, horse and sheep thieves.

The situation became so acute that prospectors in the hills, travelers, and isolated ranchmen were constantly in danger of attack.

If ranchmen sided with the outlaw element, they were classed with them, even if only passively so. If they showed antagonism for the tough element, their stock would be stolen and the lives of themselves and family be constantly in danger.

As law in the state laying to the east became more efficient, the toughs and gunmen were being constantly shoved west, and New Mexico and Arizona Territories became the dumping grounds.

People of today living under the peaceful conditions which now exist cannot imagine the changes which the past fifty or sixty years have brought.

In the early eighties, many troops of U. S. Cavalry were in the field, keeping the Indians constantly on the move, but these, except in a few cases, were not hunting outlaws.

Many of the acts of outrage committed in the eighties, which were laid at the doors of the Indians, were actually perpetrated by outlaws, the acts usually done in such a way as to give color to the belief of an Indian outrage. Those outlaws were of several nationalities. Some came from no man's land, and Indian Territory now Oklahoma. Louisiana furnished its tough Negroes, and half breeds, while Texas, Old Mexico, and Kansas, each added its quota.

Such were the conditions in the early eighties, so tough that local Constables, Sheriffs, their deputies, and deputy U.S. Marshals were helpless; these officers knew the outlaws and where to find them, but as they outnumbered the Officers some ten to one, was the principal reason for creation of the State Militia. The Militia did police and other duties, as the following orders from the Adjutant General's office will show.

"Santa Fe, New Mexico. January 1st, 1880. To his Excellency Lionel A. Sheldon, Governor and Commander-In-Chief of the New Mexico Militia. At present we have thirteen Companies of Militia which are armed and drilled, as Cavalry. These are needed for the pursuit of Indians, and bands of outlaws. In 1882, two years before, short scouts were made against Indians and outlaws under Captains Blain, Marmon, Fountain, and Captain Younge. Signed Colonel Fountain."

On February 9th, 1883, Colonel Max Frost of the second

regiment was ordered to take the Santa Fe Company of Militia as a guard to escort the noted desperado Milton Yarberry to Albuquerque, where he was executed for murder.

On the 6th of February, 1883, the following petition endorsed by Colonel Rynerson of Las Cruces, New Mexico, was received by Honorable Lionel A. Sheldon, Governor of the Territory of New Mexico.

This petition signed by some sixty-five residents of precinct No. sixteen Dona Ana County, "known as Colorado" request, "that as for some time large bodies of lawless men have been raiding on our livestock, and owing to their numbers we feel that the ordinary Judicial Power is insufficient to cope with the evil, we Citizens being in dread of our lives should we offer assistance to our neighbors to recover their stock.

"In view of these facts, we petition your Excellency to commission a number of men under competent authority, and for a period of about ninety days to follow such thieves, and protect us and our properties while in pursuit of our legitimate business."

This petition on February 6th, 1883 was referred to Major A. J. Fountain with instructions to investigate same, and act in his discretion as to the use of the Militia for the protection of the people.

Major Fountain and his command acted at once, and Doroteo Sais, the partner of John Kinney, one of the worst men in the Territory, was captured and killed while trying to escape. The "Kinney Gang" was mostly captured, and entirely broken up. Kinney and several others, being sent to the Penitentiary for long terms of imprisonments, the report of same is as follows. Note: This is the same Colonel Fountain who, with his young son, disappeared some forty years ago while driving his buckboard and team between La Luz and Las Cruces. It was commonly supposed they were murdered. Their buckboard and team were found near the point on the White Sands, but to the present time, their bodies have not been recovered.

Colonel Fountain states that his objective point for this scout was the vicinity of Kingston in the Black Range of New Mexico where Colonel Fountain had information that some fifteen notorious rustlers were gathered. He knew from this information furnished that they would resist arrest. He held warrants for most of them, including the following: P. Johnson alias "Toppy Johnson" and Tom Cooper alias "Tom Kelly" who had a large number of indictments pending against him in Lincoln County; John Watts, Tom Grandy, Charles Thomas, James Colville, "Supposed to be a titled Englishman," Hank Brophy, William Leland alias "Butch," Nat Irwin "Tex," and a great many others. Colonel Fountain and his men arrived at Nut Station and were met by Cartwright and Forsythe of the Sierra Mining Co, also a deputy Sheriff named Gilson, and two guides sent from Hillsboro and Kingston. Upon the information furnished, these outlaws would resist the "Greaser Militia" as they termed them.

Colonel Fountain had been specially cautioned to look out for Tom Kelly, alias "Cooper," John Watts, Hank Brophy, "Tex," Butch and Charles Thomas. The residents of the town of Kingston and Hillsboro agreed that the men above mentioned were the real leaders of the outlaws. Before Colonel Fountain left Nut Station he received word that John Watts, Butch, Tex and two others were in Lake Valley. The colonel arrived early in the morning and arrested Butch without any trouble. John Watts was seen to mount his horse and flee, but he ran into Captain Van Patten's men who were following Colonel Fountain's troop. Watts was ordered to halt, and when he drew his Winchester, a dozen carbines were leveled, and he surrendered. Colonel Fountain told them he had warrants for their arrests for cattle stealing and if they tried to get away they would be shot, but if they went along quietly they would be delivered in safety to the Sheriff of Dona Ana County. Tex was in town when Colonel Fountain arrived, but succeeded in making his escape, and the Colonel was afraid that Tex would carry the news of his approach to Kingston and frighten the men he was after, so he decided to hurry on. When he left Lake Valley, he mounted the two prisoners on one horse, and presently all arrived at the cienega known as Daileys, formerly McEvers ranch.

There, everybody got down and started to get breakfast, the two prisoners dismounting with the others. Watts, one of the prisoners, wanted a drink of whiskey, saying he could get one at a shack nearby, but was told he could not leave the camp. It was still dark, and having finished breakfast, the men began saddling their horses, and someone asked, "Where are the prisoners?" Almost instantly a shot was fired, the men grabbed their arms and ran in that direction. The man who fired the shot shouted, "There they go up that road." A volley was fired in that direction, probably thirty shots; then following swiftly up the road, where in a distance of some two hundred yards lay the bodies of Watts and Butch, both dead.

Colonel Fountain now moved on to Irwin's ranch. Margarita Sierra, who was along, identified this as the place where cattle stolen from Dona Ana had been sold.

The ranch was now deserted, but there were fresh horse tracks in the vicinity. Taking a shortcut, Colonel Fountain and his men pushed on to Kingston. They met a man on the trail who informed the troop that the rustlers were at Johnson's butcher pen about a mile from Kingston in the mountains.

A shortcut taken by the guide took the command through some very rough country, and arriving at Johnson's no one was found at home; the only living thing was a very much worn out horse; the rustlers had fled to the mountains.

Colonel Fountain now headed for Kingston, where he

received a message from Mr. Brownson, Supt. of the Sierra Mining Company at Lake Valley, informing him that trouble might be expected from the friends and sympathizers of Watts and Butch at that place, and wanted men for protection of life and property.

Colonel Fountain sent a small squad under Captain Salazar, and told him to report to Supt. Brownson. When they arrived in Lake Valley they were directed to guard three prisoners who had been captured by Officers of the Mining Company.

One of these was a man named Shannon, who had tried to incite a mob to attack the soldiers; he was marching up and down the street armed, and calling upon everyone to come and avenge the deaths of Watts and Butch. He was arrested, but repeatedly announced his intention of escape, but was often warned by his fellow prisoners and by his friends not to make the attempt. He foolishly persisted, however, and broke and ran from the guards, who fired upon him when he was about a hundred yards away. He was instantly killed.

La Ley de Fuego.

The End

Black Jack Musgraves

by
N. Howard Thorp

In the fall of 1885, there rode up to a ranch called the Bar 02, on the San Francisco river in western Socorro County, New Mexico, three tough looking hombres, fully armed, and riding exceptionally fine horses.

Dismounting at the ranch-house, they mentioned their names and said they were in pursuit of a bunch of stolen horses.

The men who were supposed to have stolen the horses were the two Musgraves brothers, one of whom had adopted the title of Black Jack. The third man of the party being followed was thought to be a man named McGonigal, but of this they were not sure.

The Musgraves were supposed to have some Indian blood in them and worked through the southern part of New Mexico and along the lines of Texas and Arizona, and when hard pressed by the authorities took refuge in Old Mexico.

The horses the posse was after had been stolen in Lincoln

County, New Mexico, and were the best horses that some of the big ranches owned.

The posse, started out by these ranchmen, "one of which was a Sheriff," were told to follow the outlaws' trail and not return without the horses. As to the disposal of the thieves—should they overtake them—that was up to the trailers, and regarding them no questions would be asked. Mounted on the best horses obtainable, the handling of the thieves when caught was entirely up to them.

The posse said they and been trailing the horses for over a week, and from the abandoned campfires found and other indications, did not think they were over a day behind them.

They stated as they were not familiar with the country they wished a guide, as between the Frisco river and Clifton, Arizona, "where they thought the thieves were headed for," was, they understood, a very rough and broken country, and they did not want to lose any time by taking wrong trails.

There is a question among old timers as to who the guide who went with them was. Some say it was a Bar 02 hand, others, a man from the W.S. outfit. As the W.S. outfit bought out the ranches and cattle of the Bar 02, both or either of the stories may be right. Anyway, early the next morning after their arrival, the party of three with their guide left the Frisco river over the old Indian trail, and late the same evening rode into Clifton, Arizona. They hunted up the town Marshal, who said he was well acquainted with the Black Jack gang, and that Black Jack had a Sweetie living in Clifton and, if he was in the neighborhood, would undoubtedly pay her a visit. He was sure Black Jack had not been in town for several weeks, but if the posse would leave someone to identify the stolen horses he would arrest Black Jack should he turn up.

The Marshal advised that the rest of the posse go up Blue River, and at the McKeen ranch—near where the main trail going west crosses the river—they might learn something of the men they were after. They accordingly started and rode up the river until night overtook them and they had to make camp. From what the Marshal told them, it was almost certain that if the thieves did not intend to come to Clifton, they would cross the Blue river above the McKeen ranch.

The posse got to the McKeen ranch early the following morning; found McKeen was not at home; but Bob Bell, who was holding down the ranch, gave them breakfast. Bell told them three men had crossed the creek the day before, following the trail to the Navajo reservation. He happened to see them watering their horses, but was some distance away; and from where he sat his horse the men looked like Indians. As the horses had started up the brushy trail, he could not make out any of their brands. For the reason that he thought they were Indians was why McKeen had gone to Alma on the San Francisco river, so as to warn the ranchmen to look after their stock.

We told him we had heard that Black Jack had a holdout near the Zuni reservation on Rausensocker Creek. Bob told us there was at one time a settlement of Mormons there until the Indians ran them away.

The posse now took a trail some fifteen miles west of Blue River, over some of the roughest country laying out of doors.

The posse later found they had taken the right direction but the wrong trail, as over the right one, as it afterwards proved, Black Jack and his partner were making their way to Clifton. After a day spent in righting their way over the rough country, the posse was glad to eventually find some smooth country, and about sundown arrived at a bluff and a trail which descended into a canyon. Down in its depths they could see a grove of cottonwoods, so decided they had reached Rausensocker's ranch.

They tied their horses in the brush, away from the trail, and spreading out sneaked up towards the house, which appeared to be an old cabin some two hundred feet from the trail with a stout corral adjoining, but no stock within, however. They could see horses grazing along the creek.

The posse waited, crouching in the brush, to see if there was anyone in the house, when at the end of a half hour a man appeared from within, and started picking up some stove wood, then turning, went back into the house. All waited impatiently another half hour or so and at last decided that the man they had seen was the sole occupant of the house. It was decided that it was best to bring the horses near the house. The Sheriff and his deputy now left a man in charge of them, with instructions that if the man who was within the house made a break to get away while they were approaching the same, the outside guard was to shoot him down.

The Sheriff and his deputy now disappeared into the brush and were not again visible for a half hour or so. Then one of them showed up above the house. Evidently taking no chances, he was keeping a big tree between himself and the door of the house.

In the meantime, the other deputy had crept up to the very door of the house, and the man within, "now evidently starting to go after wood," opened the door and found himself looking down the barrel of the deputy's gun, seemingly curious to see what was in it. Throwing up his hands he was backed into the room by the man holding the gun.

The other deputy, upon seeing what had happened, ran to the door, and the man left with the horses brought up to the house.

The horses which had been stolen were now unhobbled and put into the corral. When questioned, the captured man said Black Jack and his partner had gone to Clifton. The deputy said he was sorry he had missed them, but the prisoner grinned and said, yes, it was too bad.

The Sheriff and his deputy took turns guarding the prisoner and dispatched the third man to the corral to sit up with the horses and guard them against a possible reappearance of Black Jack.

A good supper was prepared by the prisoner, who afterwards, being handcuffed to the Sheriff, slept in the house. Everyone waked early, and uncuffing the prisoner he cooked breakfast. After breakfast, horses were saddled and the prisoner was handcuffed to his saddle horn, but loosely enough so he could handle his bridle reins.

Very late at night the posse reached the ranch from which they had started on the Frisco river, and though they had not got Black Jack and his partner, they got one of his men and, more important still, all the horses.

Sometime later, a Detective for the Southern Pacific railroad of Mexico heard there was a very badly wanted desperado named Smith at a ranch in the mountains near Clifton, Arizona; also that there was a gang of train robbers and cattle thieves living in that vicinity led by Black Jack Musgraves and his brother.

One day Smith went into Clifton for supplies. These outlaws happened to meet him and told Smith if he mentioned that they were there they would kill him.

At the same time, it seems, Smith had no intentions of giving them away, but when they threatened him it made him mad, and as soon as he got to Clifton he told the Sheriff where they were hiding, stating the gang got their meals at a ranch on a trail leading down from their hideout.

Smith said there was a big pile of rocks by the side of this trail, and if the Sheriff posse would hide behind it they could capture or shoot the last one of the outlaws with no danger to themselves.

The officers took positions as told, but it being a bitterly cold night, as soon as they saw smoke coming from the chimney of the ranch house they went there and decided to make the arrests as the men came into the house.

As the outlaws turned the point in the trail, the posse standing in the doorway of the house opened fire. Black Jack and his brother George Musgraves were killed outright, but the rest of the outlaws escaped among the rocks and brush.

The End

Dalton Gang

by
N. Howard Thorp

Contrary to general belief, the Dalton Brothers and their gang did not start their roguery in Oklahoma but in New Mexico, so they may be classified with the elite, who in the past have made bandit history in the cactus-ridden state of New Mexico.

The story of the Daltons—like that of most bandits and train robbers—has been much enlarged upon, and like the whispering school for scandal has increased in volume in the telling.

The supposed mental processes of a bandit have often been described, but I have never known one whose first deed of violence was not actuated by the immediate need of money.

Such indeed was the cause of the Daltons' first gunplay, the loss of the cash capital in hand.

Born in Missouri, the three brothers, Bob, Grat, and Emmett Dalton, at an early age went west. Grat left the others in New

Mexico and established himself in Paso Robles, California. What Grat followed for a living is not generally known, but it is said he worked as a cowhand on one of the numerous haciendas near Paso Robles. It must have been some peaceable pursuit as his name does not seem to have appeared in print.

The three brothers split up on the San Francisco in New Mexico, where after working a few months Bob, Emmet Dalton, and three friends, George Newcomb and George Bryant and Bill McElhanie, started east with little money in their pockets. Arriving eventually at the town of Santa Rosa, they lined up at the bar. Bob Dalton, seeing a faro game in progress in the rear of the saloon remarked, "Watch me take it in." He strode to the faro table and sat down. It was not but a few minutes when he returned to his friends, broke. One of the others tried his luck with the same result. Finally the kid brother, Emmett Dalton, commenced playing and he too lost everything he had. By this time, the three who had lost their rolls concluded they had been up against a crooked game, and Charley Bryant suggested they get their money back. Ten guns jumped into sight, and Bob Dalton called, "Hands-up!" The five hold-ups approached and surrounded the dealer, lookout, and other players. "We are taking what we lost," said Bob, and swept all the gold, silver and paper money in sight into his pockets, and all five backed towards the door.

Once outside they jumped into their saddles, and a moment later were flying out on the trail with posses close on their heels and hot lead whining past their racing horses. This was the way the Daltons got started on their mad career, and whose depredations eventually covered several States.

As a real holdup, this little incident was comparatively harmless, yet it marked the first chapter in the history of the world-famous Dalton gang, probably the most spectacular and widely roving band of outlaws on the whole frontier. They were the last of the notorious holdup crews.

They were a badly scared bunch of youngsters that beat the posse out of town, and they had started something which they were compelled to finish. For reasons hard to determine, this little holdup in Santa Rosa stirred up a tremendous lot of excitement, and distorted tales of the holdup went ahead of them as far east as their home state of Missouri, and lovers of desperados and glamorous characters likened them to the James boys, Quantrell, and other Missouri-born outlaws. Nevertheless there was a loud clamor for their arrest, and numerous rewards were offered for their capture.

Following their escape from the Santa Rosa posse, five badly scared young men, amazed at the excitement they had created, decided to split up and await the time until the hue and cry was over.

Bob Dalton went to California to visit his brother Grat in Paso Robles; McElhanie and Newcomb went to Guthrie, Oklahoma; Emmett Dalton and Charley Bryant rode east and holed up at Riley's ranch near Kingfisher, Oklahoma.

Then presently out in Alila California a southern Pacific train was held up, and the express car looted. The robbers escaped, but a five thousand dollar reward was offered for their capture, and the cry arose that it was "The Daltons did it!"

Grat Dalton was arrested in Fresno, California, and jailed on suspicion and it was a year before he escaped and again joined the gang. Bob was almost caught but on a race horse made his escape, and with Bill Powers and Dick Broadwell continued on to Riley's ranch in Oklahoma.

Over on the Canadian river, Emmett Dalton and Charley Bryant had dug a tunnel in the clay banks, thatched with weeds, and made a hideout that became headquarters for the Dalton gang throughout its wild career. Here they stored their food, and feed, and built a brush corral for their horses. Here they rested between raids, and here they gambled and divided the spoils. This was home.

The Daltons looted only Express cars, passengers were never bothered, and only during the last few months of the gang's existence did they begin robbing banks.

Until they met their Waterloo in Coffeeville, Kansas their luck was remarkable, and many a wild yarn was circulated regarding this gang of swift and silent riders, who raided and robbed, then faded away into the western night.

Hundreds of amateur "bad men" boasted of membership in this famous band of outlaws, especially while they were working in eastern New Mexico, and the Panhandle of Texas, but at no time did the gang consist of more than ten men: Bob, Grat and Emmett Dalton, Charley Bryant, Bill Powers, George Newcomb, Charley Pearce, Dick Broadwell, Bill McElhanie, and Bill Doolin. Bob Dalton was the leader of the pack, and this leadership was never questioned by the hard-boiled desperate outfit that rode at his heels.

Bob Dalton, who at one time was a deputy United States Marshall, planned the Whorton train robbery, which definitely established the gang as renegades in the eyes of the law. A Santa Fe train was signaled down at Whorton. Hardly had the brakes ceased grinding when the engineer and fireman were covered by six-shooters and told to throw their hands up, while back in the express car the messenger was also covered, and had to turn over the keys to the safe. Fifteen thousand dollars in cash was the haul, and then the train rolled on, the passengers unaware that in the short stop made by the train a holdup had been staged.

With their booty tied to their saddles, the gang raced back to their hideout on the Canadian. Shortly the newspapers announced the authorities wanted the Daltons dead or alive.

In quick succession they held up two more trains, the first at Lelietta, and another at Redrock, netting them some twenty thousand dollars. For three years their raids made the lives of federal officers a hell on earth.

Next, word was whispered about that a big money shipment on the "Katy" was to be stopped at Adair.

The train pulled into the station on time, but the gang hid in the bushes, made no move. It was clever strategy by the railroad officers, for the express car was empty, and in a darkened day coach behind it were a score of officers armed to their teeth, awaiting the attack that did not come. This was one of the smoothest traps laid by the railroad company to ensnare the bandits. The whispered reports of the large shipment of money was made by the company to those whom they knew would report it to the Daltons.

Hidden in the brush, the watchful Emmet had noticed the black coach and told of his suspicions to Bob. "Ambush!" Bob remarked. The gang made no move, and the train pulled out. A little while later, a second section arrived at the station and the train crew was paralyzed when eight men with leveled guns made for the express car. This Adair holdup was the richest haul of the Dalton gang, and the railroad officials howled their heads off when they learned that the band had eluded their trap and later succeeded in making this rich haul. After dividing the spoils they split up, two went to Texas, and the rest to California and New Mexico.

The End

The Dalton Gang's Last Hold-Up

by
N. Howard Thorp

As the Dalton gang started its mad career in New Mexico, it seems fitting they should be followed to the end of their days of banditry, though their demise happened in another state. As stated, after the train hold-up the gang scattered.

Through that mysterious means of communication known to the underworld as the grapevine telegraph, as soon as Bob Dalton had conceived the idea of another means of getting rich, the mob were again called to meet at their "Hole in the Wall rendezvous."

Before the Adair robbery, the Daltons had robbed a few small banks, but with little success. The robbery they now contemplated promised a return so great that Bob Dalton figured it would be big enough to make them all independent for life.

Coffeeville, he stated, would be the Dalton's last robbery . . . which it was.

Five men were of the party that went to the little Kansas town on the morning of October 11th, 1892. With the three Dalton boys, Bob, Grat, and Emmett, rode Bill Powers, and Dick Broadwell. Silently they hitched their horses in an alley near the central plaza or park. It was nine forty when the gang split, Bob and Emmett heading for the First National bank, and Grat Dalton, Powers, and Dick Broadwell walking towards the door of the Condon bank, just across the street. Then trouble began. A teamster named Charley Gump, who had been lounging in front of a dry goods store, awoke. Gump took one look at the five men and fled down the street. "The Daltons!" he screamed. "Hey—by damn—the Daltons I seen them!"

A shot from Bob Dalton's gun struck his hand, where upon the terrified Gump screamed the louder.

Quitting the Gump party the two bands of outlaws entered the banks.

In the First National, a white faced cashier with Bob's gun pointed at his head opened the vault, and a few minutes later Bob and Emmett dragged twenty-five thousand dollars in currency out of the bank's doors.

Coffeeville was now thoroughly aroused. The frantic cries of Charley Gump brought them crowding into the plaza, and they sent a shower of lead whistling around the two bandits, as the Daltons jumped down the bank steps and fled through the rain of bullets to the temporary safety of the alley. Here they waited for their three partners, crouched behind their horses. "I wonder," said Bob to his brother, "what has happened to the other boys?"

In the Condon Bank, Grat and his partners were having trouble of their own. As they entered the bank they lined the customers and employees with their guns; then Grat turned to Charley Ball, the cashier, and pointed to the safe.

"Open her up," he commanded. Ball's nerve did not desert

him. He licked his lips and glanced at the clock. It was nine forty-two. "I can't," he declared, "not until nine forty-five. It's a time lock."

"We'll wait," said Grat.

It is said Charley Ball's hesitation saved the bank twenty thousand dollars, and caused the death of eight men in the next five minutes. The robbers and bankers lying flat on the floor heard the bullets of the enraged Citizens on the outside as they concentrated their fire on the bandits within the bank. Grat eyed the clock, and at nine forty-four a tremendous gunfire smashed through the windows, riddled the woodwork, and whistled a murderous song over the prostrate men. Another fusillade of shots followed, and Grat Dalton's nerve broke. He hollered to Powers and Broadwell to come on, and fled through the door of the bank.

At that moment the town seemed to go crazy. The Citizens were wild with excitement, and in the run for their horses Grat Dalton was shot through the heart. The alley and their horses were their last chance of safety. Bob's gun now began to speak, and a man named Baldwin dropped with a bullet in his head. It barked once more, and then again, and two more of Coffeeville's Citizens clutched at their throats as they fell to the ground. Bill Powers, with one foot in the stirrup, reeled to the ground as a bullet hit him in the chest. Dick Broadwell, his face covered with blood, clutched the horn of his saddle. "Well-I'm-hit-bad," he gasped, and hanging desperately to his horse, galloped hurriedly out of town. They found him the next day a couple of miles distant, his face buried in the dust of the Kansas prairie; but his horse and saddle were not found. This horse had been raised on the Canadian river, and in the general horse work which occurred there the following spring, this horse, carrying his saddle, but with bridle and saddle blanket missing, was corralled and as the horse was never claimed, was turned loose again to die of old age. The saddle I believe was later claimed by a relative of Broadwell, which—by the way—was not his right name.

Back in the alley a bullet shattered Emmett's right arm, another buried itself in his groin paralyzing his leg. Bob was huddled on the ground, his body riddled with lead, he was dying, but somehow his kid brother swung him up into the saddle. "Don't bother, kid," said Bob, "save yourself, I'm done for."

The boy shook his head and answered no. And then, not over six feet away, a man named Carey Seaman with only his head and shoulders showing over a high board fence, trained a double barrel shotgun on Emmett's defenseless back and pulled the trigger. There was a roar, and a double load of buckshot tore into the youngster's body. Quietly Emmett slid off his horse.

But as Emmett fell, Bob Dalton, his eyes glazing, fired one more shot. It was the last shot fired by the Dalton gang, and the aim was perfect, the bullet drilling a small black hole squarely in the center of Carey Seaman's forehead.

Many sentimentalists have written much stuff trying to exonerate the Daltons for their many misdeeds, but personally I can present no excuses for them. They had their chances like other men of their time to make good, and chose—as they thought—the easiest way, and in consequence paid the price.

It seems remarkable they carried on their depredations as long as they did, but the unsettled conditions of the country in those times greatly added to their chances of avoiding arrest. Then there was a sort of glamour surrounding the outlawed bandits of those days, and they were protected and advised of the arrival of officers, often by the minions of the law themselves, as they did not care to argue certain questions involving right or wrong with them. Emmett the Kid brother did not die, and of the famous Dalton gang he was the only member to survive. The Doctors patched up his shattered body, and the law sentenced him to life imprisonment in the Kansas Penitentiary. After serving fifteen years, a petition signed by thousands of people was presented to the Governor of Kansas, who taking into consideration Emmett's good behavior while a prisoner and the fact that he was only a kid when he got into trouble, finally pardoned him from the Penitentiary. I hold no grief for those who are professional hold-ups, but a kid like Emmett Dalton's admiration for an elder brother is quite easily understood, for Bob Dalton certainly had plenty of dash and nerve, and in the eyes of the kid was enshrined as a hero. As his later life after his release proved, the Governor of Kansas made no mistake in granting Emmett a pardon, nor did he ever give his friends, who signed the petition for his release, grounds for regret.

The End

The John Greer Gang

by
N. Howard Thorp

Late one evening just before the passenger train was leaving Carrizozo in Lincoln County New Mexico, a young man—evidently a cowpuncher—stepped on the rear platform of the passenger train, which was bound for Alamogordo. Passing through the Pullman he seated himself in one of the forward seats.

No particular attention was paid him, as he resembled a cowhand in his best cloths treating himself to a ride.

The train passed Three Rivers, and Tularosa, and a couple of miles north of Alamogordo the Stranger arose from his seat, and pulling a six-shooter faced the passengers, and calmly said, "Ladies and gentlemen this is a hold-up, dig up your valuables and as I pass down the aisle put everything you have of value in my hat, which I hold in my left hand. My partner who is on the rear platform has you all covered, and anyone who fails to do as I say will be sorry."

Proceeding in a leisurely way the bandit soon arrived at the rear of the car with his loot, consisting of pocket books, silver, rings and a few good watches, not a great deal, probably not over two thousand dollars in value.

As the train pulled into the outskirts of Alamogordo the bandit dropped off the rear platform of the Pullman, and disappeared in the darkness. Although this was a single handed job, the thought which he had instilled in the minds of the passengers by the remark, "You are all covered by my partner who is on the rear platform" undoubtedly had its effect, as facing the young robber they did not look back, or they would have discovered he was alone.

It has always been supposed that Greer's younger brother and John Gates "Alias" Frazer, was stationed at the point where Greer got off the train, fully intending to hold-up the express and mail car attached to the train, but for some unexplained reason this miscarried.

Riding west from Alamogordo the gang split up. Gates, one of the Greer gang, was surprised, and arrested at Deming, being held for the Tucson Arizona Officers on a charge of burglary of considerable extent. Riding into Deming the two Greer brothers went to the jail where they encountered the deputy sheriff. They threw down on him, disarmed him, and ordered him to turn John Gates loose. He told them he did not have the cell keys, that the Sheriff Dwight Stevens who was uptown had them. Leaving his younger brother to guard the deputy, John Greer went in search of the Sheriff.

Deming in those days was a little sleepy cow town, its one principal street started at the Harvey House on the railroad and struggled south towards Mexico. The street, lined with little houses and saloons slept, and was only awakened when a bunch of cowboys came in from the surrounding ranches—and as they called it—"took the town in."

With his chair tipped against the outer wall of a saloon and sound asleep, the recently elected Sheriff Dwight Stevens was suddenly awakened by John Greer's gun being poked into his stomach, and the advice given to walk ahead of Greer to the jail was obeyed.

With Sheriff Stevens and the deputy covered, the keys were produced, and Gates was freed. In passing the Sheriff—who was still covered by John Greer's gun—Gates remarked he had "always wanted a pearl handle six-shooter," so promptly relieved the Sheriff of his gaudy gun.

Locking the Sheriff and deputy in the jail, the Greer brothers and Gates got their horses, and rode out of town. This was on election day of 1910. The evening of the day these three left Deming they rode into the corrals of the V Cross T Ranch. Here they were presently surrounded by a posse which had taken their trail.

When surrounded, the three raced out of the corral shooting, killing Tom Hall, a famous trailer, and Al Smithers, formerly an Arizona ranger, the posse in return killing John Greer, young Greer and Gates escaping.

They were trailed to the rough country, north and west of Cooks Peak, and in Arabe Canyon were so closely pressed they had to quit their horses and a-foot, take to the brush. Young Greer climbed a cliff and concealing himself, made it so hot for the posse with his saddle gun, they were glad to retreat, but took Greer's and Gate's saddle horses with them.

It has been the custom for western riders to ascribe almost every bank robbery and train hold-up occurring in New Mexico to the Black Jack gang. In many instances—such as the hold-up of the automobile containing the payroll of the Chino Copper Company—they occurred many years after Black Jack's gang had broken up, and himself hanged at Clayton. The robbery of the Chino pay car was committed by the Greer gang led by John Gates "Alias" Frazer. There is little to describe. These three men stopped the automobile, and reports say, got away with thirty thousand dollars.

As this was the usual amount carried to meet the payroll, it is presumed the gang got about that sum. It is also known that it was buried, but none of it has ever been found, though many fortune seekers have sought it.

In tracing down this hold-up I have run across two different versions, so will not mention—at this time—either, but will refer to the possible location of the buried money taken from the car.

The loot was in canvas sacks, and after being taken, the car which had contained it was shooed on its way.

About half a mile south and half a mile east from where the car was stopped, some months after, was found the remains of a campfire, a letter addressed to young Greer—which had probably been carried in a hip pocket, and dropped out as he mounted his horse—some burnt matches, and an empty whiskey bottle. This is near the point where Gates said—before his death—the money had been buried.

In part of his statement, Gates referred to the fact that he had a pint of whiskey wrapped in his slicker, and after getting the money they carried it to a distance, buried it, and built a fire, then made some coffee, and roasted a goat's leg they had got from a herder and finished the bottle of whiskey. He remembered leaving the empty bottle near the fire when they rode off. This all tallies with what—with the exception of the money—was afterwards found: campfire, bottle, and letter.

We will now return to Young Greer, and Gates, who had fought off the pursuing posse in Arabe Canyon near Cooks Peak.

Afoot, they were in a desperate plight, and decided to split up, as singly they could the more easily escape detection. They traveled at night, young Greer heading east for the Sacramento Mountains, and Gates for El Paso. Although a diligent search was kept up, nothing was heard of them for some time.

Finally a man walked into an El Paso Pawn shop and tried to pawn a six-shooter. The man who ran the shop had been notified—like all El Paso pawn brokers—to watch out for a six-shooter of a certain number and make. The gun offered for pawn tallied in every way with furnished description of gun wanted. The man on some excuse was detained, the police were called, and without knowing whom they were arresting, took to jail John Gates "Alias" Frazer. The gun was the one he took from Sheriff Dwight Stevens of Deming at the time the Greer brothers liberated him from jail.

Identified as one of the men who was in the fight at the V Cross T Ranch in which Tom Hall, Al Smithers, and John Greer were killed, he was taken to Socorro, New Mexico, and accused of the shooting, convicted and hung.

It was a question of someone having to be found guilty, though one of the posse, who was at the fight, said John Greer—who himself was killed—was the party who actually killed the two officers. Quien sabe.

The End

The Wild Bunch of the San Francisco River, New Mexico

by
N. Howard Thorp

The outlaws who had drifted from the towns of Tombstone, Morenci, and Clifton, when the Earps and other peace officers made it too hot for them, rode north and east to the Blue River, following it up until they came to where the San Francisco river empties into it, and in a few miles crossed the line into New Mexico and arrived at the little town of Alma. Black river was also a great hold-out for them. Many of these men—all former cowhands—went to work for the W.S.S.U. double circles, Lyon and Campbell and other outfits, eventually aiming to get to the hole-in-the-wall gang of Wyoming.

In the spring of 1885 old Geronimo the Apache was raising all the devilment in eastern Arizona and western New Mexico possible. An Apache Indian has the faculty of disappearing from sight on a level mesa where there is apparently no cover or other object to conceal him from your view; also he can reappear in the same mysterious manner, from nowhere. He also has the faculty of being able to see what is going on behind him without moving anything but his eyeballs. People who have these accomplishments are hard to handle.

One squaw captured by the sixth Cavalry in command of Captain Hammond, and brought to the W.S. ranch for safekeeping, proved to be the wife of the great Medicine Chief Geronimo, and whom the boys at the ranch christened "Biddy," a hard looker, but built on generous lines, and probably a good beast of burden. The Troops had been pressing the Indians so close the old girl had played out, and was left on the trail. This is the same band that killed Luce, Orwig, and Young Lyons, all ranchmen of the Alma district.

A few miles below Alma the Frisco river enters a box canyon, the end of which is where White Water Creek empties into the main stream. At this point there is a wide place where one may get down from the high cliffs to the river. In all this five miles of canyon this is the only possible place of descent. This was a favorite spot of the Indians to way-lay travelers.

The Cavalry at one time ran a bunch of Indians into this box canyon and as it was late in the day, placed heavy guards at each end. All night long they kept their patrols and fires going, waiting for morning when they expected to put an end to at least one bunch of Apaches. During the night the Indians had scaled these cliffs, and with a crude rawhide harness had pulled their horses up with them and made their escape. One seeing the walls of this canyon would say such a feat was impossible, but nevertheless it so happened. Enough concerning the Indians. I have only mentioned this incident to show what a resourceful lot the ranchmen of the early days had to contend with.

Jasper Tomason, who was called Jap for short, had worked for the W.S. outfit since the brand was originated, had lately been "sittin" courting one of the Meader girls; Jap had drawn his pay and signified his intention of marrying her, so we were all surprised to hear that she had suddenly married another suitor named Potter. Now Potter was endowed with worldly goods, but in looks could not compare with Jap. The first thing anyone knew was the news that Jap had killed Potter. Jap was now under arrest at Cooney, and when the outfit rode over to try and get him out of jail on bond, they found him and the deputy enjoying a drink at the local bar.

At the hearing at the Justice court, it seems that after the girl had married Potter, Jap still continued his attentions, and Potter threatened to shoot him. When the case was called, the Judge, who had been very drunk, did not appear, and after a thorough search he was found asleep in a ditch. After washing himself in a nearby creek, he assumed an air of great dignity and strode into the courtroom. Calling the court to order, he bound Jap over to the Grand Jury and was sent to Socorro, New Mexico, and there given a life sentence. After two years of leisure he was pardoned out by Governor Prince.

The country at this time was infested with cow thieves, and trouble for the big ranchers began, so they enlisted the services of all the tough cowhands who came along.

About this time, the W.S. ranch put in as foreman a man named Golden, a big stout fellow, a good rider, and all-around hand. The day after Fred Golden took charge, a chuck-liner, "one who rides from ranch to ranch getting free board" who gave the name of McNeil, rode up and stayed all night, bringing four horses in the Hashknife brand. He explained having them through the fact he had been working for that outfit, and took the horses in on wages. When the home outfit started the roundup, they left him at the ranch under the eye of old Charley.

In a few days when returning to the ranch, the outfit was met by old Charley, who told them McNeil had left, and stolen the best stallion on the ranch who at night was always locked in the barn. The ranch started men horse-back in every direction, and at last two of the riders found where McNeil had tried to lead the stallion up an almost impossible trail. And the horse had slipped back and fallen several hundred feet to his death. McNeil was next heard from in Utah, where for train robbery he was sentenced to the Penn for twelve years.

In 1888, old Charley the ranch hand of the W.S. outfit was murdered by a man named Penny in a saloon in Cooney, New Mexico, owned by Penny and Shelton. After the Justice court had sent Penny to Socorro for trial, with the assistance of Mr. Ferguson, one of the best criminal lawyers in the Territory and an able interpreter, a verdict of not guilty was obtained, the prisoner being turned loose. Next Penny turned up in Bisbee, Arizona, where he had been elected Justice of the Peace. About this time the bottom fell out of the cattle market, and the T. Bar ranch was offered for sale. Mr. Black of the Y. outfit bought the cattle while Mr. Porter took over the ranches. The T. Bar cattle were turned over to the buyer on the forks of the Gila river, near a ranch owned by a man, Cox.

The V. Cross T. and D.D. Bar wagons were camped near together when a puncher named Grostette walked over to the V. Cross T. wagon to make two brothers who were working for that outfit retract some remarks they had made about his sister. The names of the two brothers have slipped my memory, but when Grostette offered to whip them both in a fistfight they opened fire and killed him, but not before he had mortally wounded them both.

One day three heavily armed men rode up to the W.S. bunkhouse and asked for the boss. They said they were after a notorious horse thief known as "Black Jack" who was supposed to be a half-breed Indian, who stole horses along the border states, and when pursued by the law usually held up somewhere on the San Francisco and Blue rivers. This Black Jack was not the man Ketchum, who was also known as Black Jack, and was afterwards killed.

In 1895, cattle were a fair price and little rustlers sprung up like spring grass. The W.S. outfit had at this time recorded some seventy brands, in order to protect the W.S. brand, brands into which the home brand could be easily changed. The foreman of the double circle, Cole Railson, met and after a good deal of private conversation recognized the foreman of the W.S. outfit was a gentleman he had formerly known in Montana, though at the time of the meeting, Fred Golden confessed his right name was Boyd Rochfort, much more aristocratic than the name Golden under which he had been going. After this meeting, Fred quit and went to Bisbee, Arizona but did not survive long.

In 1906, on account of the hard range, the W.S. outfit purchased large holdings near Springer in Colfax County. The boss of the W.S. outfit had a wonderful grey saddle horse named Rattler, and what was known as the best buggy team in western New Mexico. One evening two men rode up to the ranch and asked to stay all night; no one at the ranch knew them. They repaid the kindness by stealing three of the above mentioned horses; one of the buggy team they did not get. These two men were the notorious brothers, the Ketchums, Tom the elder who was known as Black Jack and his Brother Sam. They stole the grey saddle horse at night out of the stable, but could only catch one of the team, Major, who was loose in the pasture. They rode Major until he gave out but the saddle horse they rode into Wyoming and sold him to some of their friends in the Hole-in-the-Wall.

Jim Lowe, and a man who called himself McGuiness, next showed at Alma. As Perry the old hand was then leaving the W.S., McGuiness was given the job of foreman, and kept his partner,

Jim Lowe, with him. Tom Caphart also was working there and a fellow—who on account of the color of his hair—was termed Red. When the cattle of the W.S. were shipped to Springer, all the above mentioned men went with them, and on their arrival there quit. About this time the train was held up and robbed at Folsom seventy miles east of Springer.

When the posse following the robbers came up with them, a man named Franks not only whipped them but killed three and wounded four of the posse, then carried his wounded companion away on horses.

One of the wounded men who, although only shot through the arm, was Sam Ketchum, who when overtaken by the posse, quit cold and surrendered. Franks got away and for a long time was not again heard from. Franks had been shot twice through the body and wounded in two other places, but managed to ride three hundred miles to southern Lincoln county. Franks proved to be, when finally arrested, the W.S. foremen McGinnis.

The End

Socorro, Courtesy Palace of the Governors (MNM/DCA #11435)

With this mixed population of cowboys from the nearby ranches, miners and teamsters any one of them boisterous and turbulent by nature, coupled with the fact that during this period there were forty-four saloons within the city limits, Socorro was according to Old Timers a very lively town. A vigilance committee was organized as a necessary aid with which to supplement the forces of law and order. Killings and lynchings were the order of the day, the advent of the railroad in the early eighties served to bring in more of the undesirable element.

Facsimile: "Socorro, Early History up to 1900," Lorin W. Brown, May 25, 1939, NMFWP, WPA #231, NMSRCA

Henry Coleman, "Bad Man"

by
N. Howard Thorp

Henry Coleman—which was not his right name—came from Texas where he was born. His family was one of the best in the Lone Star State.

One of his brothers was a U.S. Senator, another a very prominent attorney, and a Texas County bears the old family name.

Henry somehow started life on the wrong foot, and when he became of age, or slightly after, rode to New Mexico, where he first became notorious in and around Deming, New Mexico.

At that time he had three companions, one of whom now lives not a great way from the settlement of Quemado, and is a ranchman there. As he still lives, we will call him Long John, which is not of course his name.

These four men started by buying cheap cattle south of the Boca Grande river, which south of Deming is the dividing line of the United States and Mexico. They worked south as far as Palomas Lakes, La Ascencion, Corralitos, and Aguas Calientes.

These cattle, they would drift into the United States and peddle around Silver City, Lake Valley, Las Cruces and other towns. But this method proved too slow, and profits too small, so from buying they took to rustling the Mexican stock, and presently were returning to Mexico with bunches of American bulls they rounded up and which south of the line brought good prices.

One day Coleman, accompanied by one of his men, went to Silver City to get some checks cashed, when he ran into four men from whom he had previously stolen cattle. All were mounted. The men accused Coleman of stealing their cattle, and the fireworks started. Coleman killed two of them, wounded two others, and made his getaway. From then on he became unpopular, and subsequently confined himself to the theft of Old Mexico cattle.

Coleman, while on a trip to the State of Chihuahua, was caught with a bunch of stolen cattle. He killed the Mexican who first interfered with him, quit the cattle, and just as he thought he'd got away, he unfortunately ran into a bunch of Federal Rurales, who, as he was a gringo, arrested him on general principle, and took him several days journey to the jail in Juarez. His partner Long John, learning of his arrest, and hearing that a charge of murder had been lodged against him, knew he was in a serious fix, with the chances he would be stood up against an adobe wall and shot. Knowing that all cowboys—in those days—were regarded with suspicion if seen in Juarez, Long John determined upon a rescue. He borrowed from a young lawyer friend a suitable outfit which disguised the fact he was a cowboy.

Unfortunately, John's friend was small, while John was some six feet four inches in height and build in proportion. A friend of mine, who saw John riding a horse and leading another across the International bridge from El Paso to Juarez, said it was a comical sight.

John wore a black derby hat much too small, a frock coat with sleeves almost to his elbows, the bottoms of his trousers several inches above his ankles, and with a bright red tie. Riding with a dignified air he approached the Juarez jail. Like all Mexican jails, the cells were on three sides, the fourth side being a high adobe wall, leaving a large open corral or yard in which all stray stock was put, and during the day the prisoners were allowed to exercise there.

John circled the enclosure a time or two, and seeing a guard slipped him some money and told him to give a letter, which he handed him, to Coleman.

The letter told Coleman to stand close to the wall and watch for a rope coming over the top. Presently Long John rode his horse behind the wall and threw the end of the rope over. Coleman slipped his foot through the loop, and John's horse pulled him over. They left town on the run, shooting towards those who were quickly in pursuit, and took the Rio Grande river a mile below the bridge, and wet as rats gained the American side. This rescue almost became an international complication, though after a time the excitement subsided. Warned to keep away from the border, Coleman pulled out, and going to Arizona married a woman named Clara Oliver, who with her young brother, Don Oliver, Coleman moved to a ranch he established on the Canyon Largo, in New Mexico. This was in the years 1915 and 1916.

Coleman now got around him an active bunch of cattle rustlers, but eventually Coleman and his old partner Long John fell out, and became deadly enemies. Returning to the Canyon Largo ranch after the delivery of a bunch of stolen cattle, Coleman found that his wife and her brother had been shot to death. Suspicion fell upon Coleman, but when called into court, he had no difficulty in establishing a good alibi.

There was a neighbor of Coleman's living some six miles from the Largo ranch, by the name of Barbiny, and from talk circulated, suspicion fell upon him as the murderer. At any rate I am convinced Coleman was sincere in his belief that Barbiny was the murderer, and accordingly swore out a warrant for his arrest. The Sheriff of Socorro county and his deputies arrested Barbiny, and the same night stopped at Coleman's ranch for supper while on their way to Socorro with their prisoner. The party of four men was told to get down and come in. As Barbiny, the last to enter, came within the door Coleman shot him dead. He accompanied the Sheriff to Socorro, where he gave bonds for his appearance later. When the case came up, Coleman claimed he shot in self defense. He said that as Barbiny crossed the threshold of the door, he started to pick up a Winchester which leaned against the doorjamb, and that he, Coleman, sensing his intentions of killing him, shot first.

While the trial was going on in Socorro, Coleman and the District Attorney were both stopping at the Chambon hotel, "now the Park," and if it had not been for bystanders, the chances are that Coleman would have killed him. Coleman managed to beat the case.

About this time a new district Attorney was appointed, who lived in Magdalena. He received so many complaints from ranchmen about a gang of cattle thieves who were stealing their stock, that the district attorney decided to act. He knew by name all the rustlers. One at a time he called them in, stating he wished no more than a friendly talk. "Now boys," he said, "I have been appointed district attorney. I know you are all guilty of cow stealing, but from now on you must quit. We will forget the past and start with a clean sheet. Are you willing to or not?" With the exception of Henry Coleman and one other, they all agreed to quit.

Reports continued coming in to the district attorney's office of the cattle stealing operations of Coleman and one other man. A warning was sent to him, but it seemed to do no good.

The district attorney sent for Coleman to come in, but he refused unless allowed to come fully armed and demanded the district attorney make certain promises, all of which the office refused.

Coleman at this time was out on bond on another case, and when it was called did not show up, whereupon the district office had a warrant for Coleman's arrest issued, and it was given to the Sheriff to serve. It is a pretty well established fact that Henry Coleman had the Magdalena country officers up a tree—pretty well scared—and they were taking no chances with him. The Sheriff, a Mexican, and his deputy went on a hunt for Coleman, and on the way picked up three Americans who all had it in for him. These, the Sheriff deputized to go along. It seems they had some trouble in locating Coleman, but at last ran across him at what was called the Old Goat Ranch, southwest of Salt Lake in the western part of Old Socorro county. As all were scared of him, as soon as the posse saw Coleman, they began shooting. Coleman's horse became frightened, and began bucking and fell with him in an old ditch, never giving him a chance to draw his gun. During the shooting a bullet found its way through Coleman's leg, and cut an artery. He lay out all night and bled to death, none of the posse daring to go near him until the following morning.

The End

"Butch" Cassidy, Alias Jim Lowe, or Sallie Parker

by
N. Howard Thorp

ontrary to the usual belief that Butch Cassidy was a product of Wyoming, we find he was born and brought up in the Servier Valley, seventy-five miles west of Hanksville in the little town of Circleville, in Piute County, Utah. As a boy he seemed to have been a good looking girlish young fellow, and his companions nick-named him Sallie; this alone should have driven him to show what a hard Citizen he really could be. His family name was Parker, and his younger sister was assistant Post Mistress in Circleville.

Butch Cassidy, as he later was called, was the brains and directed some hundred or more bandits whose operations extended practically over the entire west.

One hideout of the different gangs Butch controlled was west of the Indian Creek settlement and the Colorado River in Utah. The men, who at different times "holed-up" at this point, had a boat hidden in the brush along the Grand river, so if hard pressed they could cross over and reach the rough Henry Mountains.

The southernmost hideout was near Alma, on the San Francisco River in western Socorro County, New Mexico. As this hide-out was not many miles from the Mexican border, likewise the northern hideout of these outlaws—the Hole-in-the-Wall in the big Horn basin of northern Wyoming—was but three days ride from the Canadian line. These different gangs of outlaws, some under the leadership of Kid Curry and others under Butch Cassidy, worked in harmony, and it was seldom known which of the different groups committed certain train robberies and bank hold-ups, which for years was the means of support of these desperate characters.

Until one realizes the vast desert reaches "still existing" of western Colorado, southern and western Utah—particularly the Colorado of the Grand River section and Blue Mountain country, western and northern Arizona and western New Mexico—one cannot believe it possible that these characters kept out of the hands of the law for so many years.

Take for example the Sheriff of the little Mormon town of Monticello in southwestern Utah, the County Seat of San Juan County. This town was presided over by Bishop Jones. Now the Sheriff of this county stood in with all outlaws and kept them informed of any danger which might threaten. He kept a lookout for strangers who might be detectives, or Officers of the law, on the trail of bandits.

As an example, showing the protection which Officers of the law in many instances afforded these bandits, I offer the following. One day two Officers drove into Monticello, and inquired of the Sheriff if he had seen anything of any of the Kid Curry gang, as there was a big reward offered for their arrest. The Sheriff immediately sent word to two outlaws who were in town, "Kid Jackson" and

"Peg Leg," to pull out at once, as two Detectives were camped just south of the settlement; but instead of leaving, Jackson and Peg Leg rode at night to the Officers' camp, ran off their horses and shot up their tent, so the two Officers had to "hoof it" back to town and hire a team to take them to the railroad.

This man had been Sheriff for many years, and when he eventually lost out he had influence enough to have a man appointed who was a member of the Mormon Church and whom he could trust to protect his friends among the outlaws. No wonder the Blue Mountains and all southern Utah as far as the Nevada line was a favorite winter resort for most any criminal who owned a horse and saddle.

This state of affairs was also made possible through the fact that as Sheriffs were in the minority they thought it policy to play in with the desperados, and save their own skins.

After Butch Cassidy and his gang robbed the Montpelier, Idaho bank out of a large amount of money, they took it to their holdout—which I have already referred to—fifty miles east of Hanksville, Utah and buried it. It was commonly reported that while at their holdout, they used twenty dollar gold pieces for chips when playing poker.

In the course of ten years these outlaws held up some forty trains and over fifty banks; it is also estimated they stole some twenty thousand head of horses and cattle. Here is an instance showing how cheeky they were. One evening three men got off the stage at Hillsboro, New Mexico and entering the hotel got their supper. The same night they stole two race horses owned by a man who lived near town, led them to the livery stable where they stole saddles and another horse and saddle for the third man. Well mounted, they rode to the Hillsboro bank and entering, broke open the safe and stole every cent it contained, reported to have been over thirty thousand dollars. Although known to have been some of the Butch Cassidy gang they were never caught, although the sorrel horse stolen from the livery stable was some weeks later returned. Butch Cassidy himself at this time was not in the country, though it was generally known that the robbery was committed by some members of his gang.

At a point near Folsom, New Mexico on the Colorado and Southern Railroad, a train was held up and robbed of a lot of money; the bandits who did this were all members of the Butch Cassidy gang. Many other robberies I might mention, but have not here the space.

One time a Pinkerton detective arrived at one of the ranches near Alma on the San Francisco river, hunting some bandits who had robbed a train at a place called Green Mountain, Wyoming. The train it was proved had been held up by some of the gang who were now working for the W.S. cow outfit near Alma. In this robbery the express car had been detached, and the safe blown open. An enormous amount of money had been taken, over a hundred thousand dollars. Included in the money stolen was a large package of ten and twenty dollar bills, consigned to a bank in Oregon. These bills were new and unsigned. A number had been traced to the bank of Silver City, and from there traced back to the store at Alma, and the detective said he had come to investigate the matter.

When the outlaws blew the door of the safe off, the explosion blew off the corner of a package of bills, so all the bills showed the same corner missing. The proprietor of the Alma store said he got the bills from a man named Johnny Ward. When found, Johnny Ward acknowledged having passed the bills and said he got them from a man named McGonigal for two horses he had sold him. The detective did not arrest Johnny Ward, as he was satisfied he came by them honestly. He took the numbers of the bills and said he would try to find McGonigal.

Presently the detective drew out a photograph and showed it to the boss of the W.S. outfit, asking if he could recognize any of the men in the picture. The boss stated that one of the men shown was Tom Caphart, and another was Jim Lowe.

The Pinkerton man wished to know if the boss had ever heard Jim Lowe called by any other name. He answered no. The detective then stated that the man known as Jim Lowe was in reality Butch Cassidy, and that Tom Caphart was known as Franks. The ranch boss told the detective that Jim Lowe was the best man who ever worked on the W.S. ranch handling cattle. Nevertheless, the detective replied, there was hardly a State south of the Canadian line that did not want him, and there was a large reward offered for his capture. He was well known as the brains and leader of the best organized gang of outlaws ever formed in the west, and even the Company he represented would be willing to pay twenty thousand dollars for him. The detective stated it was the custom of these outlaws when they had committed some big robbery or holdup for the parties who were engaged in it to seek employment at as great a distance from the scene as possible, and remain working under other names until all excitement had died down. The next job was always done by a different gang and in a far distant part of the country; but it was always carried out by the organized gang of which Butch Cassidy was the head.

He further stated that the gang undoubtedly had inside information as to money shipments, time, and amount, as in all their various holdups they had never as yet held up the wrong train or bank; this was what was causing all Officers and the U.S. Secret service men as well so much worry. He said no one had the slightest idea where Butch Cassidy had disappeared to after his last robbery of some years before, and he was surprised when yesterday he saw him in Alma. The detective was asked if now that he knew where Butch Cassidy was would he attempt to arrest him. He smiled as he replied, "I'm not such fool to attempt it on his own ground. If I tried to arrest him here, I would need a regiment of Cavalry to help me." Shortly afterwards, Jim Lowe and Tom Caphart, realizing that as times were changing the game was about up, and taking considerable money with them, left for South America.

The End

Bad Man Moore, Alias Johnny Ward

by
N. Howard Thorp

Bad Man Moore, as he was known, was born in eastern California, and even among those California vaqueros—of which there are none better—Moore was known as one of the finest ropers in the State.

Those were the times when fifty and sixty foot raw-hide ropes or "riatas" were used; not tied to the horn of one's saddle as is done pretty generally in the west today; but after the animal was roped, a couple of wraps or dale gueltas were taken around the saddle horn to snub the animal you had caught.

When Moore was twenty-five he killed in cold blood his young brother-in-law. The young man being very popular, a posse was quickly formed and Moore, riding in the lead—but at a safe distance—hit the trail east. The posse made Moore hot-foot-it as far as Elko, at the foot of the Bull Run Mountains of Nevada, where, seeing they were losing ground, turned back. The day following that upon which the posse quit the trail Moore saw a horseman approaching from the north, and probably supposing it was someone looking for him, killed him, without ever finding out what the stranger wanted. This happened in an isolated place in the foothills of the Bull Run Mountain. If the man was ever found, no one ever knew how he met his death.

Skirting the Great Salt Lake to the north, a month later Moore rode into the then great cattle town of Cheyenne, Wyoming. He shortly went to work as a cowhand for the Swan Land and Cattle Company, at that time the largest in the State, claiming over a hundred thousand head.

Moore was a great worker, and as already stated, a top roper as well as a natural leader of men; so it was not long before he was made range foreman for a the company, and later District manager.

Moore was a very handsome man with his erect carriage and his long mustache, but there was one distinctive feature, which once seen was never forgotten and would remain with him through life. It was a cast in his left eye, which he usually kept about half closed, and although he wore his hat on the left side of his head with the brim pulled down, one could not miss seeing it.

Moore worked for the Swan Land and Cattle Company a couple of years; then, for some unknown reason, killed a negro who was working for him and had to quit Wyoming in a hurry.

He appeared one day at the L.X. ranch on the west side of the Panhandle of Texas on a ridden down horse, hunting work. His leadership with men soon made him foreman and later manager. He next started a ranch of his own, at Cold Water Springs situated in no man's land, now included in Oklahoma. He had several L.X. hands working with him, stealing his company's cattle. Over half the cowhands working for his outfit were outlaws, badly wanted men.

An amusing incident happened to Moore's outfit. A large party of surveyors appeared on the L.X. range, fully armed, and with chuck wagon, hack and saddle horses. They were sent to make a preliminary survey for a railroad and were very secretive concerning their business. One evening late, they pulled their outfit up close to the L.X. wagon and camped. The next morning, over half of Moore's cowhands were missing. Concluding from their appearance that the surveyors were a bunch of Texas Rangers, the outlaws during the night had saddled horses and departed for points unknown. Moore never encouraged a stranger to hang around, either the ranch or the wagon, and always gave the impression of being distant and reserved; but with his hands he was one of them.

Moore worked five years for the L.X. outfit and, having feathered his nest, quit work and sold out his no-man's-land ranch for some seventy-five thousand dollars.

Taking two of the hands—who were in on the cattle stealing—with him, he located a ranch in the American Valley, in the extreme northwestern part of New Mexico, just north of Luna Valley. Adjoining the ranch which Moore had taken up was one owned by two partners; this ranch had a splendid spring of water, which Moore wanted, as it controlled a large open range. Several times he made offers for it, but each time the owners refused to sell. Moore was an exceedingly high tempered man, bull-headed, and not easily thwarted in anything he attempted.

Finding that all attempts to get possession of the adjoining ranch were futile, he rode there alone, and awaiting a favorable opportunity killed the two owners and left them where they fell.

This act again put him on the dodge, and changing his name to Johnny Ward, rode south to the little town of Alma and went to work for an English outfit who ran the W.S. brand. Here was where so many of the "Wild bunch" worked, though not until

McGinnis, one of their hands, was arrested as a train hold-up was the company aware that from Butch Cassidy down, all their hands belonged to the same gang that worked from Alma, New Mexico to the hole-in-the-wall country in Wyoming.

To show what a curious twist there must have been in Moore's brain, I will mention the following incident, which happened before Moore had—on account of his two last killings—to quit the American Valley.

Word was received at his ranch that just across the State line in Arizona a man had killed another, and the family of the murdered man wanted a posse to go and get the murderer, who was barricaded in a log house not far distant. Moore got a few men together and took the trail at once. Arriving at the cabin, Moore called to the man to come out and surrender. A shot from within the house just missed Moore's head. He again called to the man within, telling him to come out. Another shot was the reply. All right, shouted Moore, if you won't come out I'll go in after you! He accordingly picked up a large rock and broke the door in, grabbed the man, and pulled him outside. This took a lot of nerve, for at the time Moore did not know the murderer had used his last cartridge. The man had a rope put around his neck and was swung up to a nearby tree.

Moore, though having killed several men, when another man committed a murder he was willing to see justice, as he saw it, done. Moore worked for the W.S. outfit for several months, until on account of the arrival of various detectives at Alma, thought it best to move on.

These detectives, one of whom was Charlie Siringo, were after evidence to convict Kid Curry of a northern train robbery through the tracing of paper money stolen at the time; though Moore thought they were after him, so accordingly disappeared.

Much more could be told of Moore, but these events

happened out of the State while he was on his way leaving the country, so we will confine ourselves to happenings in the State. Moore made his way on horseback north and west, crossed the Canadian border, and came to the Pacific coast. We next hear of him in Juneau, Alaska where Charlie Siringo, while on some other business, saw him. He had opened a saloon and prospered, though was eventually killed there in a fight.

The End

Curley Bill, "Outlaw"

by
N. Howard Thorp

John Chisum came from Texas to the Pecos valley in New Mexico in the year 1867, bringing with him almost a hundred thousand head of cattle. His home ranch was at Bosque Grande on the Pecos river.

His brand was a long rail on the side, while for an earmark he gave the jingle bob—ear cut so it hangs down like a bell.

A little later than the advent of Chisum, Major Murphy started a store and ranch at Lincoln, Lincoln County, New Mexico. Along in the seventies Major Murphy tried to break in on the beef contracts, which Chisum formerly held with the Government; this then was really the start of the Lincoln County war.

When these two outfits fell out, Chisum employed a number of gun men to protect his cattle from thefts by the Murphy men, and at the same time to steal with brand cattle from the herds of Murphy; this is about the time the killings began.

Murphy was a good Politician and controlled all the votes in his district; so the appointment of the Peace Officers were almost without exception outlaws.

Curley Bill and Jim Wallace were two of the fighting men employed in this trouble. After Pat Garret was elected Sheriff, he had the principal people who were connected with this war—who had not been killed off—indicted.

Before warrants could be served upon them, Wallace and Curley Bill—whose real name was William Brocius—rode west, and under assumed names went to work for the English outfits who owned ranches on the San Francisco river in western New Mexico.

Jim Wallace, sailing under the name of Tucker, stayed on the San Francisco river but Curley Bill, after resting awhile went west, and crossing the line entered Arizona where the New Mexico warrants were at that time of no service.

In the eastern part of the Cochise County, Arizona, lay the tough little mining camp of Galeyville, almost on the line between Arizona and New Mexico. A little to the west of Galeyville lay a hard little burg called Charleston. These two places were almost entirely inhabited by stage robbers, cattle thieves, and holdups. Peopled, as these two towns were, and situated within a day's ride of Old Mexico, they became ideal places for Curley Bill's future industries.

In those days there was no port of entry between El Paso, Texas and Nogales, Arizona, a distance of some four hundred miles, and the only Mexican Custom House—outside of these places—was on the San Pedro river, whose source is in Mexico and flows from there into the United States.

Cattle were plentiful and sheep in Mexico; there were few line riders so it was very easy for smugglers to cross the line from either direction. The Mexicans smuggled Mexican silver and dope into the United States, and then smuggled goods back into Mexico; the profits were large, as the duty on merchandise entering Mexico was very high, and so was the export duty on silver.

There were very few ranches at the time I speak of, along the Mexican border of Arizona and New Mexico. What few there were had not many cattle, and most of them were glad to be able to buy Mexican cattle whenever they could, and no questions asked.

A party of these Galeyville rustlers would make a raid into Mexico and bring their stock out through Guadalupe, Skeleton Canyon, and through the San Simon Valley, selling what they could along the route, and driving the balance across the State line into New Mexico where they were usually sold on the Blue and San Francisco rivers.

In the spring of 1881, Curley Bill, John Ringo, Old man Hughs, and his son Jim Hughs, and Joe Hill—who'd changed his name when he left Texas—Tom Norris, and several others brought a big stolen herd from Old Mexico, and sold them at San Carlos to the U.S. Government for beef for the Apache Indians and Troops stationed there.

Not long after this Curley Bill and John Ringo heard of a bunch of Mexicans who were crossing the border with a pack train of mules loaded with Mexican silver and headed for the Blue River of New Mexico. As the pack train entered Skeleton Canyon, Curley Bill and his gang waylaid and killed the Mexicans and stole the silver. It is said there was so much of it that it was buried in the Canyon, and has been hunted for by different parties ever since.

When Fred White had been elected Marshall of Tombstone, Curley Bill and some other rustlers went there for a celebration. Marshall White tried to arrest Curley and in the scuffle for possession of Curley's gun was shot. It so happened that Virgil Earp was with White when he was killed, and afterwards Curley

Bill surrendered to him. At Curley's trial, Earp stated that when Marshall White tried to take Curley's gun, he, Earp, threw his arms around Curley, and while White jerked the gun away from Curley it was accidentally discharged and killed White. Earp at this time was very friendly with the cowboys and rustlers, and was immediately appointed to succeed White as Marshall. After Curley's trial and acquittal he rode east and across the line into the Chiricahua Mountains in New Mexico where Elliott had a mining camp; this was some forty miles east of Galeyville and became quite a hide-out for the rustlers and holdup men both of New Mexico and Arizona.

After awhile Curley Bill again showed up in Galeyville. I quote the following from an old newspaper, the *Arizona Weekly Star* of May 26, 1881; the following notice was received from its correspondent in Galeyville.

The notorious Curley Bill, the man who murdered Marshall White at Tombstone last fall, and who has been concerned in several other desperate and lawless affrays, in southeastern Arizona and New Mexico arrived in town last night from Elliott's mining camp across the line in New Mexico, has at last been brought to grief, and there is likely to be a vacancy in the ranks of our Border Desperados. The affair occurred here at Galeyville last night.

A party of eight or nine cowboys, Curley Bill and his partner Jim Wallace, among the number, were in town enjoying themselves in their usual manner when deputy Sheriff Breckenridge of Tombstone, who was at Galeyville on business, happened along the street. Wallace made some insulting remark to the deputy, at the same time flourishing his revolver in an aggressive manner. The deputy did not pay much attention to this "break" of Wallace, but quietly turned around and left the party.

Shortly after this, Curley, who had a friendly feeling for Breckenridge, insisted that Wallace should go and find him and apologize for the insult given. This Wallace did, and the latter accompanied him back to the saloon where the boys were drinking. By now, Curley had drunk enough to make him quarrelsome, and was in one of his most dangerous moods, and evidently desirous of increasing the record as a man-killer.

He commenced to abuse Wallace who, by the way, had some pretensions himself as a bad and desperate man generally. Wallace went outside the door of the saloon where they were drinking, Curley Bill following close behind him. Just as the latter stepped outside Wallace, who meanwhile had drawn his revolver, fired. The ball penetrated the left side of Curley Bill's neck and passing through came out the right cheek, but not breaking the jawbone.

The other members of the cowboy party surrounded Wallace, and threats of lynching him were made by them. The law-abiding Citizens did not know what course to pursue. They did not wish any more bloodshed, but were in favor of allowing the lawless element to "have it out" among themselves.

But deputy Breckenridge decided to arrest Wallace, which he succeeded in doing without meeting any resistance. The prisoner was taken before Justice Ellenwood, and after examination into the facts of the shooting, he was discharged.

The wounded and apparently dying desperado was taken into an adjoining building, and a Doctor summoned to dress his wound.

After examining the course of the bullet, the Doctor pronounced the wound dangerous, but not necessarily fatal, the chances for and against recovery being about equal. Wallace and Curley Bill had been partners and friends and so far as is known there was no cause for the quarrel, it being simply a drunken brawl.

A great many people in southeastern Arizona and western New Mexico will regret that the termination was not fatal to one or both of the participants.

Although the wound is considered very dangerous, congratulations at being freed from this dangerous character are now rather premature, as men of this class usually have a wonderful tenacity of life.

The Earp party who were now on the dodge for killing Frank Stillwell, reported they had killed Curley Bill; but at the time they were supposed to have done so Curley was in Old Mexico and did not return until two months later. In confirmation of the fact that Curley had not been killed by the Earps, a reliable merchant and rancher living at Safford said that several weeks after the Earp party reported they had killed Curley Bill, Curley came to his home and said he had just got back from Mexico and he was leaving the country.

He said further that he was headed for Wyoming where he was going to get work and try and lead a decent life, as he was tired of being on the dodge all the time.

The merchant gave him a good saddle horse to ride away on.

A Mr. Vaughn living in Tombstone said that ten years later Curley Bill came through Benson on the train, bound for his old home in Texas, and stopped off long enough to visit the Post Master, whom he had known in his earlier days in New Mexico.

Another story is that after arriving in Wyoming he joined the Hole-in-the-Wall gang, and afterwards left for South America with Butch Cassidy—"quien sabe?"

The End

Elfego Baca carrying the gun he had stolen from Pancho Villa, for which Villa offered a reward of $30,000. Courtesy Palace of the Governors (MNM/DCA #087485)

Elfego Baca

by
N. Howard Thorp

In 1882 the rustlers in Texas, no-mans-land, and Indian Territory, "Now Oklahoma" became so bold and were stealing and robbing so constantly that the deputy U.S. Marshals in Indian Territory made a concerted effort to clean house.

Most of these desperate characters fled to Texas, where the Texas rangers killed many. Some got into Old Mexico, and a large portion came through with trail herds to western New Mexico, where some of them got work, and were the nucleus of what was known as the wild bunch. These were not fair representatives of Oklahoma and Texas people, but were the lower order of illiterates.

Their thought was that New Mexican natives were the same as the Peon class of Old Mexico, which of course was far from the truth, as many of the natives can trace their genealogy for generations back to the people of Spain, while in the majority of cases the Oklahomans and Texans, who came here with the herds, would have trouble knowing who their ancestors were for more than a generation or two past. These trail-hands' whole attitude was drive the Mexican out. It is a hard proposition to drive a man out of his own country, as many of these strangers found out.

Into this setting, at the age of nineteen, rode young Elfego Baca, late of the county seat of Socorro, New Mexico. Elfego— it being election year—had come to the San Francisco River soliciting votes at the different plazas for Socorro friends.

Don Pedro Simpson was at the time Sheriff of Socorro County, whose vote was about seventy-five percent Mexican. The fact that Pete Simpson was called Don Pedro immediately turned all newcomers against him.

At the time of Elfego Baca's arrival at the upper Plaza on the Frisco, a drunken cowboy named McCarthy, having filled up on Mr. Milligan's bad whiskey, was riding up and down the main street, recalling the fact that he was Citizen of the great Republic of Texas, and as the Alamo was in some way connected with Mexicans, gave vent to his feelings by shooting up the town.

Elfego Baca, who was a deputy Sheriff, seeing that the wild McCarthy was endangering people's lives, and the local authorities would take no action, proceeded to disarm the cowboy and place him under arrest.

Word soon went to his friends at the nearby ranches, and a mob rode into town determined to take McCarthy away from Baca and teach Baca a lesson.

There was no doubt concerning the outcome. Baca killed one of the mob, wounded another kept his prisoner, and drove the entire mob down the street, their haste being influenced by well directed shots, kicking up the dust behind them. The local Justice of the Peace—afraid of the Texans—refused to hold court. The desire of Baca and everyone was to try McCarthy on the spot and so avoid having to take him to the County seat of Socorro.

Eventually Baca brought his prisoner from the middle Plaza where he had taken him for safekeeping, a Justice of the Peace was found, and court opened. All the cowpunchers and saloon loafers following Baca and his prisoner, the courtroom was so crowded that not over half the people could enter. The verdict rendered was drunk and disorderly with a five dollar fine.

Elfego Baca was thoroughly disgusted with the court's decision and went down the street and entered a cabin, "presumably to rest."

Four men appeared on the scene who claimed they had an order from the presiding Justice to arrest Baca for shooting a man at the time of McCarthy's arrest.

The four men proceeded to the door of the cabin which Baca had entered. Hern, who was in the lead, knocked on the door and asked if anyone was inside. Getting no reply he kicked the door and hollered, "You blankety blank Mexican, let me in."

He got a reply; a bullet fired through the door took Hern in the stomach. Hern cursed, and falling backwards was dragged around the corner of the house.

Two of the four men were so badly frightened they fled; the one who dragged Hern out of danger laid him on the ground. A man known as Old Charley, hearing the shots, came galloping down the street and pulled up in front of the cabin door. He was shot at twice, both bullets passing through his peaked hat. Charley was leading a saddled horse belonging to an English ranchman named French.

After the two shots through his hat, Old Charley had business away from there, and at once, but the lead horse balked. French, seeing the trouble, ran and grabbed the reins of this horse, but in the excitement lost his hat, it falling off just in front of the cabin door. The deputy Dan now agreed with the mob that Baca should at once be arrested, but, personally, he had to have some sleep, as he explained he had been up the entire night before.

The Englishman, French, now determined to retrieve his hat and made a dash for it. While he was picking up, Baca fired three shots through the hat's brim, or "leaf" as French called it.

The mob got behind adobe walls and poured bullets into the jacal; still, whenever any of the mob showed a head or arm, he was met by a bullet from Baca. The attackers thought maybe the best way would be to take the cabin by assault, but this idea was given up.

Presently a lighted stick of dynamite was thrown, blowing off one room of the house, but fortunately for Baca, not the room he was in. From behind the adobe walls the mob were concealed, and kept up an incessant fire.

The little house was not of stone, logs, or adobe, but what is called a chosa, poles stood on ends and covered with mud. It had over one room a little gable roof with a small window in the end. Why Baca was not killed no one could imagine, for up to this time at least three thousand shots had been fired into the house, but that he was very much alive was shown whenever anyone showed themselves.

After a particularly fierce fusillade by the storming party, Baca's fire ceased, and one and all thought his measure had been taken.

Night coming on, sentries were posted to prevent his escape, and during the night Hern—the man who had been shot while demanding admittance to the cabin—died. During the night several of the sentries fell asleep on duty, and had Baca so desired, there was nothing to have prevented his walking out of the door and going where he pleased, though he probably was asleep.

Early the next morning, Mr. French, the Englishman, curious to know if Elfego was still in the cabin ran as fast as he could past the cabin door to the salute of Elfego's guns. French was now thoroughly satisfied that Baca was still alive.

While all this excitement was going on, several Mexicans made a hurried trip to Socorro to get help from the Officers.

All kinds of inducements were offered to Baca to surrender, in the most highfalutin Spanish, the mob not seeming to realize that Elfego could speak better English than the majority of them.

Presently the mob tried to set the house on fire, and threw blazing branches on the roof; but it being covered with a foot or so of dirt refused to burn.

The second day's sun was going down when a buggy containing three men drove up rapidly from the direction of Socorro. From the buggy stepped an American, Mr. Rose, who was a deputy Sheriff. He said he had come in response to a message from Elfego Baca, brought by the Mexicans who accompanied him. Now, Socorro is over a hundred and twenty-five miles from the plaza where the shooting had occurred; both the messenger and the Sheriff returning must have made fast time.

The local deputy, Dan, who had been drunk and asleep while all these events were occurring, was now very much in evidence, telling what he had done to enforce the law. Rose did not pay any attention to him, but asked questions from others regarding the affair. Dan was mad in being ignored, but returned to Mr. Milligan's for liquid consolation.

Mr. Rose now tried through the friend of Elfego, the Mexican who came with him, to communicate with Baca. After Baca recognized the Mexican's voice, he agreed to come out.

Baca said he would come out on the following conditions: everyone was to retire from in front of the house but Rose and the Mexican friend; he would then surrender to them. When these terms were acceded to, Elfego came out. Not through the door as expected, but through a little gable window in the end of the house.

Elfego was stripped to his pants and had a gun in each hand, glancing on each side as if afraid of some treachery. Elfego walked up to Mr. Rose, who disarmed him.

The deputy, Dan, still pretty drunk, now appeared and formally turned his prisoner over to Mr. Rose, thereby satisfying his injured dignity.

When asked, Baca explained he had escaped by lying on the floor, which was a foot or more below the level of the ground.

This fight of one man against a mob of over eighty, "As testified to in court during Baca's trial," was remarkable, holding out for over thirty-three hours, the honor certainly was with Elfego Baca, and even his worst enemies cannot but admit his nerve and bravery.

The End

The Manzano Gang
Interview with Elfego Baca

by
Janet Smith

"I never wanted to kill anybody," Elfego Baca told me, "but if a man had it in his mind to kill me, I made it my business to get him first."

Elfego Baca belongs to the six-shooter epoch of American history. Those were the days when hard-shooting Texas cowboys invaded the territory of New Mexico, driving their herds of longhorns over the sheep ranges of the New Mexicans, for whom they had little liking or respect. Differences were settled quickly, with few words and a gun. Those were the days of Billy the Kid, with whom Elfego, at the age of seventeen, made a tour of the gambling joints in Old Albuquerque. In the words of Kyle Crichton, who wrote Elfego Baca's biography, "The life of Elfego Baca makes Billy the Kid look like a piker." Harvey Fergusson calls him "a knight-errant" from the romantic point of view, if ever the six-shooter West produced one.

And yet Mr. Baca is not a man who lives in his past.

"I wonder what I can tell you," he said when I asked him for pioneer stories. "I don't remember so much about those things now. Why don't you read the book Mr. Crichton wrote about me?"

He searched about his desk and brought out two newspaper clippings of letters he had written recently to the Albuquerque Journal on local politics. The newspaper had deleted two of the more outspoken paragraphs. Mr. Baca was annoyed.

I tried to draw Mr. Baca away from present day politics to stories of his unusual past, but he does not talk readily about himself, although he seemed anxious to help me. Elfego Baca is a kindly courteous gentleman who is concerned to see that his visitor has the coolest spot in the room. He brought out books and articles that had been written about him, but he did not seem inclined to reminiscing and answered my questions briefly. "Crichton tells about that in his book" or "Yes, I knew Billy the Kid."

Finally I asked him at random if he knew anything about the famous old Manzano Gang which I had frequently seen mentioned in connection with Torrance County.

"There were ten of them," he said, "and I got nine. The only reason I didn't get the other one was that he got over the border and was shot before I got to him. They used to go to a place near Belen and empty the freight cars of grain and one thing and another. Finally they killed a man at La Jolla. Contreros was his name. A very rich man with lots of money in his house, all gold. I got them for that. They were all convicted and sent to the Pen."

Mr. Baca settled back in his chair and made some remark about the late Senator Cutting whose photograph stood on his desk.

I persisted about the Manzano Gang. "I wish you'd tell me more about that gang. How you got them, and the whole story."

"Well," he said, "after that man Contreros was shot, they called me up at my office in Socorro and told me that he was dying. I promised to get the murderers in forty-eight hours. That was my rule. Never any longer than forty-eight hours."

Mr. Baca suspected certain men, but when a telephone call to Albuquerque established the fact that they had been in that city at the time of the killing, his next thought was of the Manzano Gang.

Accompanied by two men, he started out on horseback in the direction of La Jolla.

Just as the sun was rising, they came to the ranch of Lazaro Cordova. They rode into the stable and found Cordova's son-in-law, Prancasio Saiz, already busy with his horse.

"Good-morning." said Elfego. "What are you doing with your horse so early in the morning?"

Saiz replied that he was merely brushing him down a little.

Mr. Baca walked over and placed his hand on the saddle. It was wet inside. The saddle blanket was steaming. He looked more closely at the horse. At first sight it had appeared to be a pinto, white with brown spots. Mr. Baca thought he remembered that Saiz rode a white horse.

"What happened to that horse?" he asked.

The man replied that the boys had had the horse out the day before and had painted the spots on him with a kind of berry that makes reddish-brown spots. "Just for a joke," he added.

"Where's your father-in-law?" asked Mr. Baca.

Saiz said that his father-in-law had gone the day before to a fiesta at La Jolla and had not returned.

"I understand you're a pretty good shot," said Sheriff Baca. "You'd better come along, and help me round up some men I'm after for the killing of Contreros in La Jolla."

Saiz said that he had work to do on the ranch, but at the

insistence of Mr. Baca he saddled his horse and rode out with the three men.

"About as far as from here to the station," went on Mr. Baca, "was a graveyard where the gang was supposed to camp out. I rode over to it and found where they had lunched the day before. There were sardine cans and cracker boxes and one thing and another. Then I found where one of them had had a call to nature. I told one of my men to put it in a can. Saiz didn't know about this, and in a little while he went over behind some mesquite bushes and had a call to nature. After he came back I sent my man over, and by God it was the same stuff—the same beans and red chile seeds! So I put Saiz under arrest and sent him back to the jail at Socorro with one of my deputies, although he kept saying he couldn't see what I was arresting him for."

Mr. Baca and his other deputy proceeded in the direction of La Jolla. Before long they saw a man on horseback coming toward them.

"He was running that horse like everything. When we met I saw that he was a Texan. Doc Something or other was his name. I can't remember now, but he was a pretty tough man."

"You a Sheriff?" he said to Mr. Baca.

"No," replied Mr. Baca, "no, I'm not a Sheriff. Don't have nothing to do with the law, in fact."

"You're pretty heavily armed," remarked the man suspiciously.

"I generally arm myself this way when I go for a trip in the country," answered Baca, displaying his field glasses. "I think it's safe."

"Well, if you want fresh horses, you can get them at my ranch, a piece down the road," said the Texan.

Mr. Baca figured that this was an attempt to throw him off the trail, so as soon as the Texan was out of sight, he struck out east over the Mountains for Manzano. Just as he was entering the village he saw two of the gang coming down the hill afoot leading their horses. He placed them under arrest and sent them back to Socorro with his other deputy.

It was about two o'clock in the morning when Mr. Baca passed the Cordova Ranch again on his way back. He roused Lazaro Cordova, who had returned from La Jolla by that time, and told him to dress and come with him to Socorro.

"The old man didn't want to come," said Mr. Baca, "and kept asking 'what you want with me anyhow?' I told him that he was under arrest and on the way to Socorro I told him that unless he and his son-in-law came across with a complete statement about the whole gang, I would hang both of them, for I had the goods on them and knew all right that they were both in on the killing of Contreros.

I put him in the same cell with his son-in-law, and told him it was up to him to bring Saiz around. They came through with the statement. I kept on catching the rest of the gang, until I had them all. All but the one who got himself shot before I caught up with him.

"If you ever go to Socorro you ask Billy Newcomb, the Sheriff down there now, to show you the records. You might see the place on the way down where they buried a cowboy I shot. It's a little way off the main road though.

"That was a long time before I was a real Sheriff. In those days I was a self-made deputy. I had a badge I made for myself, and if they didn't believe I was a deputy, they'd better believe it, because I made 'em believe it.

"I had gone to Escondida a little way from Socorro to visit my uncle. A couple of Texas cowboys had been shooting up the town of Socorro. They hadn't hurt anybody that time. Only frightened some girls. That's the way they did in those days—ride through a town shooting at dogs and cats and if somebody happened to get in the way—powie!—too bad for him. The Sheriff came to Escondida after them. By that time they were making a couple of Mexicans dance, shooting up the ground around their feet. The Sheriff said to me, 'Baca, if you want to help, come along, but there's going to be shooting.'

"We rode after them and I shot one of them about three hundred yards away. The other got away—too many cottonwood trees in the way.

"Somebody asked me what that cowboy's name was. I said I didn't know. He wasn't able to tell me by the time I caught up with him."

I asked what the Sheriff's name was, and when Mr. Baca said it was Pete Simpson, I said, "The one you were electioneering for the time of the Frisco affair when you held off about 80 cowboys for over 36 hours." This is the one of Mr. Baca's exploits that has been most frequently written about.

"Hell, I wasn't electioneering for him," he said. "I don't know where they got that idea. I couldn't have made a speech to save my life. And I didn't wear a Prince Albert coat either. They didn't have such things in this country in those days."

"Is it true that you ate dinner afterward with French and some other men who had been shooting at you, and talked the affair over?" I asked.

"I ate dinner with some men afterward but I don't remember who they were now. I don't think that man French was there at all, although he must have been in the neighborhood, as he seemed to know all about it. But I don't remember him. Jim Cook was one that was shooting at me though. He was a pretty tough man, but he came near getting it."

He showed me a photograph which Jim Cook had sent him recently. The picture showed an old man who still looks as though he could not be easily trifled with. It was inscribed, "To Elfego Baca in memory of that day at Frisco."

"Did you see the letter that Englishman wrote to Crichton? He wanted to hang me. 'Why don't you hang that little Mexican so-and-so?' he asked. I said, 'Why don't you be the one to do it?' and pulled my guns, and whoa, he wasn't so eager. You know I surrendered only on condition that I keep my guns. They placed six guards over me, but they rode 25 steps ahead of me all the way to Socorro.

"Those were great old days. Everything is very quiet now, isn't it?" said Mr. Baca looking up. "I think I'll run for something this fall, but I don't know what yet."

A Southern Pacific Locomotive 28, ca. 1888, Courtesy Palace of the
Governors (MNM/DCA #14915)

Mrs. W. C. Totty
Box 677
Silver City, N.M.

Date: July 29, 1937
Words: 225

The First Train
Robbery of the Southern Pacific

In 1881 when the trains first came through here we had two passenger
trains, a day, one going East and one going West. The trains numbers were
nineteen and twenty.

One day No. 19 came through going East with Frank Webster as engineer.
At Gage four white men and a negro boarded the train, held up and robbed all
the passengers after killing Webster and the fireman.

The men were later arrested and lodged in jail at Silver City.

Shortly afterwards they escaped from jail. Three were killed in the effort
to recapture them, the other two were sent to the penitentary.

Information: B.B. Ounby.

Facsimile: "The First Train Robbery of the Southern Pacific," Mrs. W.C.
Totty, July 29, 1937, NMFWP, WPA #87, NMSRCA

The Gage Train Robbery

by
Betty Reich

In December of the year 1883, there was a train robbery on the Southern Pacific at a wayside station named Gage. The engineer was killed and the express car looted by masked robbers. The Wells Fargo people vowed revenge. At that time there was a famous Sheriff Whitehill at Silver City. Nine years he had held office and then retired. Though no longer in office, he was engaged by the company to get the criminals. The train crew could furnish just one clue. Back of the mask, one of the faces, they noted, was that of a Negro. And Negroes were few in the Southwest. A search of the ground revealed a newspaper caught from the wind by the thorns of a mesquite bush. It bore the name of a Silver City merchant. On being questioned, the merchant was able to recall wrapping it round a parcel for a cowboy cook from the L-C Ranch. Then among the hands on the great Lyons-Campbell domain, it was remembered that there had been such a one, George Washington, a Negro. Step number one! But Washington had left the country.

At Socorro he was found. Coming to the well to draw water, he was taken in swift surprise as the sheriff's persuader was pressed against his ribs. "You are the man who killed the engineer."

The ruse worked. "No! No! No! Mr. Whitehill, it wasn't me. Mitch Lee killed the engineer."

Duped into believing that his partners were all in jail, the Negro made full confession. The robbery was planned by Mitch Lee, and carried out by him with the aid of Frank Taggart, Kit Joy and the cook. All belonged to the L-C outfit. Taggart was trailed over into Arizona and captured. Lee and Joy had also gone across the line and were found hiding out at a lonely ranch house along the Frisco River. When the man hunt ended, Mr. Whitehill's four desperadoes were locked safely inside the old adobe jail in Silver City.

While awaiting trial, they were allowed to exercise in the jail yard. Dick Ware was guard. For some unholy reason, his prisoners were obsessed with a desire to play under the gallows. There, where Dick Remine and "Parson" Young had recently come to the end of the rope, they would climb upon the scaffold and hold broad-jump contests. One morning Lee and Taggart got into an argument over the tracks and appealed to Ware to settle the matter. As the guard bent over, Lee leaped upon his neck and overpowered him, while Taggart took his gun and keys. Marching Ware ahead of them, they captured the night watchman who was then asleep, and locked both men in a cell. Taking all guns from the jail office, they unlocked the other prisoners. One Mexican boy and one white boy went with them, the others staying behind.

At the Elephant Corral, a livery stable, they took horses—all the horses—and paraded down Main Street, shooting up the town as they rode with wild yells for the Pinos Altos Mountains. Only a short ride distant lay Cherry Canyon and the roughest kind of country, where pursuit would be difficult and capture more than improbable.

One man watched them. He was driving a wagon, and quickly unhitching his horse, he followed them at a safe distance until sure of their intention. Then riding back to town, he informed the citizen's posse, which was already forming. But the robbers did not reach the mountains. It was on the rolling slopes near the location of the present cemetery that they made their stand.

The first to fall was George Washington, cleanly drilled between the eyes. Next a bullet took off the top of the Mexican's head. Lee and Taggart, seeing that flight was impossible, abandoned their horses and hid among the scrubby junipers. Joy was already lying in a shallow wash behind some bushes. Through a winter's day the shooting continued. Lee, shot through the abdomen, lay mortally wounded, and Taggart with all his ammunition gone, at length surrendered. Joy, after killing a citizen named Joe Le Fur, escaped. The white boy surrendered. When the dead and wounded were loaded on a wagon to be brought to town, someone suggested a hanging. The suggestion was taken up with much alacrity. Instantly ropes appeared, and soon necks were inside nooses. The wagon was driven under a bough, and paused while the rope was thrown over. The wagon went on. Booted legs struggled a while in mid-air, and then hung still. What Bret Harte called the "weak and foolish deed" was done. The outlaws had died with their boots on, and not ingloriously. It was a fine day's work. And it helped to establish a tradition.

The white boy, when captured, made no resistance. Innocently tendering his gun to the officers, he showed them that he had not fired a shot with it. Thus he beat the noose. It was not until later that they discovered that the mechanism had jammed on the first attempt!

As told by Ross Calvin in "Sky Determines."

Villa Raid

by
Betty Reich

When Francisco (Pancho) Villa raided Columbus, New Mexico, March 9, 1916, it was a prosperous little town (3 miles north of the Mexican border in Luna County) that had a wide trade territory.

During the raid the Ravel Hotel was burned. This hotel was operated by a Mr. W.P. Ritchie. Mr. Ritchie was killed and his body was badly burned. There was also an unidentified man killed in the hotel. He was registered in the hotel register but the register burned and no one knew who he was. Mr. Ritchie's daughter, Edna, was the only person beside himself that knew the combination of the safe. She was so frightened that she could not open it. The Mexicans took Mrs. Ritchie's rings. A Mexican boy that she judged to be about twelve years old held a gun in her ribs and shouted, pronto, pronto! while other Villistas beat her on the hands with the butts of their guns because she could not get her rings off quick enough. After the raid she got her rings back by mail but she never knew who sent them or their history after they were stolen.

The Mexicans were searching for Sam Ravel, a merchant of Columbus, with whom, it was reported, Villa had unsatisfactory business dealings. They did not find him for he was in El Paso but they did find his younger brother, Arthur, in town. As two of Villa's men were escorting him down the street—one on each side of him—they were shot by Americans and young Ravel escaped. Some people say that he ran all the way to a ranch several miles from town; others say that he hid under a pile of hides.

A.D. Frost, who operated a hardware store in Columbus, left his home with his wife and baby during the raid. They did not take time to dress but went in their night clothes. They went out the back way and were not seen by the Mexicans until they started their car, then they became a target for the raiders. Mr. Frost, who was driving, headed for Deming. In a few minutes he slumped over in the seat and was not able to drive. Mrs. Frost got out and pushed him into the other seat and drove into Deming. It was found that he had been shot in the shoulder and three bullet holes were found in the back of the driver's seat.

The Paige family hid in an outhouse during the raid. Three times the Mexicans set fire to their house and each time Mr. Paige put the fire out as soon as the Mexicans had left. Eighty bullet holes were found in their piano. There were some portraits hanging on the walls that Mrs. Paige had painted. The Mexicans shot around the faces of these until the faces fell out.

Mrs. Garnett Parks was the telephone operator at Columbus. She stayed at her post with her baby between her knees and phoned Deming for aid, which did not get there in time to be of much assistance. Both she and the baby were cut by flying glass but neither one was shot.

Juan Favela was the man that warned Columbus of Villa's approach. He was at that time, and still is, an employee of the Palomas Land and Cattle Company—a cattle company south of Columbus in Mexico. He rode a horse to death bringing the news to the army headquarters in Columbus.

Few persons in the town were aware of the approach of Villa. However, they knew that Villa was in the vicinity and there had been many rumors but the residents felt secure with the 13th Cavalry guarding the border and the town.

After the raid more than 60 Mexican bodies were found in Columbus. These were taken east of town, oil was poured over them and they were burned. Almost every house in town had bullet holes in it.

Within a short time there were 15 or 20 thousand American soldiers stationed at Columbus, business had increased rapidly and the population had grown accordingly. Today, Columbus is a very small village with very little sign of its former prosperity.

As told by Mr. and Mrs. A.J. Evans, Jesse Fuller and L.L. Burkhead.

Villa's Buried Treasure

by
Betty Reich

lmost everyone knows the story of Pancho Villa, the Robin Hood of Mexico.

An assassin's bullet ended his career in Parral, Chihuahua, Mexico, on July 20, 1923. There have been many tall tales told about the notorious bandit, many of which are almost pure fiction. For instance, there is the buried treasure story. This yarn has sent many people into the hills looking for loot that Villa and his men were supposed to have cached for a rainy day.

Narrators of the treasure stories have overlooked the fact that the Villa revolution was a brother act. The second member of this partnership affair was Hipolito Villa, Pancho's younger brother.

Hipolito is living, and if buried treasure was scattered about he would be out with a pick and shovel now. For Hipolito needs money for living expenses, just like everyone. That's why he is working at the unromantic job of assistant agent of the federal forestry office in Chihuahua City, Mexico.

Hipolito Villa still owns Rancho Fresno, 15 miles west of Chihuahua City. He retired to this ranch after his last uprising in 1924, when he gave the federal government some uncomfortable moments by taking up arms to avenge the assassination of Pancho.

Hipolito was known as a dangerous man during revolutionary days. In later years he has been so meek that he has just about faded out of the picture. That explains why persons who sell maps showing the location of Pancho's buried treasure make the mistake of over-looking the fact that one of the Villa partners is still alive.

The only buried treasure that persons close to Hipolito say they know about is the $258,000 he put in the first paving and sewer system Juarez (Chihuahua, Mex.) ever had. He took that money from the Juarez gambling concession to improve the city.

Hipolito never took graft and he was not a robber, his old followers declare. They say that when the Villa government collapsed, Hipolito took $36,000 that came from the gambling hall and went to Havana in December 1915. It wasn't long before he was broke. Now he is working at a white collar job and wishing those buried treasure stories were true.

As told by John Casey.

When Villa Raided the Town of Columbus

by
Betty Reich

When Villa raided the town of Columbus, March 9, 1916, he stationed his machine gunners on a small hill, which has since been known as Villa Hill, about 300 yards southwest of the business district of Columbus and west of the army camp. The 13th Cavalry was stationed at Columbus to protect about 65 miles of the border, as affairs in Mexico were very unsettled.

At that time Mr. A.J. Evans, owner of the Ford garage, lived with his wife and four children in a small house at the foot of this hill on the east side.

On the night of March 9, Mr. Evans was awakened by the sound of men going past his house. He looked out of his window and saw Mexicans passing in a stooping position. They were so close that he could have reached out and touched them. In just a few minutes he heard some of them run into a wire fence. Mr.

Evans awakened his wife and whispered to her not to scream but that there were Mexicans all around them. About that time the first shot was fired and then no one would have heard her if she had screamed because every Mexican in Villa's band began shooting and shouting, "Viva Villa! Viva Mexico!" The machine gunners on the hill began shooting over their house into the army camp. They were aiming at the place where they knew the army guns were locked up for the night.

A good many bullets went through the roof of their house but only one went through the house below the ceiling. This was a soft-nosed bullet used by the Mexicans, which entered the south wall and did a great deal of damage to the house but hurt no one. The Evans had a Ford car in their garage in the yard but they knew they would be shot before they could reach it.

They were more afraid of American bullets than they were of the Mexican bullets, because they knew the Americans had better ammunition. The whole family—the oldest child was nine and the baby was six months old—got down on the floor on the west side of the house (next to the Mexicans) and stood a mattress up between them and the American bullets. It was very cold and they were dressed only in their night clothes. Mrs. Evans knew where the children's shoes were and she got these in the dark and put them on them so they would be ready to leave the house if they got a chance.

No one entered their house. None of the doors were locked, just the screens were fastened; once they heard someone rattle one of the screens but no other effort was made to enter the house.

From the empty cartridges on the ground it appeared that some of the Mexicans had shot around the corner of their house at the Americans.

Every time there was a lull in the shooting they could hear a Mexican somewhere nearby playing a violin.

When the Mexicans set fire to some of the buildings in the business district it became as light as day in their house and one of the children whispered to their mother to put out the light. The children had been told to keep quiet when they were awakened.

The family was afraid to look out of the windows lest they attract the attention of the enemy. However, about daylight they gathered courage enough to look out and they saw American soldiers pass and capture the hill.

After the raid the American flag was placed on this hill and it was guarded by soldiers.

As told by Mr. and Mrs. A.J. Evans.

Description of a Military Reservation
Columbus Military Reservation

by
Mrs. Mildred Jordan

"Viva, Villa!"

"Down with the Americans!"

With these shouts a revolution crazed band of several hundred Villistas sneaked across the border onto the little town of Columbus back in March 1916, and by daybreak sixteen Americans and nearly one hundred bandits had been killed.

Ever since that bloody night there has been a fierce debate back and forth about whether Pancho Villa himself took part in the raid.

Some say yes, some say no. It is said that Villa led the raid but that he actually operated a machine gun on the main streets of Columbus. Investigation showed Villa was responsible for the raid. One woman who had been held prisoner by Villistas was saying that he planned to wipe out the Americans and would raid Columbus.

It was reported Villa was riding a big horse, the only man in the raiding party who did have a big horse. Footprints of a big horse were found and there were reports from persons who thought they saw Villa, but no proof.

Charles DeWitt Miller of Albuquerque killed, W.F. Murphy riddled with bullets. Jolly Garner, brother to the Vice President, John Garner and Ben Aguirre, Mexican border officers, were sleeping in a hotel the night they raided Columbus. They were in the thick of the battle.

Dawn found the streets of Columbus strewn with dead and wounded. The dead Villistas were hauled outside of town, where a great funeral pyre was built. The bodies were burned, making a gruesome bonfire. Columbus feared a raid, yet was not prepared for it when it came.

At the present time the town remains a quaint little Western town, located on the sandy plains near the Mexican border about four miles from Las Palomas, Mexico. Border officers are still located in the little town. There are many old ruins of buildings, some with walls partly standing while only the floors remain of other buildings. The country surrounding the town is of sandy plains and barren mountains, very little vegetation.

As told by Mrs. J.J. Burr.

PROCLAMATION $5,000⁰⁰ REWARD

FRANCISCO (PANCHO) VILLA

ALSO $1,000. REWARD FOR ARREST OF CANDELARIO CERVANTES, PABLO LOPEZ, FRANCISCO BELTRAN, MARTIN LOPEZ

ANY INFORMATION LEADING TO HIS APPREHENSION WILL BE REWARDED.

CHIEF OF POLICE
Columbus
New Mexico

MARCH 9, 1916

Facsimile: "Proclamation $5000.000 Reward Francisco (Pancho) Villa," (poster) March 9, 1916, History file #26 Pancho Villa Raid, NMSRCA

Pancho Villa, Famous Mexican Chieftan and his staff, Courtesy Palace of the Governors (MNM/DCA #185038)

Betty Reich
Dist. # 4
Deming, New Mexico
April 30, 1937

Villa's Raid on Columbus

262 words

Mr. L.L. Burkhead of Columbus, New Mexico (3 miles north of the international border line between the United States and Mexico on State Road No. 11) who was postmaster at Columbus in 1916 at the time of the Villa raid had an interesting souvenir made of this event. It is a metal watch fob in the shape of the state of New Mexico. On one side is a map of New Mexico with a star marking the location of Columbus and with the words:

> Souvenir of
> Villa Raid
> on
> Columbus N.M.
> March 9th
> 1916

On the other side are the words, "9 citizens & 7 soldiers of 13th cavalry killed Town looted & burned Raiders driven into Mexico after 2 hr. fight leaving more than 80 dead."

There were several thousand of the watch fobs made but there are very few left in this part of the country.

SOURCE OF INFORMATION:

L.L. Burkhead
Columbus, New Mexico

Incidents of the Early Southwest

by
Mrs. W. C. Totty

In 1882 a large smuggling train consisting of five mules loaded with stolen silver and gold from Dog Springs, New Mexico, came through what is called the San Louis Pass. They crossed the Animas which is located in the southern end of Hidalgo County (then a part of Grant County) and came through to Skeleton Canyon.

During the night two Rustlers known as Billie Grounds and Dick Hunt came upon them, and killed all of the men, and took the gold and silver.

One of the mules got away which was never found. There was something like ninety thousand pesos in all of the gold and silver.

Billie Grounds and Dick Hunt hid the silver in one place and put the gold in behind some ledges. For some time after the robbery neither of the men was heard of.

In 1884 Verge Butcher of Duncan, Arizona, who was a brother to Billie Grounds, came to see me and asked if I would go with him to Skeleton Canyon in search of the money.

In those days finder was keeper so naturally I was anxious to go. We looked for many days, but never found a thing.

Many people have looked since, but no money has ever been discovered. I believe the money was removed from Skeleton Canyon as I later read a letter from Billie at El Paso, his mother at home, wherein he gave her the location as: "I'm sitting on top of Look Out Mt. I can see the Organs, Cooks Back, Tres Hermanos, and the Floridas. I also can see the smoke from the Smelter. This money, Mother, is buried North West of El Paso."

To this day the money has never been found, but people still search Skeleton Canyon in hopes of unearthing the treasure.

Related by B.B. Ounby, Lordsburg, New Mexico.

Billie the Kid
Interview: Louis Abraham of Silver City

by
Mrs. Frances Totty

Mrs. Bill Antrim was a jolly Irish lady, full of life, and her fun and mischief. Mrs. Antrim could dance the Highland Fling as well as the best of the dancers.

There were very few American boys in Silver City when the Antrims lived here, therefore the few American boys that were here ran together all of the time. The Antrim house was the place where the boys gathered most of the time.

Mrs. Antrim always welcomed the boys with a smile and a joke. The cookie jar was never empty to the boys. From school each afternoon we made straight for the Antrim home to play.

My mother was dead, and my father had a Spanish woman for a cook, her food never tasted as good as the meals that Mrs. Antrim cooked. I ate many meals in the home of Billie the Kid and I know that I was welcome.

Mrs. Antrim was as good as she could be, and she made every

one welcome in her home. When she died in 1873, she was buried in the City Cemetery. There was not a hearse in Silver City then so my father's Surrey was used to carry the body to the cemetery.

Billie and I as well soon learned we had lost a dear ally and friend, as well as his mother. A cousin of Mrs. Antrim came back from the East a few years ago and placed a monument at her grave.

I have often been thankful that she never had to know of the trouble Billie became involved in for it would have broken her heart. How thankful I am to know that that good woman never had to face that heartache.

Billie's home was an ordinary good American home. Good parents, and a good environment in the home. Billie's father came to Georgetown and settled. There he died.

Mr. Antrim, Billie's stepfather, was a mining man at Georgetown. Billie Bonney's mother married Mr. Antrim and the family moved to Silver City in 1870. Here Billie lived until he was arrested by Sheriff Whitehill.

The story of Billie the Kid killing a blacksmith in Silver City is false. Billie never was in any trouble at all, he was a good boy, maybe a little more mischievous at times than the rest of us with a little more nerve.

When the boy was placed in jail and escaped he was not bad, he was just scared. If he had only waited until they let him out he would have been alright, but he was scared and he ran away.

He got in with a band of rustlers at Apache Tejo in the part of the county where he was made a hardened character.

Ed Moulton, a miner and friend of Mr. Antrim, was like a father to Billie, for he had known the family for a long time and was in their home but Billie never did kill anyone over Mr. A. Moulton.

Mr. Antrim was a man of good character, and was highly

respected here until his death. Joe Bonney, Billie's brother, left here and was thought well of until he turned gambler, and went to his death in Colorado with his boots on. These two boys of a good and happy family, good boys when they were youngsters came to a tragic end for what reason no one knows.

Narrated by Louis Abraham.

Devil Dick's Career and His Ignominious End

by
Frances E. Totty

"As the Santa Rita train rolled into the little junction point and cow town of White Water, New Mexico, I arose and got together my traps, glad of the chance to stretch my legs and fill my lungs with the freshest and finest of fresh air on the earth. Besides the water tank, station and section houses, there was nothing but the small unimportant general store and post office and a few condemned boxcars converted into dwellings for the section hands and their numerous families. I inquired of a fellow traveler who appeared to be familiar with the country if I might purchase cigars at the emporium across the way and was informed that practically everything was to be had there, from needles to dynamite, as well as any information about the country I might desire, the proprietor-postmaster and justice of peace being a well-informed party, indeed.

"Having purchased what had the general appearance, but

which in no other way resembled cigars, from this man of many titles, I stopped to note a couple of dispirited cowponies with dusty flanks and business-like accoutrements. Having exhausted all possibilities of interest in the general store, I started back to the shady side of the depot, as the only other loafing place of interest.

"While the train from Chino Copper Mining Company camp was loading its daily transfer of mail, express, etc., my attention was attracted to a party of eastern people who were getting into a ranch wagon: evidently a house party from some nearby ranch. The party was in high spirits and appeared to be expecting a good time. One of its members, an extremely tall and leisurely young man especially attracted my attention, as well as that of a couple of booted and chapped cowboys, like myself, resting in the only shady spot available. The older man was a little dried up native with the looks of a lifetime in the saddle on the open range. The other, a younger man, very red headed, was evidently very amused, like myself, by the appearance of the tall member of the ranch house party. Finally, their supplies and baggage being loaded the wagon drove off and simultaneously the train of Silver City departed, leaving the station almost deserted save for a few other passengers waiting the departure of our train for the camps.

"As there was still some time to wait I became interested in the conversation of the older cowpuncher whom Red Head called 'Doc.' He was evidently in a reminiscent humor. I interrupted him long enough to offer cigars, which they took without comment and which I accepted was permission to remain to listen. Doc continued: 'This Devil Dick I was telling you about was before your day, Red. Nobody ever heard his real name, but he was well known all over this country and Arizona. Man he was some bad hombre and when he was aroused by liquor the tall timbers was a popular resort for most everybody, I tell you. He come into this country when I was a kid with my first pair of chaps and us young fellows rode mighty quiet in the vicinity, and the older ones too, for he had a record for holdups, murders, and such like before he came and it shore kept accumulating right along. There wasn't many Sunday School prize winners here then, neither. He just about run things to suit himself, I tell you. He never wore a glove on either hand and always pulled both guns at the same time and when he pulled they generally went off simultaneously and someone fed the graveyard right now. He was some pest while his desire lasted and his demise was shorely looked for a heap.

"'It was so sudden when it happened and the last man you'd a thought of was the man that pulled it off. That tall dude here awhile ago reminded me of the fellow. He was a long lanky hombre and when the stage dropped him off in Old Town in front of Ike's saloon and hotel we was free in our remarks, eastern dudes being so scarce in them times out here. He hung around a few days, a sort of quiet and harmless fellow and nobody even thought of him again except to make fun of the way he moved around, sorta like a turtle for his longness—and they got to calling him 'Hurry up Harry.' After a while he wandered off into the hills with a dinky, little double barreled shotgun, eastern clothes and all. Said he was out here for his health and so we'd forget him only when he rode in from his camp for supplies.

"'Old man Hopkins lived over the river and his gal, Sally, taught all the schools there for many years—and what she learned them roughneck kids must have been some doings, for she didn't have sense to come in from the rain and all the boys called her 'Silly Sally' behind her back. She shore had some giggle. Ike had a little fellow tending bar for him, with some kind of foreign sounding name, French or Irish or something. The best we could make of it was 'Sklip' so we called him 'Shorty Sklip.' He got beau-ing Sally around considerably and he never had much competition, neither. One day he hooked up Ike's old scarecrow ring-tailed team and he and Sally started for Hot Springs meaning to stay for a dance that night. Me and the puncher was riding that night and heard what happened. Shorty and Sally stopped at Dobe Mex's booze joint on the Deming road. Sally said she wanted a drink of water, but Shorty told me afterward that she took some beer that he ordered and he orter remember because it was $2 a bottle, when they had it, which wasn't often.

"'Maybe that was what caused the trouble. Anyway Dare Devil Dick come smiling along and he sees Sally drink and begins hollering for beer before he quits his bronc. Dobie Mex says he ain't got any beer and Dick gets to singing and says he will split the bottle with Sally and have a kiss for good measure. Lem McCloud, wagon boss for Diamond P's and some more punchers were sitting around. Them fellows weren't anxious to mix with Dick no how, but the play come up to strong, for Sally was a good little girl and hadn't no bad habits, except giggling and going with Shorty Sklip. Lem and the boys had their guns on Dick no sooner than he'd leaned toward Sally. I guess Dick thought that he had this country gentled to eat out of his hands, but he overlooked Lem's crowd and he hadn't pulled any woman stuff before. Anyway Lem and his bunch kept him covered until he got out of sight and they'd took all the medicine out of his guns likewise.

"'He made some remarks, when he was going, about the details of Lem's funeral which we all believed was shore prophesizing, including Lem for he was so nervous that night at the dance. But Dick never showed up that night and we never heard of him again for weeks, barin' a holdup over near Silver City about two days afterward that had all the earmarks of his doing that kind of a job. Dick was wanted all right but the wanting wasn't confined to any one party, Sheriff or otherwise, that is bad enough for them to express that want to Dick, personally.

"'Anyhow things was quiet and we got used to seeing Lem in

real life same as usual, when the big thing was pulled off and Sally was in it again.

"'She sure was a bad omen in Devil Dick's horoscope, all right. She and Shorty and Long Dave Brown drove by the Diamond P's one day on their way home from some frolic; Lem threw his saddle on the rig and got in, meanin' to spend the night at Old Town and bring a bronc back to the ranch. It played out on him the last time he was in town and he borrowed a horse and turned it loose at the ranch. Well they got to the Picture Rocks where the trail turns down toward the river and first thing they knew they were close enough to read the V. C. brand on Devil Dick's big bay horse and both of his guns were weaving fancy pictures in the atmosphere they were reaching for with all hands aloft. And say Dick was figurin' on startin' a brand new graveyard with Baldy and Shorty and Lem and Long Tom throwed in as head stones. He'd gave poor Sally some scare about her future prospects too, for she keeled over in a dead faint. Pronto—and then is when it happened. Somebody coughed that wasn't in the original party and at that particular moment curiosity was shore justified, coming as a change from them prognostications of sudden death and destruction of Devil Dick's. Anyway all eyes, including Devil Dick's, turned toward the sound immediately. There was a big boulder about ten feet from the trail and just up the slope and 'Hurry Harry' and his shotgun was laying across it and pointed to the place that it would do the most good to save the situation. And man it was shore some welcome sight. That long gent was appearing over the rock like a full moon over the mountain on a dark night and when he got unlimbered and stood at his full height his shoulders were just about in line with Dick's head and him sitting horseback. And that was just as steady as that rock it was setting on. What the eastern gent was doing at that particular spot is hard to figure out, and that question wasn't agitating the other part of the public much then. Nobody ever thought to ask him about it. Suppose he was just ambling about his usual way—sort of an instrument of God, I reckon. But when Devil Dick saw him, a sort of puzzled look came over his face as though he had seen him before, and then sudden he wilted and his face got greenish white and his hands and arms trembled so he could hardly hold them up. He shore looked like he was seeing a ghost. As it turned out I reckon he thought that he was.

"'It seemed like he'd held up a stage a year before over near Tucson, and being so close to civilization he wasn't taken no chance on anybody identifying the holdup and so he just shot up the whole bunch and this Harry's young brother was one of the victims. Harry got his through the right lung, but come to after some time and managed to crawl and drag himself about five miles to a Mexican's shack and they nursed him back in shape to travel. He got them to keep quiet about him being in the holdup and he'd been roaming around the country hoping to get a chance at the fellow that got his buddy. And he shore never wasted no opportunity. Lem was a deputy, although that wouldn't have made no difference at the time. But it made it all seem regular and lawful like, for they hanged Devil Dick to a juniper tree that looked like was shore growed there for that purpose. Long Dave said that the reward was for Dick dead or alive and he reckoned he'd be easier to take back dead as the hack was so crowded, anyway. And shooting was too good for that varmint. Harry wouldn't take any of the reward so they split it amongst them, and Sally got a silk dress for her wedding and some more women fixings with her share. Sent all the way to Santa Fe for it. NO, she didn't marry Shorty. A fellow from Texas got her and she left with him. Never come back no more.'

"Just at this moment the conductor shouted 'all aboard,' and I made a rush for my train and didn't get a chance to thank the old cowpuncher for the entertainment. But his story filled my mind all the way to the camps and the bare hills took on a new interest and appearance.

"I thought of the many untold happenings and tragedies that have taken place on the rugged trails in this land of eye for eye and tooth for tooth."

From Malcolm Macleod. Printed in the Silver City Independent, June 22, 1915.

Early Days in the Southwest

by
Frances E. Totty

My people came to the Mesilla Valley in the early days. They lived at Fort Seldon when they first came to the valley. They had a meat market and ran the ferry across the river. We stayed at the fort a short time then moved to Mesilla or the present Old Mesilla.

In 1873 the worst cold spell came to the Mesilla Valley that was ever known in history; there has never been such a spell since in the valley. The stock froze; grapevines that had been in the valley for more than a hundred years were killed. My father didn't sell any meat for days and days as he couldn't cut it, as after a beef was killed it froze so hard a knife was of no use whatever.

Many of the families decided to leave the Mesilla Valley and go to Las Mimbres. Some twelve families left Old Mesilla in their *carritos*, which were two-wheeled carts, the only mode of travel that the people had at that time. The party settled on the Mimbres River at the present site of Old Town, thirty-five miles northeast of Silver City beyond Faywood Hotsprings.

The families cleared off plots of ground for cultivation. They were making a success of farming and rejoicing that they had come to the Mimbres Rio. The Apaches were waiting for the time to get some good horses and to slaughter their unexpecting victims. Victorio, deciding that his tribe needed some new mounts, raided the colony drove off all the cattle and horses and killed every member of the settlement. Old Town for some time was vacant, but later other settlers came into town.

News soon reached the small town of Mesilla of the disaster that had befallen their relatives and friends. There were many who had planned on going to the Mimbres, still in Mesilla, that were rejoicing that they were still alive, and many were sorrowing for those that were gone.

My father in 1876 decided to come to this district of the southwest; he settled at "Bras Springs," the present Burro Springs, so called by the Spanish people because the black tail deer came to the springs for water.

When we came here there wasn't any Lordsburg or Deming. Silver City was a small village of around two hundred people, and Ralston, the present Shakespeare, was a stopping place. Burro Springs was the only water in the immediate territory, and was a stopping place for man, beast, and the devil himself on his way to Mogollons. We sold water, food supplies, mining supplies, and kept rooms for the travelers.

We looked on the desperado type as protection in those days. Curly Bill and other such characters were always welcome to such outlying places as when these men were staying at the place we never expected any trouble and we felt that we were safe from the Indians, for the Indians respected these supposed to be gunmen.

Curly Bill was a handsome man; his reputation might have been bad, but he had his good points as well. The bad man of the yesterday was not bad by nature, as a rule. They were victims of circumstances. In most cases they were men who were mistreated and abused by some party until they were cornered and forced to kill to save their life or property. Rather than let the law be their judge they would hide out, and sooner or later be forced to kill again; then it wouldn't be long until they would be an outcast from society and a desperado.

Curly Bill as we knew him was quiet and when he came to the Springs stayed off to himself. He was called Curly from the fact that he wore long hair. He never did us any harm, but always seemed to be our friend. As to whether he was connected with the "San Simon Gang" I very seriously have my doubts, but I do know that he worked for Harvey Whitehill, and was loyal to the man.

Curly Bill was at our place one time just after we had returned from Apache Tejo with some of our cattle that had been stolen. We had recovered all of our stock, but five cows. Curly sat listening to our misfortune shaking and nodding his head. The next morning Curly left the Springs and five days later came in with our five cows, and that is the way the supposed to be bad man did his friend a favor. There wasn't any talking to be done; they believed in action and talking later.

When Curly left this part of the Southwest in 1885, he was supposed to have gone into Arizona and gotten into trouble and killed, but this is false for I sold cattle to him after the World War. After the war we couldn't find buyers for our stock and buyers were begged to buy, and were enticed in every way possible to look at our stock. A group of buyers were over at the corrals, by the McComas Tree, looking at our cattle. I noticed one of the buyers from California looked familiar to me. We eyed one another for some time; finally the fellow came over to me and said: "Did you know Harvey Whitehill?"

I quickly replied, "I did and I know you." He smiled and nodded his head. He had been able to start life over after he was reported killed, and he wasn't the only bad man who was killed to become leaders of the country. The country was so sparsely settled that they could go into a new place and start a new life.

Russian Bill and King that were hung at Ralston were not desperados, but bullies: they would go into town and get drunk and shoot up the town. One time while shooting up the town King was shot through the back of the neck. Russian Bill used the old Indian method of putting salt on the wound and pouring whiskey on over the salt. The first application burned like the devil, but later the whiskey deadened the pain.

King finally came to after Bill had kept hot rock all around him for several days, and kept up the use of salt and whiskey. After King completely recovered the two men decided to give the town of Ralston a day to remember.

The two men went to town and got drunk. Sandy King picked a quarrel with Harry Mess, a clerk in the Carol Brothers store and shot his finger off. King was arrested and guarded by Jack Rutland behind the saloon. Russian Bill stole a horse and went to Deming where he was arrested and returned to Ralston. Both these bullies were now prisoners for Jack to guard. One night Russian Bill was singing "Climbing Those Golden Stairs" and the men decided that when Jack brought his prisoners in with their blankets they would give the men a chance to see Saint Peter, and sing "Climbing Those Golden Stairs" to him for they were tired of their pranks.

The men took the blankets that the two men slept on and threw them over the heads of Russian Bill and Sandy King. They took the two men down to the old hotel and hung them. These men weren't men that were respected as outlaws, but men that tried to run over people. They weren't rustlers or killers, as so many of the men that made the frontier a safe place, but a modern bully. . . .

Related by J.C. Brock, Age app. 75.

Main Street, Lordsburg, New Mexico (no date), Courtesy Palace of the Governors (MNM/DCA #152065)

Rough on Rustlers
Silver City and Lordsburg Coach Held-Up, The Rustlers Disgusted with Their Luck
(Reprinted from the *Silver City Enterprise*, 1882)

by
Francis E. Totty

One Saturday afternoon Marriage's coach on the Lordsburg line was stopped by three rustlers a short distance the other side of Mt. Home, and sad to relate the coach did not contain a single passenger nor any express packages of any kind. To say they were disgusted would not half express it.

One of them remarked that it was the first time in his varied experience of fourteen years that he had been so flatly disappointed and said unless times got better they would have to give up their chosen profession or seek a new field for their labor.

The driver conversed with them for some time and asked why they did not hold him up the day before. They said that it was because he had a lady passenger and they did not wish to frighten her.

It is very evident that the New Mexico bandits' code of

etiquette has been revised recently, as it is not long since they held up coaches regardless of its occupants. However, their business is expanding and they can afford to be more liberal.

The 'Frisco traveling men should make note of this revision in the etiquette of rustlers, and on their next trip bring their wives along as a safeguard.

The average rustler does not fear a whole arsenal of guns and ammunition, yet under the new code they will weaken under the gentle and benigning influence of a woman's presence.

The driver recognized the Clifton and Lordsburg stage company's brand on two of the horses ridden by the rustlers, and it is presumed they are the ones taken out of the team some two weeks ago when the stage was held up between Clifton and Lordsburg.

From the Silver City Enterprise, 1882.

Jicarillo Bob Took the Pot
Farmington, New Mexico

by
Mrs. Frances E. Totty

On Saturday night of Sept. 24, 1887, in the back room of Jicarillo Bob's place a poker game was held with Jicarillo Bob present to see everything was fair.

The men at the table were Tom Sinabaugh, a cattle-dealer and Albert Potter, Omaha Throup, and Pop Williams, gamblers. The game had been going along for some time without much excitement, with no very large winnings, when suddenly Pop Williams who had thrown down two cards, offered to go it blind for fifty-five dollars.

The others saw him, and a crowd that had assembled at the bar moved over to see how the thing would come out. All the others drew three cards each.

Williams ran his cards over carelessly, called for a drink, and with a cigar in one corner of his mouth said, "I'll bet fifty dollars." All the others stayed in, and on the showdown no one manifested a disposition to raise it; there appeared that there were five aces on, Pop Williams having three and Potter Albert two. This discovery came very near resulting in war.

At the suggestion of Jicarillo Bob, the pot was left up and a new deal was had, he taking the extra ace and tearing it up.

After the new deal Albert called for four cards, Sinabaugh for three, Throup for three and Williams for two. There was now more than four hundred in the pot. As Albert offered to bet fifty dollars, the others felt they would have to see him; when it came around to Albert again he concluded to raise the terms a little, and he put up a hundred dollars.

This caused old man Sinabaugh to draw out with the remark that the water was getting a little too deep for a man with a little pan. The other saw the raise and called—down came the cards and almost simultaneously with their appearance was the crack of a revolver and Potter fell out of his chair, while Pop Williams, gun in hand, reached over and swept in the pile of money.

On the table in front of where Albert was lying were five cards, three of them aces; while in front of Williams were two aces, one of the duplicates of one in the hands of the man under the table.

So much interest was excited by the inspection of these two hands and the sweeping in by Williams of the money that no one noticed Albert slowly rising on the other side of the table. Jicarillo Bob was the first to catch a glimpse of him, but he had only time to cry out to Williams when Albert's revolver was discharged and Williams fell with a bullet through the head.

Every man in the room except the proprietor then broke for the door, but before all had gone out, Bob's voice was heard saying that the dispute over the game had left no one to claim the stakes and he as landlord would therefore take possession.

Displaying two big repeaters as he said this, he was just in time to reply to a shot from the weapon of Omaha Throup. Neither man was hit and for a minute they stood facing each other. A bystander stepped in between the two men, and the crowd edging forward quickly separated the two men.

Then a council of war was held and it was agreed that the money not claimed should go to the house; the two survivors of the game received their stakes back.

The next morning Albert and Williams were buried just out of town. At the head of their graves two boards were placed—that at Albert's grave bore the inscription "Three Aces" and that at Williams' grave having "Two Aces." The coroner's jury returned a verdict that both men came to their death from natural causes, super-induced by overeating. "A good way," one citizen said of covering up the fact that they were hogs. It was never decided which one had the extra ace but the fact that in Albert's pocket another ace was found and in William's belt there were two more, it was inferred that both were cheaters.

Source of Information: J. R. Kinyon.

Jail Escape and Capture of Bandits— Mitch Lee

by
Francis E. Totty

I n the spring of 1883 six men held up the Southern Pacific and robbed, then escaped from the country surrounding Deming over to near Silver City, where they were captured. The jail in Silver City was an old adobe structure that anyone could escape from if they really tried, for the walls had broken bottles on them to keep anyone from climbing them and there were not many real prisoners in the jail.

The robbers decided to escape from the jail and soon saw that they could climb over the walls. They climbed over the wall and made the owner of the Livery Stable saddle them some horses and they left the town behind, but they were seen by a man on a wagon who gave the alarm and the posse was soon after the men and overtook them at the cemetery.

Several of the men were captured and hanged at the cemetery and one, Kid McCoy, was brought back to town as he told the posse that he hadn't fired a shot. When he was brought to town they found that the gun was jammed and he couldn't fire the gun if he wanted to shoot. Mitch Lee escaped and went to the home of Thompson where he asked for food. Mr. Thompson lived on the Gila and told Lee not to return as he did not want him around. The same night Lee returned to the home of Thompson and climbed on the roof. Thompson shot him in the leg and captured him. He brought his prisoner into town and took him to the office of Dr. Slough.

Mr. Lee's leg had to be removed and he would not take anything to ease the pain, so Dr. Slough said that he was as rough as he could possibly be. After the leg was removed Lee was returned to jail and later to prison.

Source of Information: Louis Goforth.

Holdup of Santa Rita Payroll, Greer Brothers

by
Francis E. Totty

"In the late summer or early fall of 1911, about four miles south of Santa Rita, which is 16 miles east of Silver City, the two Greer brothers and a third party held up J.M. Sully and Jim Blair. Mr. Blair and Sully were bringing the mine payroll from Deming to Santa Rita. The men fled in the direction of the Kneeling Nun.

"Mr. Sully and Mr. Blair went to Santa Rita and gave the alarm. A posse was formed at once consisting of J.M. Sully, Jim Blair, Lon Portwood and Reese Jackson. The posse overtook the bandits in the hills. The Greer boys hid behind some rocks and took the drop on the men in the posse. When they had the posse covered the Greer brothers ordered the men to unarm. After the posse was unarmed, they were ordered to sit down and remove their shoes. The boys then collected the shoes and guns and ordered the men to turn and march back to Santa Rita barefooted, a walk of about

426

three miles through rocks and cactus. The men said they turned over every stone on the mountain trying to avoid the stickers and sharp rocks. They were in a rush to get to the office to report their failure to capture the men, yet their efforts were in vain as they were all so tender-footed.

"The bandits left Grant County and went to Deming, Luna County, where one of the members of their gang was in jail. The jailer was overpowered and the keys taken from him. The boys opened the jail and took their partner out and left town going northeast.

"Willie Bellah and I were herding cattle in Donahue Canyon when we heard shots in the hills. Thinking that it was some of the cowboys, we called back but the shooting continued.

"Will remarked, 'Say, take your six-shooter and do a little answering to those fellows.'

"I grabbed for my gun, and in my haste shot too soon, the bullet entering the neck of my horse and killing him instantly. The horse fell on top of me. Willie jumped off his horse and uncinched the saddle and pulled both saddle and me from under the horse at the same time.

"Hearing the shot I fired, Smithers, a ranch detective, came down from the hills and investigated. Hearing of our troubles he called other men out of the mountains. They were hunting the Greer boys and their gang, and a few miles back they had found where the men had stopped and cut one another's hair. The posse went with us to our corral to get fresh mounts.

"Dwight Stevens, Sheriff of Luna County, was leading the posse. They overtook the gang at Double Adobe Ranch house. He stationed Tom Hall and Smithers to guard the front of the house, the other members of the posse surrounding the house.

"The gang, deciding that things were getting too hot, decided to shoot their way out. They came out the front door shooting.

Tom Hall shot one of the Greer boys and wounded him in the leg. The boy escaped into the canyon but was later captured and tried. The other Greer boy, Tom Hall, and Smithers were killed.

"The bodies of Smithers and Hall were taken by horseback to Engle and then sent by train to Deming. Tom Hall was at one time a citizen of Grant County, but after getting in an argument with Tom Lyon's men, he left here and settled in Deming."

Related by G.I. Goforth (age 55).

Fountaine Murder

by
Frances E. Totty

"In February 1896 we were living at the Gold Camp, thirty-five miles from Las Cruces. Judge A.B. Fall had charge of the camp, and lived there most of the time. One afternoon, the day that Col. Fountaine was supposed to have been killed upon, A.B. Falls came by the house in a light spring wagon going to Las Cruces. Just past our house was a hill that the road went over. When Mr. Falls came to this hill his horses balked and after an effort to get them to climb the hill he unhitched and brought the horses back to the corral, which was on the opposite side of our place from the hill. Judge Falls then took a small team of mules and hitched to the wagon and went on toward Las Cruces. This happened just about dusk or what would have been sundown, but as the day was bad and the sun wasn't shining we all knew that the Judge had important business in Las Cruces or he wouldn't try to drive the thirty-five miles after dark; but I do know that A.B. Fall could not have killed Col. Fountaine as many believed because thirty-five miles is a long ways to travel, much less to the White Sands.

"As I remember the case, Col. Fountaine went to Lincoln County as Prosecuting Attorney against some cattlemen that had been rustling; among the men were Robert Railey, Jim Gillon, and a fellow by the name of McNew. There had been several threats against the Col. if he did go to push the case, and his wife pleaded with him to not go; but the Col. seemed to think that it was his duty to go and push the case through; finally his wife told him to take their nine-year-old son Henry with the remark, 'They surely won't molest you if you have the child along.'

"When the two left home, Mrs. Fountaine, a Spanish lady, wrapped both Col. Fountaine and Henry with a Spanish shawl, as she was afraid that they would catch cold.

"When the buckboard was found that the Col. was traveling in these two shawls were found spread out behind the seat. Where the bodies of the two were buried has never been made positive, but many think the skeletons found in the Sacramento Mountains were them. When Col. Fountaine and Henry did not return at the time Mrs. Fountaine expected them she became worried and sent out the alarm. A number of posses went out to hunt the bodies because there were a number of men under suspicion besides Oliver Lee.

"Sam Bernard, Kingston, who served on the Grand Jury of the case has heard a man say that he heard Jim Gillon say, 'I cannot kill the boy' and Bob Railey replied, 'I sure can.' Whoever killed the two placed the two bodies across the backs of the horses and followed them on other horses to where they were buried, but the trail never could be followed.

"Bob Railey's wife lives at Jarilla, New Mexico now; she was a sister to Jim Gillon and Bob Railey was good to her and the children because he was afraid of her brothers, but he was a brute. I have seen him beat horses until they fell, then stomp and kick them in the eyes and pour dirt and sand into their ears, and a man that would treat a dumb animal that way will do anything. McNew later killed Bob Railey.

"Col. Fountaine was a brilliant man, one respected by law abiding citizens; he was a social leader in our district. We had many dances in those days and Col. Fountaine was the best dancer by far; he taught we who attended all of the new steps and at every dance there was a short time set aside for the Col. to teach some new steps in dancing or teach a new pupil. Col. Fountain and Eugene Van Patten were fast friends and seemed to enjoy the dances more than anyone else there. In the early days we not only danced the square dances, but the Spanish dances as well, and the Col. taught all of the Spanish dances. Col. Fountaine was a Mason; this order offered a reward for any information as to his death, but all was in vain. Col. Fountaine may not have been a God fearing man but he was a good man. He was brave and courageous, and had a desire to serve his fellow man in a respectable way. On his way back from the trial he knew that he was being followed by three men, but not who they were, for he told the mail carrier from Tularosa that he had been warned at Tularosa to not go on and that he had seen three men following him.

"It has never been found out who killed Col. Fountaine, and probably never will, but the countryside was certainly in an uproar about the fact, and his killing was not the only mysterious killing of the early days."

Information Source: Alberta (Skidmore) Cowan was born in Illinois in 1867 and came to Dona Ana County in 1882, having lived ever since that time in Southwest New Mexico. Living at present in Silver City.

Rustlers: Hanging at Shakespeare

by
Mrs. W. C. Totty

In the early days the rustlers were organized into a company. Their Captain was V.Z. Boon, and First Lieutenant Bud Stiles. There were about seventy-five members and they ruled this country.

The rustlers never worked together. On a small job there would only be one or two while on a large job five or six. When the rustlers stole they always went in for large jobs as getting five or six hundred cattle in one night.

There was also what we call the Petty Thieves, who just stole saddles, blankets, horses and such.

In the year 1881 a man by the name of Sandy King, known as a petty thief, lived in Shakespeare. One night Sandy was drinking and went over to the Carol Brothers store and picked a quarrel with Harry Mess, the clerk. During the quarrel Sandy shot the little finger off of Mess's right hand. The officer put Sandy in jail.

About a week before this Russian Bill (known as a petty thief throughout the country) had stolen a Knox Brothers horse. Russian Bill was arrested by Dan Tucker in Deming. He was brought back and lodged in jail at Shakespeare. Jack Rutland was the jail keeper.

One night the Rustlers came to town and formed a mob. They went to the jail and took Sandy King and Russian Bill to the old Shakespeare Hotel and hung them, thus disposing of two petty thieves.

A short time before the hanging of Russian Bill, I had a horse, Old Charlie, stolen from my corral. I reported the thief to Captain Boon of the Rustlers who asked me if I had any idea who got the horse.

I replied, "I suspect Russian Bill." Boon said, "You wait two or three days and the horse will return."

A few days later I was surprised to see my horse standing in the corral.

The story of Rustlers being mean, killers, and drunkards is false. They were kind, good-hearted, and full of mischief. They were generous with their money; rustling was a business with them, and they were on the job all of the time.

When they came to town they would cut up, fire their guns at the people for action. At one time there was a Chinaman settled here from the coast. He was endeavoring to establish and run a laundry.

One night I heard someone yelling, "Murder! Murder! Help!" I started to dress and see what the trouble was when father said: "It's nothing but the rustlers teasing the Chinaman."

The next morning I went down to see what happened, and the old Chinaman was scared stiff. He said, "I thinka—I gotta white man friend—and last night they come and shoot the works. You wanta buya—me—a—outa. I do not lika here—I mova fast." I didn't buy him out but he soon left town.

The Santa Rita Holdup

by
Frances E. Totty

The Greer brothers, thinking that Jim Blair and Mr. Sully were returning to Santa Rita with the mine payroll, held the two men up in 1911 and took all the two men's personal valuable belongings. When the bandits found that the payroll was late getting to Deming and the men were returning to Santa Rita to wait for the payroll, they threatened to kill the men. The two finally convinced the bandits they wouldn't gain anything by killing them. The bandits decided to let the two men go and escaped into the foothills of the Burro Mountains south of Santa Rita.

When Mr. Sully and Jim Blair reached town and told of their misfortune, Lon Portwood, deputy, Horace Moses, mine superintendent, and Reese Jackson, G.O.S. cowpuncher, noted for tracking horses, decided to try to capture the bandits.

The trail took them into the roughest part of the mountains, the part especially noted for caves and hideouts of the rough people. When the men came up to the cave called "Robbers Roost," so called from the fact it was a bandit hideout, a voice called, "Where do you think you are going, Micky?" The hidden party was speaking to Mr. Jackson and addressing him as Micky because he was Irish.

The three men realizing that they were in danger tried to joke with the bandits in the Roost; but in vain the men joked, for the bandits demanded them to drop their guns and remove their shoes.

The three men had to beg for their lives for a day. One of the Greer boys fired at Lon Portwood, but the other Greer boy told him to not waste his shells. The three men were released barefooted and told to return to Santa Rita.

Grudgens' Tombstone

by
Victor Batchler

I t was in June, 1938, that I heard the following story. Its accuracy is entirely founded on the man's veracity who told it to me. But I believe that it is for the most part correct. Of course, were I to ask other old-timers about the feud between William Grudgens and Tom Woods, perhaps they would give me an entirely different slant on the matter; depending on which side they believed in strongest. This story was told to me by Owen Norris, who lives on his ranch in Bear Canyon, about sixteen miles to the northwest of Silver City, New Mexico.

We, Owen and I, took a party of dudes into the canyon of the Middlefork, starting from the Bear Mountain Dude Ranch, about four miles north of Silver City where I happened to be working at the time in the capacity of dude wrangler. We drove the saddle horses about thirty miles to the north the first day, where we were met by the dudes and made camp on the Sapello, which is a small river that flows into the Gila River to the west. The Sapello (pronounced sah-pale-yo) was so named because there is an unusual number of frogs on the banks of the stream, and the Spanish word "sapello" means frog. As this camp site was nearly the end of the traversable road, we packed all the supplies, bedding and personal equipment of the dudes on some horses and pack mules, saddled our own horses and the dudes' saddle horses and started out. As it was only about a twenty-five mile ride to our campsite, about five miles up the Middlefork, we made it in one day and camped just before dark.

We passed the old Heart Bar Ranch, which is located about a half-mile below the junction of where the Middlefork runs into the Westfork. Both of these streams are upper tributaries and headwaters of the Gila and flow through the western and southwestern portions of Catron County. There is a Forest Service Telephone line that goes to the Heart Bar Ranch and no further.

Through the entire route of our journey, there abounded some of the most beautiful scenery I had ever seen. The Gila Wilderness Area is classified by the U. S. Forest Service and New Mexico State Game Department as being one of the most beautiful sections of the State of New Mexico. Also there abounds more game than almost any other section of the state.

The fishing was good, and for the first few days we spent nearly all our time fishing and swimming and generally resting up from the trip, which was a little arduous to the dudes, but was an extremely short, pleasant ride to Owen and I. About the third day, the whole party decided to visit the Gila Cliff Dwellings, about five miles away, in a little side canyon that flows from the south into the Westfork. On our way, we passed Grudgens Cabin.

Owen made some mention of a tombstone with a strange inscription near the cabin, so we all started looking for it. I found it just a little ways back of the cabin on a little slope. A crude picket fence enclosed the grave, and at its head there was a large, granite tombstone with the strange inscription:

TO THE MEMORY OF WILLIAM GRUDGENS
MURDERED BY TOM WOODS
AUGUST 21, 1887

No one thought much about the strange inscription until after we had visited the Cliff Dwellings and were on our way back to camp. Then one of the dudes ventured to ask Owen if he knew any of the history that lay behind the tombstone. "Sure I do," replied Owen, and in as correct a fashion as possible I will outline the story in Owen Norris' own words:

"The Grudgens family lived in that cabin fer quite a few years. They had a few friends and more enemies. 'Though it was never proved on 'em, a lot of people suspected Bill Grudgens of stealin' cattle. It was certain that he had a good place to hold 'em until the brands healed over. He could have fenced up any one of a bunch of box-like canyons he had close to his place, and a bunch of stolen cattle would have been hard to find in a rough country like that. Grudgens was a kind of a strange man, because he never welcomed visitors around his place. Quite a few times he had ordered men off his place and wouldn't let 'em come close to his cabin. This made him a lot of enemies, and made people think that he was coverin' up something. Naturally, as there wasn't much to steal in the country besides cattle or horses, it made some people think that Grudgens' place was where some missin' cattle had been taken. They had searched the surrounding country, and had been afraid to search Grudgens' Ranch because they were afraid Bill Grudgens might let loose some "lead" right close to any trespassers.

"Tom Woods lived a few miles below Grudgens' place, down on the Gila. He told some of his neighbors he had been missin' a few head of cattle and that he suspected Grudgens of stealin' 'em.

However, not desirin' to invite any trouble, he had decided to take his loss and steer clear of Grudgens. Probably he never would have started any close investigation if his son, a boy of about twelve, and a Spanish-American cowboy had not struck the trail of a bunch of Woods' cattle that they could see had been driven off in the direction of Grudgens' Ranch. Woods' wife was a Spanish American woman, and although there was quite a bit of prejudice against a man of Anglo-Saxon blood marrying into the Latin race at that time, Tom Woods had many friends and was well-liked throughout the surrounding country. He was a hard worker and was honest in all his dealings.

"Woods' son and the cowboy trailed the stolen cattle onto Grudgens' Ranch. Grudgens or whoever stole the cattle must have been waitin' for anybody followin', for the boy and cowboy were killed from ambush.

"Back at his ranch, Tom Woods got alarmed when his son and the cowboy did not return home that night, and early the next mornin' buckled on his revolver and grabbed his rifle and set out on the trail. In the middle of the mornin' he found the place where the bodies had been buried. He was heartbroken when he saw that one of the bodies was that of his son. He returned to his ranch and sent word to neighbors to help him carry the bodies back to his ranch, where he gave them decent burial.

"That same day, he rode to Grudgens' Cabin intendin' to kill Bill Grudgens, because there was no doubt in his mind but that Grudgens was the man who had murdered his son and the cowboy.

"Grudgens' wife told Woods that her husband had left the country and would not be back for some time. Woods didn't believe her, and spied on the cabin for days in hopes that he would see Grudgens return. Finally, he found out that Grudgens had really left the country.

"For two years Tom Woods trailed Grudgens over the States of New Mexico and Arizona, but Grudgens, who now lived in fear that Woods would some day find him, kept out of the way.

"Finally, Woods got a tip from some source or other that Grudgens was comin' home to see his family. Woods laid in ambush near Grudgens' cabin for several days before Grudgens came, and finally, when he was just about to give up hope, he was rewarded by seein' Grudgens ride up to his cabin. A little while later, Grudgens stepped out the door and outlined himself perfect in Tom Woods' rifle sights. A bullet struck and killed him instantly and Woods shot him several times after he had fallen to make sure he'd killed him.

"Grudgens' family sent to Silver City fer a Tombstone, and bitterly directed that the inscription be cut into the rock so that everybody that saw the tombstone would know that Tom Woods was a murderer. What they'd oughta put on that rock was how Bill Grudgens was one of the murderin'est, black-hearted scoundrels that ever lived," finished Owen.

Early Days in Magdalena

by
Victor Batchler

*I*n early days, and even as late as 1916, Magdalena was one of the toughest towns in the West. The branch line of the Santa Fe R. R. that ran up from Socorro carried more cattle away from Magdalena than any other town in the United States. For a hundred miles north, south, southwest, west and northwest, ranchers drove cattle in large herds to Magdalena for shipment. Cowboys, wild as the fierce wind off the ranges, stalked its streets with whiskey under their belts and looking for excitement. Their cowponies' hooves drummed staccato accompaniment to the roar of their sixshooters as they rode in at full speed, yelling and livening up the town.

Two other elements added to the general excitement and continuous bloodshed and warfare: The sheepmen, who were continually at odds with the cowmen, and who were sided by nearly all the Spanish-American element, and the considerable population of miners who worked at various mines in the Magdalena Mountains and at Kelly, a mining town that once boasted a population of nearly five thousand. The miners, especially on payday, loved a fight for their own propensity to indulge in battle. The fact that a large percentage of these were Irish undoubtedly softened a few skulls by shillelaghs.

It has been said that were all the men killed in Magdalena laid end to end, one could walk on dead men from the upper end of the business district comprising two blocks, to the depot, nearly 250 yards away. The local saddlemaker, Thomas Butterfield, recounts, "When I first came to Magdalena, it was such a wild town that I was afraid to go home nights, and made my bed in the saddleshop. There was always shooting and yelling after sundown, and nearly every night there was a pitched gun battle, or a fight with knives, clubs, or fists. Bullets sung around my saddle shop and were always smashing windows. It got to where I just left the windows broken. It didn't do any good to replace them.

"I never will forget the time when I was walking down the street with a fellow toward the saddleshop and I was talking with him about selling him a saddle. The next thing I knew, somebody shot this fellow and he dropped right in the middle of the conversation and before I could collect a down payment on the saddle. I turned around and ran so fast that provided anybody had had an airplane to keep up, they could have played cards on my coat tail."

Gambling ran full blast, and times have been seen when there were six or seven men around a poker table with four or five thousand dollars in heaped up greenbacks and poker chips in front of each man. Ranches have been won and lost at the turn of a card. Probably one of the most unusual and dramatic poker games in the history of the town was when a rancher had his ranch mortgaged and nearly every cent he had in front of him in a game of stud poker. There were thousands of dollars in the pot, and this rancher had an ace of hearts in the hole, and a king, jack and ten of hearts showing face up, with one more card to fall. Three or four more players had large pairs and possibly better than pairs. The rancher with the possible royal flush calmly called a large bet and said to the dealer, "Give me a queen of hearts, and I'll get the rest of what I've got." It wouldn't be hard to imagine just how he felt when the next card came off to him and it was the queen of hearts. That pot probably was one of the biggest in the history of poker in Magdalena.

The Apache Kid

by
Clay W. Vaden

The life story of the Apache Kid, one of New Mexico's most picturesque outlaws, though not so well known as that of Billy the Kid, is just as exciting and it is gradually being pieced together by old timers of this colorful section of the great Southwest.

The Kid's widow still lives on the Mescalero Indian Reservation near Alamogordo, New Mexico, as do two of their daughters, but the widow's lips have disclosed little of the activities of this Indian to whom were attributed numerous killings, many of which old timers now believe were committed by renegade white men.

Charlie Anderson, of Kingston, New Mexico, former Deputy Sheriff, has recently disclosed the fact that he was among the posse who killed the Apache Kid and buried him near Monticello, in Sierra County. They did not claim the $5,000.00 reward offered for him because they were not positive at the time that the Indian they killed was the notorious Apache Kid and Federal Officials made so much trouble for anyone in later years who killed a redskin that they felt the least said about it the better.

The Kid's death cleared the mystery of the two killings. A brakeman had been shot from a train and investigation brought not the least clue to his killer then, but the brakeman's key was found on a string tied around the Apache Kid's neck. An old timer was shot through the head. Nearby were found the tracks and the pistol of another miner, who was arrested, convicted and his case was on appeal when the personal affects of the dead miner were found in the Kid's possession.

Old timers say that the Apache Kid was the son of the old Chief Nana and was rescued from the back of his dead mother by William Paxton who still lives at Elk. The squaw was killed in a fight between marauding Indians and a band of cowboys. Mr. Paxton hoped to exchange the Indian boy for two white girls who had been captured by the Apaches. The exchange was not effected but the Kid was sent to an eastern Indian school, where he learned to speak English. During his later years of hiding he often came to town in various disguises as a Mexican, an Indian or a paleface.

His widow asserts that the Kid never killed unless he was driven into a corner. In 1883, a girl of Indian and Spanish blood was captured and carried away by the Kid. She and her mother were gathering piñon nuts on a mountain near Three Rivers. She declares her captor was always kind to her and her children.

When officers and cowboys had been crowding in upon him in the mountains where he was making his last stand, shortly before he was killed, he realized death was near and took his squaw to a mountain peak where White Mountain could be seen and told his wife that was near her home and for her to return there if he should be killed.

Their eldest boy was with the Kid when he was killed, but escaped and joined his mother.

Mrs. A.E. Thomas, a former teacher at the Mescalero Indian School, said that the older children, accustomed to a free animal-like existence, pined away and died. Marian Sims, a well-to-do Indian relative of the Apache Kid's wife, furnished a house and bought a piano for her and the girls, but they were more content living in a wigwam. He send one of the girls away to school but she walked back, a distance of more than 100 miles, traveling by night.

A Pioneer Souvenir of
Outlaw Pilar

by
Clay W. Vaden

Among the many souvenirs of the early days in the southwest is a piece of rope, approximately five inches in length.

This bit of rope, which recalls the life of the early days of the OLD WEST, belongs to E.J. Fender, pioneer resident, of Hillsboro, New Mexico, and is a part of the rope used to hang Pilar, a Mexican outlaw, at Silver City, in 1887.

Pilar was accused of many crimes, among which was the kidnapping of a 14-year-old girl which proved his undoing.

Fender and his wife, who were residing at the Dennis and Black sawmill nine miles from Silver City, were among the first to see Pilar after he had kidnapped the girl from the Mimbres mill in 1885. When seen he was riding horseback with the girl tied to the horse to prevent her escape.

Not long after Pilar passed the Fender home he met Deputy

Sheriff Tom Hall who stopped and questioned him. This was in the vicinity of Pinos Altos. As Hall turned to ride away, Pilar shot him, and in the excitement the girl broke her bonds, and escaped to Silver City where she was given protection. Pilar escaped.

In addition to being charged with the death of Hall, Pilar was also accused of having killed two men at Mule Springs and a teamster who was hauling ore from "The Old Man Mine" west of Silver City. In the latter murder, Pilar and his accomplice were thought to have waylaid the teamster, tied his feet together and cut his throat in order that they might steal his team.

Pilar not only was wanted in New Mexico but also had a price upon his head in Old Mexico, where it was alleged that he had murdered four families. When it became too "hot" in New Mexico for Pilar, he crossed into Arizona where he was captured.

At Flagstaff, Pilar was identified by a negro who had traveled with him, and an officer entered a saloon where Pilar was playing Monte and ordered him to surrender.

Pilar knocked the officer's gun from his hand and attacked him with a knife. The negro, who had followed the officer, entered the fight and overpowered Pilar, who was arrested and held for New Mexico authorities.

He was returned to Silver City where he was tried and sentenced to be hanged. Andrew Laird was Sheriff and "Doc" Belt was deputy at the time.

Fender, who was present at the hanging, cut the five-inch piece from the rope used in the hanging, and cherishes it as a rather gruesome relic of "THEM GOOD OLD DAYS WHEN THE WEST WAS REALLY WILD AND WOOLLY."

Joe Fowler Hold-Up-Man and Criminal

by
N. Howard Thorp

I n November of the year 1884, Joe Fowler, a deputy Sheriff of
Socorro, N.M., was running wild in Socorro, New Mexico,
there being some twenty murders of which he was accused.

As to where Joe Fowler came from, there are a great many
different stories. I have heard three different ones as to his place
of origin, though the most probable one was that he was an ex-
cowboy who on account of his meanness had been run out of
Texas. In the early eighties many another before him had come
from other States, seeking refuge in New Mexico. There is also a
question as to whether or no Joe Fowler was his right name, but
that is a matter of minor importance.

Such small crimes as stealing ore from the mines, cattle and
horse stealing, and holding up not only people but stages for a time
was overlooked, as he seems to have had the people of Socorro
completely Buffaloed.

Most of the murders accredited to him were committed after his victims had been arrested and disarmed, usually on trumped-up accusations; for it seemed Fowler was in demand among unscrupulous politicians for doing away with any who opposed them, so naturally these parties wished to keep him in office.

On one of Fowler's stage hold-ups a very ludicrous thing happened. Fowler and one of his gang left Socorro, Nov. 20, 1883, and rode to San Antonio; then crossing the Rio Grande and passing the little town of San Pedro, continued east a matter of five miles, to where the old stage road runs down a steep hill through a cut in the hills; there they took their stand, and awaited the westbound Ozane stage.

Fowler it seems was riding a young horse—that he had just stolen—which happened to be gun-shy; this it seems Fowler did not know.

As the stage approached, the two hold-ups dashed up on either side of the four-horse team and with six-shooters drawn ordered the driver to stop. Fowler's gun must have cocked, at all events it was discharged; his horse began bucking and threw Fowler off, he landed in front of the wheelers and behind the lead team, his hat going in one direction and his gun in another. The other hold-up, seeing the predicament of his partner, put spurs to his horse and fled. The driver then whipped up his horses, and with Fowler a-foul between the horses was dragged and bumped along until finally he had to release his hold and fell beneath the coach.

As the hold-ups had handkerchiefs over their faces, they could not—in the dim light—be identified, but for several days afterwards Fowler lay in bed, and when he did again appear he was on crutches. He had ridden home on horseback.

From the following incidents we may assume that the value as placed by Fowler on a human life was eighteen dollars.

In the faithful discharge of his sworn duties as deputy Sheriff, he arrested an inoffensive citizen at Socorro, N.M. He then herded him to jail in Socorro. Searching him, Fowler discovered that he was the possessor of the sum of eighteen dollars.

On the principle that dead men tell no tales, Fowler took an old forty-five Colt's six-shooter, and calling the man to the bars of his cell, shot him through the head, afterwards throwing the old gun into the cell beside the victim. The following day, after due deliberation, the coroner's jury rendered a verdict of suicide. Later the gun proved to be one that had been taken from a former prisoner, and the only person having access to the safe where it was kept at that time was Joe Fowler, Deputy Sheriff.

Another of his hoydenish pranks was committed on a man having a wooden leg. Meeting him on the street Fowler declared he did not like the looks of the wooden leg, so shot it to pieces, then another idea entered his crooked brain: I will have to shorten the other leg also, and proceeded to fill that one also with lead; the poor fellow had to have it amputated.

However, the better element in Socorro were by now getting fed up with his crimes and were about ready to call a halt.

One evening while drinking, Fowler and his gang entered the principal hotel in Socorro, and after a great deal of cursing in the hotel lobby, proceeded to the bar room. As they entered the door a drummer for some eastern wholesale firm walked to the bar and ordered a cigar. Fowler, looking for someone to pick a row with, pulled his gun and ordered the drummer to take a drink of whiskey. The drummer tried to explain that the reason he took a cigar was because he had stomach trouble and could not drink anything intoxicating.

This did not suit the redoubtable Fowler, who remarked, "I'll cure your stomach trouble," and drawing his knife plunged it into the unfortunate's stomach, killing him almost instantly. Fowler's friends hurried him away and locked him in jail for fear, after this cowardly murder, he might be lynched.

Finally the better element of Socorro stepped into the saddle and decided Fowler must go. A few days after Fowler had committed this murder, in some mysterious way everyone in town was told to assemble between eight and nine o'clock when a meeting would be held to decide what disposition was to be made of Fowler.

It was whispered that Fowler's friends intended spiriting him away, but the best element of the town was determined to take the matter into their own hands, and once and for always put an end to his activities.

There are many causes in the west for crowds to assemble: a horse race, a fire, a fight, or a frolic "dance"; but more people got together this night than probably ever before had assembled in Socorro. A thousand quickly increased to double that number; not only the square in front of the courthouse was filled but the tops of the low adobe houses nearby were covered with curious spectators.

A group of men, possibly a dozen, entered the courthouse and the doors closed after them; the crowd outside waited expectantly to see what would happen, for from the word which had gone forth, some sort of an open air trial was looked forward to.

After a half hour or so the committee came out, dragging the most contemptible and miserable object imaginable. All Fowler's bravado was gone, he was howling and begging for his life, a craven and a coward, forgetting entirely that twenty-odd others he had murdered.

The rest of the program went off without a hitch.

Fowler was hustled into a wagon. The procession drove, rode, and walked to the edge of the town, where a big cottonwood tree overhung the road. This tree always afterward known as the Fowler tree, still stands.

The rope, put on in jail by the mob, which was around his neck, was thrown over a cottonwood limb and the wagon was driven out from underneath him. Several shots—which were supposed to be merciful—were fired into him, but they were unnecessary; by the looks of his face he was already dead from fright before they swung him loose, a horrible sight, the face of a coward.

The crowd quickly dispersed, most of them hunting different bars, as it took something strong to take the bad taste of the sight of a coward out of our mouths.

The End

Cruz Richards Alvarez, Mesilla, New Mexico, 1978, photograph by Jack Loeffler

Old Timers Stories:
Cruz Richards Alvarezd

by
Marie Carter

Cruz Richards Alvarez of Old Mesilla, New Mexico, is a man who takes great pride in his ancestry. So when I asked him to tell me something about his family history, he complied with my request and began:

"My great-grandfather, John Richards Alvarez, was a prominent London physician, who took a notion to embark for America. Since his wife was dead his two sons, Reuben and Stephen, accompanied him on the voyage.

"While they were at sea the crew mutinied. John Richards must have been a game old boy. For he took charge of the ship and brought it safe into Galveston, Texas. At a later date, however, he was beheaded by the Indians, consequently, the boys were left orphans in the wilds of Texas. Reuben, who was destined to become my grandfather, seemed to have inherited some of his father's fighting blood. For during the Mexican War, he became inspired with a desire to fight, so he joined the American army under General Scott in Mexico. On returning from the Mexican War he stopped at Presidio, Texas, which was Mexico, and met my future grand-mother."

"Love at first sight, followed by a prendorio, or engagement announcement," I suggested.

According to the old Spanish custom there should have been a prendorio, but in this case, everything went haywire. "The girl's father, Francisco Hernandez," he explained, "was a rich old guy with lots of money and cattle and thought Reuben was an adventurer with designs on the family fortune. So he told him to be gone or he would shoot him."

"Did he go?"

"Si Senora, muy pronto. But he came back. Then what do you think happened?" he asked.

"I can't imagine."

"He kidnapped the girl."

✳✳✳

. . . A few days ago, while nosing around the streets of Old Mesilla. I had the good fortune to meet Cruz R. Alvarez again. He called my attention to the old jail where Billy the Kid was incarcerated, saying:

"He was a tough customer, ruthless with his enemies, but generous to his friends, the native rancheros. His good looks, charming personality, and fine dancing, won him the admiration of the younger set who considered him a gay caballero. But he was a desperado, a gunman and a killer, who was sentenced to be hung, April 13, 1881."

"In Dona Ana County?"

"No, in Lincoln County. Colonel A.J. Fountain, who

organized the New Mexico Militia, was Billy the Kid's defense counsel," he said.

"Mr. Alvarez," I said, "I always thought Billy the Kid was shot."

"He was, but that occurred after he escaped from the Lincoln jail."

"Escaped?"

"Yes, killing both of his guards. Prior to his incarceration, April 1, 1878, he killed Sheriff William Brady and George Hineman. On July 15, 1881, Pat Garrett, the sheriff of Lincoln County, and two deputies discovered Billy the Kid at the home of Pete Maxwell, near Fort Sumner. The outlaw walked into Maxwell's bedroom and was shot by Garrett."

Cruz Richards Alvarez: Born in La Union, New Mexico, September 14, 1896; son of Mr. and Mrs. Deonicio Alvarez of La Union; graduate, Industrial Commercial Department, State College, New Mexico; teacher of Spanish in Las Vegas Normal University; teacher in Hollywood, California Secretarial School; teacher, El Paso Vocational School, El Paso, Texas; attached to American Embassy, Madrid, Spain, during World War; married and has two children, Consuelo, a girl, and Benjamin, a boy; wife was Fanny Bermudez, granddaughter of Don Rafael Bermudez, Customs Collector for Mexico in Mesilla up to 1854.

List of Illustrations

Bibliography of New Mexico Federal Writers' Project Documents

WPA—Works Progress Administration/NMFWP—New Mexico Federal Writers' Project

NMSRCA—New Mexico State Records Center and Archives

A *Holdup After Midnight*, Reyes N. Martinez, July 25, 1936, NMFWP, WPA #233, NMSRCA

A *Pioneer Souvenir of Outlaw Pilar*, Clay W. Vaden, NMFWP, August 3, 1936, NMFWP, WPA #87, NMSRCA

A *Tough One*, W. M. Emery, July 6, 1937, NMFWP, WPA #239, NMSRCA

A *Would-Be Bad Man*, Kenneth Fordyce, August 13, 1938, NMFWP, WPA #87, NMSRCA

Alameda, N. Howard Thorp, no date, NMFWP, WPA #88a, NMSRCA

Albuquerque, Marino Leyba (Outlaw), As told to me by Mr. Skinner, of Old Town, Albuquerque, New Mexico, N. Howard Thorp, no date, NMFWP, WPA #88b, NMSRCA

Alejo Herrera – Patriarch, Chihuahua District, Roswell, Georgia B. Redfield, January 4, 1937, NMFWP, WPA #186a, NMSRCA

An Incident of Farmington, In the Fall of 1895: Personal interview with Mr. W.A. Hunter, of Farmington, New Mexico, Mrs. R.T.F. Simpson, September 4, 1936, NMFWP, WPA #226, NMSRCA

An Unwanted Fugitive, W. M. Emery, November 13, 1936, NMFWP, WPA #87, NMSRCA

"Bad Hombres" of the Early Days, Elinor Crans, February 23, 1939, NMFWP, WPA #178b, NMSRCA

Bad Man Moore, Alias Johnny Ward, N. Howard Thorp, January 20, 1938, NMFWP, WPA #88b, NMSRCA

Bandits of New Mexico, N. Howard Thorp, February 18, 1937, NMFWP, WPA #88a, NMSRCA

Battle at Blazer's Mill, Otero County, Georgia Redfield, May 1, 1937, NMFWP, WPA #217, NMSRCA

Bill McGinnis, The Nerviest Outlaw of them All, N. Howard Thorp, January 13, 1938, NMFWP, WPA #88b, NMSRCA

Biography of Guadalupe Lupita Gallegos, Bright Lynn, January 5, 1939, NMFWP, WPA #227, NMSRCA

Biography: Salome Garcia, Carrie L. Hodges, October 31, 1936, NMFWP, WPA #87, NMSRCA

Black Jack Ketchum, D. D. Sharp, August 3, 1936, NMFWP, WPA #87, NMSRCA

Black Jack, "Tom Ketchum," L. Raines, August 3, 1936, NMFWP, WPA #87, NMSRCA

Black Jack Musgraves, N. Howard Thorp, December 23,1937, NMFWP, WPA #88a, NMSRCA

Black-balled, Kenneth Fordyce, no date, NMFWP, American Guide, WPA #188, NMSRCA

Bob Lewis, "Peace Officer," N. Howard Thorp, May 9, 1938, NMFWP, WPA #88a, NMSRCA

Broncho Bill, "Train Robber," N. Howard Thorp, 1938, NMFWP, WPA #88a, NMSRCA

Butch Cassidy, Alias Jim Lowe, or Sallie Parker, N. Howard Thorp, January 28, 1938, NMFWP, WPA #88a, NMSRCA

Canyons and Caves in the Guadalupe Mountains, Katherine Ragsdale, August 26, 1936, NMFWP, WPA #201, NMSRCA

Clay Allison, "Gunfighter," N. Howard Thorp, no date, NMFWP, WPA #88b, NMSRCA

Crime Did Not Pay in '73, Kenneth Fordyce, April 2, 1937, NMFWP, WPA #87, NMSRCA

Curley Bill, N. Howard Thorp, February 7, 1938, NMFWP, WPA #88b, NMSRCA

Curley Bill, "Outlaw," N. Howard Thorp, December 9, 1937, NMFWP, WPA #88b, NMSRCA

Dalton Gang, N. Howard Thorp, June 14, 1938, NMFWP, WPA #88a, NMSRCA

Dancing Cowboys, Kenneth Fordyce, March 5, 1937, NMFWP, WPA #87, NMSRCA

Description of a Military Reservation; Columbus Military Reservation, Mrs. Mildred Jordan, 6/19/36, NMFWP, WPA #102, NMSRCA

Devil Dick's Career and His Ignominious End, Francis E. Totty, Silver City Independent, June 22, 1915, NMFWP, WPA #87, NMSRCA

Dr. T. O. Washington—deceased, Kenneth Fordyce, December 5, 1938, NMFWP, WPA #189, NMSRCA

Early Days in Magdalena, Victor Batchler, May 193-, NMFWP, WPA #231, NMSRCA

Early Days in the Southwest, Frances E. Totty, February 25, 1938, NMFWP, WPA #196, NMSRCA

Early Crimes and Tragedies in Northern New Mexico, Kenneth Fordyce, April 12, 1937, NMFWP, WPA #87, NMSRCA

Elfego Baca, N. Howard Thorp, no date, NMFWP, WPA #88b, NMSRCA

Flechado Pass, L. W. Brown, 1937, NMFWP, WPA #87, NMSRCA

Fountaine Murder, Francis E. Totty, October 29, 1938, NMFWP, WPA #197, NMSRCA

Grant Wheeler and Joe George, New Mexico Train Robbers, N. Howard Thorp, December 16, 1937, NMFWP, WPA #88b, NMSRCA

Grudgens' Tombstone, Victor Batchler, November 1938, NMFWP, WPA #231, NMSRCA

Henry Coleman, "Bad Man," N. Howard Thorp, April 16, 1933, NMFWP, WPA #88b NMSRCA

His Last Wishes, Mrs. Belle Kilgore May 14, 1937, NMFWP, WPA #153, NMSRCA

Holdup of the Santa Rita Payroll, Frances E. Totty, January 15,1938, NMFWP, WPA #88a, NMSRCA

In the year 1893, Rosario O. Hinjos, no date, NMFWP, WPA #233b, NMSRCA

Incidents of the Early South West, Mrs. W. C. Totty, August 3, 1937, NMFWP, WPA #153, NMSRCA

Interview with Elfego Baca, The Manzano Gang, Janet Smith, no date, NMFWP, WPA #87, NMSRCA

Interview: Louis Abraham of Silver City, "Billy the Kid," Mrs. Francis Totty, November 23, 1937, History Library, Museum of New Mexico, Santa Fe, New Mexico H-5-4-2#1

Jail Escape and Capture of Bandits-Mitch Lee, Frances E. Totty and Louis Goforth, June 7, 1938, NMFWP, WPA #87, NMSRCA

Jicarillo Bob Took the Pot, Farmington, New Mexico, Mrs. Francis E. Totty, August 18, 1937, NMFWP, WPA #153, NMSRCA

Joe Fowler Hold-up-man and Criminal, N. Howard Thorp, November 26, 1937, NMFWP, WPA #88b, NMSRCA

Las Vegas, Malaquinas Baca, NMFWP, WPA #227, NMSRCA

Mañana, L. Raines, March 24, 1936, NMFWP, WPA #216, NMSRCA

Mrs. Amelia (Bolton) Church, Georgia B. Redfield, October 3, 1938, NMFWP, WPA #186b, NMSRCA

Murder in Mora County Mystery, Santa Fe New Mexican, August 12, 1864, 8/29/40 Boothill News, NMFWP, WPA #88b, NMSRCA

Murders in Early Clayton, D. D. Sharp, April 23, 1938, NMFWP, WPA #238, NMSRCA

Northern New Mexico's Bad Man and His Gang "Black Jack Ketchum," Kenneth Fordyce, February 27, 1937, NMFWP, WPA #87, NMSRCA

Old Albuquerque Chronicles, Elinor Crans, March 23, 1939, NMFWP, WPA #178b, NMSRCA

Old Days in Las Vegas, New Mexico, N. Howard Thorp, February 4, 1937, NMFWP, WPA #88a, NMSRCA

Old Days in the Territory of New Mexico, Desperado Milton Yarberry, The Kinney Gang, Major Fountain, N. Howard Thorp, no date, NMFWP, WPA #87, NMSRCA

Old Timers Stories: Cruz Richards Alvarez, Marie Carter, April 19, 1937, NMFWP, WPA #197, NMSRCA

Old Timers Stories, Early Day Folsom: The Killer Thompson, W. M. Emery, October 31, 1936, NMFWP, WPA #87, NMSRCA

Old Timers Stories, Mrs. Caroline Geck Weir (Husband: W. C. Weir), Marie Carter, June 4, 193-, NMFWP, WPA #197, NMSRCA

Old Timers Stories, Mrs. Mabel Luke Madison (Husband: James Madison), Interview: June 6, 1936, Marie Carter, July 12, 1937, NMFWP, WPA #197, NMSRCA

Old Town Albuquerque Chronicles: Slaves, Serfs, Peones, Elinor Crans, March 16, 1939, NMFWP, WPA #178b, NMSRCA

Original Narrative by Mr. Kello on San Juan County, Mrs. Helen Simpson July 20, 1936, NMFWP, WPA #225, NMSRCA

Outlaw Names, NMFWP, WPA #88a, NMSRCA

Pioneer, Daily Robbery, Kenneth Fordyce, March 26, 19—, NMFWP, American Guide, WPA #188, NMSRCA

Pioneer, Trouble, Kenneth Fordyce, March 5, 1937, NMFWP, American Guide, WPA #188, NMSRCA

Pioneer Story: Abran Miller, Edith L. Crawford, October 3, 1938, NMFWP, WPA #210, NMSRCA

Pioneer Story: Ambrosio Chavez, Edith L. Crawford, August 29, 1938, NMFWP, WPA #210, NMSRCA

Pioneer Story: Charles P .Mayer, Edith L. Crawford, July 19, 1938, NMFWP, WPA #210, NMSRCA

Pioneer Story: Francisco Gomez, Edith L. Crawford, August 15, 1938, NMFWP, WPA #210, NMSRCA

Pioneer Story: Interview with Ella May Chavez, Janet Smith, 7/6/36, NMFWP, WPA #228, NMSRCA

Pioneer Story: Interview with Mrs. Pauline Myer, A Visit from Outlaws, Janet Smith, August 17, 1936, NMFWP, WPA #87, NMSRCA

Pioneer Story: Mrs. Mary E. Burleson, Edith Crawford, February 28, 1938, NMFWP, WPA #228, NMSRCA

Pioneer Story: Pedro M. Rodriguez, Edith L. Crawford, August 22, 1938, NMFWP, WPA #210, NMSRCA

Proclamation $5000.00 Reward (Poster) March 9, 1916, History Files #26, NMSRCA

Raton's First Jail, Kenneth Fordyce, March 5, 1937, NMFWP, WPA #188, NMSRCA

Red River, James A. Burns, June 6, 1936, NMFWP, WPA #233a, NMSRCA

Reminiscences of Lincoln County and White Oaks by Old Sages and Stagers, Edith L. Crawford, June 14, 1937, NMFWP, WPA #210, NMSRCA

Rough on Rustlers, Silver City and Lordsburg Coach Held-Up The Rustlers Disgusted With Their Luck, Mrs. Frances Totty, September 1937, NMFWP, WPA #87, NMSRCA

Rustlers: Hanging at Shakespeare, Mrs. W. C. Totty, Enterprise, 1882, July 29, 1937, NMFWP, WPA #87, NMSRCA

Rustlers on the Range, W. M. Emery, May 10, 1937, NMFWP, WPA #87, NMSRCA

Seven Rivers – Lakewood, Katherine Ragsdale, September 9, 1936, NMFWP, WPA #199, NMSRCA

Shack Stealing, Vernon Smithson, July 17, 1937, NMFWP, WPA #153, NMSRCA

Socorro, Early History up to 1900, Lorin W. Brown, May 25, 1939, NMFWP, WPA #231, NMSRCA

Story of the Harrell War, Edith L. Crawford, June 7, 1937, NMFWP, WPA #87, NMSRCA

Taos . . . The Law Conscious, Kenneth Fordyce, July 19, 1938, NMFWP, WPA #233a, NMSRCA

The Apache Kid, Clay W. Vaden, October 24, 1936, NMFWP, WPA #87, NMSRCA

The Capture of the Outlaw Coe, W. M. Emery, 3/21/36, NMFWP, WPA #87, NMSRCA

The Clifton House, Kenneth Fordyce, February 12, 1937, NMFWP, WPA #87, NMSRCA

The Dalton Gang's Last Hold-Up, N. Howard Thorp, June 20, 1938, NMFWP, WPA #88b, NMSRCA

The Fate of a Horse Thief, W. M. Emery, July 20, 1937, NMFWP, WPA #87, NMSRCA

The First Train Robbery of the Southern Pacific, Mrs. W. C. Totty, July 29, 1937, NMFWP, WPA #87, NMSRCA

The Gage Train Robbery, Betty Reich, June 28, 1937, NMFWP, WPA #87, NMSRCA

The Harrell War, Edith Crawford, June 7, 1937, NMFWP, WPA #209, NMSRCA

The John Greer Gang, N. Howard Thorp, April 23, 1938, NMFWP, WPA #88b, NMSRCA

The Law in Their Hands, Kid Menser's Shooting in a Saloon, Kenneth Fordyce, January 30, 1937, NMFWP, WPA #188, NMSRCA

The Raid on the Granary, Reyes N. Martinez, July 18, 1936, NMFWP, WPA #233a, NMSRCA

The Santa Rita Holdup, Frances E. Totty, January 22, 1938, NMFWP, WPA #87, NMSRCA

The Stockton Gang, Kenneth Fordyce, December 5, 1938, NMFWP, WPA #87, NMSRCA

The Tragedy of Paint Horse Mesa By Colonel Jack Potter, Carrie L. Hodges, 6/28/38, NMFWP, WPA #87, NMSRCA

The Wild Bunch of the San Francisco River, New Mexico, N. Howard Thorp, March 11, 1937, NMFWP, WPA 88b, NMSRCA

Tom Tobin, Helen S. Speaker, May 19, 1939, NMFWP, WPA #189, NMSRCA

Uncle Dick Wooten, The Daylight Stage-Coach Robbery, Helen Speaker, May 19, 1939, NMFWP, WPA #189, NMSRCA

Uncle Dick Wooten, "Uncle Dick's" Toll-Road on Raton Pass, Helen Speaker, May 19, 1939, NMFWP, WPA #189, NMSRCA

Vicente Silva and His Gang, L. Raines, August 3, 1936, NMFWP, WPA #88a, NMSRCA

Villa Raid, B. Reich, May 17, 1937, NMFWP, WPA #102, NMSRCA

Villa's Buried Treasure, B. Reich June 1, 1937, NMFWP, WPA #102, NMSRCA

Villa's Raid on Columbus, Betty Reich, May 3, 1937, NMFWP, WPA #102, NMSRCA

When Chris Otto Whipped the Bad Man, W. M. Emery, 6/18/37, NMFWP, WPA #87, NMSRCA

When Villa Raided the Town of Columbus, B. Reich, May 10, 1937, NMFWP, WPA #102, NMSRCA

Wild Cow Mesa, Katherine Ragsdale, November 2, 1936, NMFWP, WPA #201, NMSRCA

Wild Times in Santa Fe, N. Howard Thorp, May 16, 1938, NMFWP, WPA #87, NMSRCA

Names Index

The Goudy Old Style typeface used throughout this book was designed by Frederic W. Goudy, a book and type designer active from 1896 to 1941. The handtooled version used in titles was designed by C. H. Becker, M. F. Benton and W. A. Parker in 1932. This book is printed on acid-free paper.

, Tennesse

Johnnie, Pistol Johnni

Pinkey, Happy Jack, Big

fiend Bill, Pegleg Dick

Dutch the Gambler (Jim F

Fox, Red River Tom, Hold

Skinny, Long Vest George,

Cockey Bill, One Armed Ji

Kelley, Lord Locke, Long L

"Shakespeare", Chuck-a-luc

Jim, Bostwick the Silent Ma

George, Blondy, Shotgun Bil

Car Bill, Little Jay, Kentuc

Frank, Shorty, Skinny the Ba

Nose Clark, Soapy Smith, Squi

rocky Faced Johnnie, Picolo

g Foot Mike, China Jack,

ns, Cold Deck George, Hop-

ebud, Sandy, (Red Oaks),

y), Red-face Mike, Dummy the

Jack, Short Creek Dave,

key Hall, Baldfaced Kid,

Gambler, ~~Smokey~~ One Armed

Maroney the Peddler,

ts, Hog Jones, Hog-foot

urricane Bill, Pawnee

otty, Big Murphy, Box

ommy the Poet, Sheeney

Elk Skin Davis, Broken

yed Rob

CPSIA information can be obtained
at www.ICGtesting.com
Printed in the USA
LVHW111605290922
729617LV00018B/144